READY TO SAIL

BY THE SAME AUTHOR

Further Offshore

READY TO SAIL

A Captain's Guide to
Boat Inspection and Repair—
Preparations of Boat and Crew
for Offshore Passagemaking

Ed Mapes

This edition first published 2008 by
Sheridan House Inc.
145 Palisade Street
Dobbs Ferry, NY 10522
www.sheridanhouse.com

Library of Congress Cataloging-in-Publication Data

Mapes, Ed
    Ready to sail : a captain's guide to boat inspection and repairs—preparations of boat and
crew for offshore passagemaking / Ed Mapes. —1st ed.
        p. cm.
    Includes index.
    ISBN 978-1-57409-271-4 (pbk. : alk. paper)
    1. Boats and boating—Maintenance and repair—Handbooks, manuals, etc. I. Title.
    VM321.M267 2008
    623.82028'8—dc22   2008048687

ISBN 978 1 57409 271 4

Edited by Tim Gregoire
Designed by Keata Brewer

Printed in the United States of America

To each and every mate that I have sailed with, thank you, for a book is only written when the author has been taught and influenced by enough people to become competent.

Very special thanks, for their support and encouragement, are due my wife Kim and son Eddie. May our time on the water together bind our family and keep us forever shipmates.

CONTENTS

INTRODUCTION xi

CHAPTER 1: FIRST IMPRESSIONS 1

CHAPTER 2: THE HULL 3
    Decks 3
    Interiors 13
    Underbody 18

CHAPTER 3: THE RIG 27
    Running Rigging 27
    Sails 31
    Standing Rigging 42

CHAPTER 4: GROUND TACKLE 55
    Hardware 55
    Anchors 56
    Windlasses 59

CHAPTER 5: STEERING SYSTEM 64
    Rudders 64
    Steering 67
    Self-steering 70
    Emergency steering 78

CHAPTER 6: AUXILIARY ENGINES 80
Routine maintenance 80
Diesel engines 82
Transmissions 93
Driveshaft 96
Stuffing box 97
Cruising range 98

CHAPTER 7: ELECTRICAL SYSTEM .101
Direct Current systems 101
Multimeter diagnostics 106
Alternating Current systems 111
Power requirements 113
Lightning 115

CHAPTER 8: PLUMBING 118
Freshwater plumbing 118
Wastewater plumbing 122
Marine toilets 125

CHAPTER 9: SHIPBOARD AMENITIES 129
Galley 129
Cabins 139

CHAPTER 10: THE ELEMENT OF SAFETY 141
Equipment 141
Safety Measures 146
Medical Kit 157

CHAPTER 11: CREW PREPARATION 161
Crew lists 162
Emergency protocols 164
Seasickness 168

CHAPTER 12: PREPARING THE BOAT FOR SEA 171

Maintenance list 171
Food stores 174
Voyage planning 176
Float plan 177
Weather 179
Documents 181

APPENDIX A 183

Checklist for Crew Clothing and Personal Gear 183
Crew Responsibility List 184

APPENDIX B 186

General Tool Kit 186
Spares for the Offshore Yacht 186

APPENDIX C 189

Inspection Checklists 189

ACKNOWLEDGMENTS 199
INDEX 201

INTRODUCTION

It was my fate, in the fall of 1988, to meet a gentleman at a boat show in Harrison Township, Michigan. While showing me around his boat, he mentioned that he needed a hand in sailing her to the Caribbean to join the charter fleet. In that instant, my sailing world began to expand past cruising, racing, and delivery on the Great Lakes. Three weeks later, we were on the Detroit River in EN-CHANTRESS, bound for Lake Erie and the Atlantic Ocean beyond.

Leaving New York Harbor and the Ambrose Light was a momentous event. My anticipation of new adventures made me wonder what was out there, and whether or not I could handle it. Little did I know that just ahead were three days of Force 9 cold front winds and the accompanying 30-foot waves as the Gulf Stream collided head-on with those northerly winds. There would be no meals, little sleep, and seemingly unending seasickness. Waves hissed as they lifted us to their crests, roaring as they swept past. The bow sliced through the dark water and threw spume aft toward the cockpit.

Whipping through the rigging, the gale produced a crescendo of sound, forcing us to shout to be heard over the roar. When the breakers approached from astern, there were only seconds to duck and hold on as warm Gulf Stream water deluged the cockpit. The lightweight autopilot could withstand only a few hours of the punishment, so we took our turns at the helm. What had I gotten myself into?

This was my introduction to offshore passagemaking. But what I discovered during those days on the edge was something unexpected. I found that once I got past the noise and cold, the nausea and the fear, the ocean was astoundingly beautiful.

The crests of those towering waves provided a panoramic view of the vast blue sea with its highlights of white foam. The night sky was full of more shimmering stars than I ever dreamed existed, and the waves' phosphorescence reminded me of snow-covered landscapes on a bright winter's day. I was delighted by flying fish, dolphins, whales, and that wonderful watery roar as our bow carved through the water, right on course for Bermuda. The immense power and benevolence of Nature were on full display.

Introduction

I discovered that our well-found yacht, properly maintained and stocked with the right gear, lent a calming sense of confidence and security. This reassurance allowed us to become more comfortable with the storm, certain that the boat could withstand whatever she had to. That unforgettable passage and the lessons it taught me became a basis for the inspection and preparation of every boat I sail. If a vessel is truly ready, she will get us to port. We survived that test, made landfall in Bermuda for a few repairs, and proceeded on to the Virgins.

I've logged thousands of sea miles since that first passage and now find myself compelled to help others discover what waits beyond their own harbor entrances.

This book is written for everyone who wants to sail the ocean. In the following chapters, you will learn a profes-sional approach to preparing your vessel, yourself, and your crew to sail the oceans with confidence. Each chapter of *Ready to Sail* explores a phase in the inspection process. An Inspection Checklist is included in an Appendix and can be used to direct your own yacht inspections. The rest of the book takes you through repairs, shows you how to assess the readiness of your boat and crew, and offers other valuable suggestions for successful offshore passagemaking.

As Irving Johnson, one of the greatest sailors to ever hoist a mainsail, said, "The man who goes to sea is bound for sure adventure." These words ring true every time I steer a course away from land. Each voyage is a new adventure and a new test. Making port is not really the end of a voyage—it's a starting point for the next. I hope your discoveries are always enchanting and leave you thirsty for more.

READY TO SAIL

CHAPTER 1

FIRST IMPRESSIONS

When commissioned to sail a yacht to an offshore destination, the delivery captain is asked to place the well-being of his or her crew under the care of that vessel. With little foreknowledge of the boat's history, we need to adopt a systematic approach, to become familiar with all of the boat's systems and equipment, and make sure that everything functions properly. This applies not only to delivery skippers, but also to anyone considering taking a vessel onto the water. It is only after a meticulous examination that I feel comfortable casting off the lines and setting sail. This is no guarantee against failures, but my goal is to ensure that the boat is in good order beforehand and all spares or replacement parts are on board.

The inspection process is quite similar to the marine survey typically done before the acquisition of a yacht, but it serves a different purpose. You're no longer trying to determine whether you should buy the boat; rather you must discover its faults and weaknesses in a much higher-stakes game—that of ocean readiness. You'll not only examine the boom, but also make sure that a preventer system is in place and ready for sea.

If the purpose of the voyage is to deliver a newly purchased yacht, the owner should have a completed marine survey, as insurance companies require a survey before financing a yacht purchase. This survey provides valuable information, and if deficiencies are noted, pay particular attention to those areas and make certain they're properly addressed. It is a mistake, though, to put complete trust in the survey alone. Perform your own inspection as usual, using the survey as another source of information. You cannot be sure that the survey identified every fault, and it's your well-being on the line offshore.

Pay attention to "workability," or the efforts made to ensure that the setup and equipment performs as it's designed to. There may be reef lines run to shorten the main sail, but if they're attached too far forward on the boom, reefing will not flatten the sail. Your decks may look like new and glisten in the sun, but there may be areas that are too slippery when soaked by seawater, and need a non-skid surface. Modern vessels with polished varnish cap rails may look beautiful at boat shows, but have no pad eyes to place snatch blocks.

Focus more on function than aesthetics when inspecting a boat about to be placed under duress. Don't stop your thought process with the mere presence of a piece of gear; go on to consider how it will function in a rough seaway.

Before beginning the inspection process, it's wise to gather all pertinent yacht information. You'll need statistics about the yacht itself to gauge performance under sail and its range under power. Customs officials, likewise, will be interested in the ship's papers. The most important items are the ship's documentation and registration papers, along with all passports.

The assessment of any boat begins as you first approach it from the dock. This is the first step of the inspection, one I call "First Impressions." It may be moot if performed by the boat owner, but an objective examination here can still reveal flaws. A simple once-over provides the initial perception of the boat's overall condition, level of maintenance, sail plan and deck layout. It's not comprehensive; rather it is a way of getting an initial feeling for the boat. The inspection checklist begins here, and I usually make some notes where indicated.

Minor cosmetic blemishes don't mean much. We are primarily interested in anything that relates to seaworthiness. Evidence of collision, for example, indicates possible structural damage that could lead to leaking of the hull, ports, hatches, seacocks or rigging. Photo 1-1 is a prime example of such damage. Evidence of neglect is a warning that vital systems may also be affected. On the other hand, a good standard of care indicates that other components have likely been well maintained.

After you've completed this preliminary scan, and noted any defects or areas of suspicion on the checklist, proceed with the inspection in an orderly fashion.

PHOTO 1-1
This collision damage is a sure sign that repairs are needed and begs the question, "What else was damaged?"

CHAPTER 2

THE HULL

DECKS

The order in which the inspection proceeds is up to you, but I find it convenient to move first to the hull, its structural supports, and the deck. Begin with an evaluation of the hull, its construction material, design, and condition. Look for rust, spider-cracks, flaking or chalkiness, as well as holes or indentations indicating collision or other significant damage. Photos 2-1 and 2-2 are examples.

Once, while battling for the lead on the last upwind leg at the Etchells North American Championships on Narragansett Bay, our starboard jib lead let go just before a tack. On an Etchells, in the heat of a race, there's no jury rig quick enough to stay in competition. It was a painful lesson in the value of a thorough inspection. Examine each point of attachment for everything connected to the deck—handrails, blocks, sheaves, water and fuel deck fittings, life raft

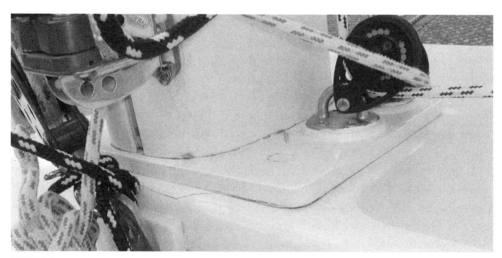

PHOTO 2-1
The cracked deck at this mast base must be repaired before sailing.

PHOTO 2-2
Due to its proximity to the forestay, this crack required extensive repair.

fittings, the toe rail, shrouds and stays, the mast, winches—everything. Each hole through the deck can become a source of leakage. If a deck fitting appears to be weathered, corroded or damaged, repair or replace it immediately.

I'll discuss seasickness in Chapter 11, but it should be noted that seawater below deck creates a damp, smelly environment that's uncomfortable to live in and contributes to seasickness. I try to prevent a wet boat by checking the deck carefully for any leaking. You should spray the deck with a dock hose, observing below for water leaking through the ceiling, ports and hatches, and down the hull. Don't just trickle the water from the hose; spray it hard to mimic the force of an ocean wave. It may take a while for water to appear inside, so don't rush it.

Rails

The rub rail, toe rail and cap rail are frequent sites of leakage that may or may not show clear signs of damage. Toe rails in particular are often used for attachment of the preventer or snatch blocks, which sustain high loads. These structures should be solid, and any worn areas demand immediate attention. I regularly have to apply silicone to the internal and external cap rail junctions to VOYAGER's hull to control leakage to the interior.

These structures are secured with bolts that penetrate the deck through a backing plate, with a washer and nut on the interior. Once access to the nuts is gained in the boat's interior, solidifying the structure is simply a matter of filling the holes with waterproof compound, inserting the bolts back through the deck and backing plate, and fastening the nuts tightly.

Note the condition of cleats located near the boat's rail. They must be strong, solidly secured, and able to withstand great loads. Their attachments are similar to all deck structures and involve nuts, washers, bolts, backing plates, and a suitable waterproof sealant to prevent leaks.

Stanchions provide support for the lifelines and are important safety structures. Check each stanchion in its entirety, from the base to the top opening of the lifelines. Examine for bending, rust, laxity or other obvious damage. The bases must be securely mounted to the deck in order to provide strength and prevent leaks below. Any gap between the stanchion base and the deck will allow water to seep in, so I make it a habit to apply a bead of silicone to all stanchion bases.

The lifelines may have hidden flaws since the plastic coating can mask an interior weakening of the core. Inspect the coating for rust, cracking, or breaks—these may indicate that the core, usually composed of braided wire, is damaged. Also check the attachment points to the stanchions, pulpit and pushpit. The pelican hooks connecting lifelines to the posts are often corroded, the threads stripped or otherwise damaged. If the stoutness of a pelican hook is in doubt, replace it.

Damaged lifelines must be replaced by new ones, obtained in specified lengths at a marine hardware store. Sagging lifelines give inadequate support, so they should be tightened by either screwing a turnbuckle or having a rigger cut the wire and swaging on new end fittings. Remember that lifelines should not be trusted as lifesavers—never rely upon them to support the weight of a sailor—but they should be dependable enough to prevent a person or gear from rolling overboard.

The bow pulpit and stern pushpit anchor the stanchion-lifeline system forward and aft. They should be solidly in place and strong enough to support a sailor's weight. It's not uncommon to stand on these structures when attending to one of the stays or a spinnaker, so examine them as you would the stanchions and look for similar flaws. Mast pulpits offer protection when working at sea so they should also be solid and able to support a sailor's weight.

Davits

A sailboat's davits are strong structures, but on most boats they shouldn't be used to carry a dinghy on the open ocean. Anyone who has witnessed the power of a wave breaking over the stern understands that a dinghy in that situation is probably a goner—along with whatever else is torn off with it. Removing the dinghy from stern davits in heavy weather is a dangerous undertaking, so it's best to stow it before the voyage, no matter how fair the forecast. The dinghy should be lashed to the foredeck or deflated and stored low in the boat. Inspect the davits, keeping in mind that they may be used as hoists for supplies and fuel or to assist someone climbing on board from the water. Pay particular attention to the lines and sheaves to gauge whether they've been damaged by exposure to the elements. Replace questionable lines and service sheaves to ensure they spin correctly.

Ports and hatches

Ports and hatches are obvious points of leakage on any boat. If the decks have been sprayed with water you may already have noticed leaking, which is common in this area—especially in older boats or those that spend a lot of time in direct sunlight. Hatches are prone to leakage due to being atop the deck. They'll leak if not dogged down tightly when the deck is wet, so secure them when water sprays over the decks or rain is forecast. Hatches can leak for other reasons, so check for cracks or crazing of the tempered glass, frame breaks, or loose framing within the deck opening.

Hatches with broken lenses are usually replaced. You can order a replacement lens from the manufacturer or have a suitable substitute cut at a specialty glass shop. Carefully remove the old lens from the frame's sealant. Lay a bead of sealant around the periphery of the frame and carefully set the new lens into position. Use a clean cloth to re-

move any excess before the sealant dries. Once the sealant is no longer tacky and the lens is solidly in place, the hatch may be closed and sprayed with water to test the repair job.

Broken frames must be repaired or replaced, and the seal between the area in question and the deck must also be resealed. The easiest procedure is to contact the manufacturer to order exact replacement frames with lenses. When repairing a broken aluminum frame, scrape the broken segments to remove debris, then clean them with acetone. I have used synthetic body putty to temporarily form a seal between the two frame segments but this compound will eventually break down. A solid repair is to screw a thin slat of aluminum into position straddling the broken frame segments.

From the inside of the boat, place the aluminum over the break and drill starter holes through the slat into the frame. Then remove the aluminum slat and enlarge the holes so that the machine flathead screws pass through easily. Apply a bead of adhesive silicone to each frame segment, bring them together, and screw the slat into position. Silicone may also be used to seal the area between the frame and the deck to make a watertight seal. Or you can remove the hatch and install new adhesive foam gasket material from a marine hardware store. After the new hatch is lowered onto the gasket material, it can be screwed into a secure position.

Ports are inspected in the same manner as hatches. Check for broken or crazed lenses, and dried, cracked, or displaced sealant. Actual breaks in the framing are very rare unless there's been a collision. A dogged port should be able to withstand strong, direct sprays of water from a hose. In the absence of broken glass or framing, leaking is usually due to degraded sealant or dried gasket material. Some brands of ports have small slots in the framing that allow water penetration, and, consequently, the interior sealant will degrade quickly.

Ports have a raised portion of the frame facing the outer hull that is mounted against gasket material, sealant, or both. An insert usually covers the inner face of the frame for aesthetic reasons. The opening window closes against waterproof gasket material glued into place around the periphery of the port opening, with a flange backing as part of the frame. The gaskets, after exposure to sunlight and water, become less pliable over time and, even when the port is dogged tightly, will begin to let water in. Simply removing the old gasket, applying waterproofing sealant, and installing a new gasket often stops the leaking.

If slots are machined into the port's frame, they will eventually leak. Use a small screwdriver to remove the old sealant, which will come out in dry, crusty pieces. To gain full access, it's best to remove the inner retaining fitting— usually secured with Velcro patches— from the port. Once the old sealant is removed from the slots (there are usually two per port) new sealant is applied. Manufacturers recommend black silicone sealant. Squirt the sealant into the slots from outside, and observe as it fills

the slot and emerges into the space inside. After the sealant has dried, dog the port shut and spray with water. Once the leak has been repaired, replace the inner retainer.

Tank fittings

On the deck, take a look at the fuel, water and waste removal fittings. Missing or improperly secured caps, or cracking of the surrounding deck structure, are problems. Caps can be replaced, but stripped threads will require replacement of the entire fitting. Ensure deck integrity by re-bedding a loose fitting. These fittings extend downward from the deck and are double clamped to hoses that lead to tanks below. The fittings are secured to the decks with nuts, bolts and backing plates. Removal of a deck fitting is often difficult because the hose below deck must be removed before the fitting will come off, and this may entail creating an opening in the woodwork or whatever material covers the work area.

Fuel and water tank vents often become clogged by spider webs or other debris, so make sure they are clean. When filling tanks, be sure that air is expelled from the vents as the tanks fill.

Tank fittings that attach to the vent or fill hoses are subject to fatigue and breakage, especially when plastic fittings are used. Check all fittings and be sure that hoses are double-clamped. A gasket often sits between the fitting and the tank, with the fitting base attached to the tank by small stainless steel screws. If the fitting is leaking, the screws may simply need tightening. If the openings are stripped on a metal tank, drill out a larger hole and tap it for a larger screw. Stripped screw holes in fiberglass tanks require that the area be cleaned, washed with acetone, and filled with epoxy resin. After curing, sand the repair until it is smooth, and drill pilot holes to accommodate new stainless steel screws.

Deck hardware

Mast bases and the attachment points for stays and shrouds will be discussed later in the book, but should be inspected during the deck exam. Cheek blocks, sheaves, line clutches and lead tracks must be solidly mounted and in good working order. Removal and reattachment is recommended if deck-mounted equipment is loose. Remember that lines under tension exert great loads, and can expose undetected weaknesses, usually at the worst possible time.

Corrosion can cause parts with moving components, such as deck sheaves, to freeze up. Moving parts should be disassembled, cleaned and treated with Teflon spray or 3-in-One oil to ensure smooth operation.

Sometimes the hardware itself is not damaged, but has simply become loosened from the deck. In this case, repair involves removing the deck fitting (and usually the headliner below deck) to access the backing plate and nuts. Apply bedding caulk or silicone and mount the fitting tightly in place. If a metal backing plate is not present, install one. Backing plates not only provide support for the nut and washer, but also distribute the load of the fitting. This makes the attachment stronger, with less chance of cracking the deck or pulling loose under high-tension load.

The main problem with deck sheaves is corrosion. They're also affected by the accumulation of salt crystals and fine dust particles, which damage the bushing or bearings by an increase in friction. If the block with the frozen sheave is held together with rivets, the only way to return it to service is to clean it with fresh water, apply penetrating fluid or WD-40, and hope that it frees up. If not, discard it. You can disassemble blocks where the faceplates are secured by screws. On blocks with a bushing, remove the bushing from the sheave, thoroughly clean it and the sheave center hole, reassemble the block and mount it into position. Blocks with roller bearing-borne sheaves must also have the faceplate removed, but be sure to remove it carefully or the bearings will scatter everywhere. The sheave and bearings are held together by a retaining plate, and come out as a unit. Pull the unit from the block and you can access the bearings and sheave. Once it's been cleaned and reassembled, mount it on deck.

Winches

There are many types and sizes of winches, but they typically work on the same principle and have similar parts.

First, make sure all the winches are mounted securely. Whether on a spar or on deck, any loose winch must be removed and repositioned tightly. A winch's primary component is the main shaft that engages the winch handle. The shaft is geared to operate with single or dual action (i.e. the shaft turns when the winch handle is cranked in one direction or in both). In a dual action winch, the gearing causes the shaft to turn at different speeds in either direction.

Pawls and springs are used to prevent the shaft from spinning in the opposite direction from which it is being turned. Therefore, after a sheet has been winched in and the winch handle is released, the winch won't release the trimmed sheet. The winch is housed within the drum and rests on a winch base containing holes for the mounting bolts. Other components are involved, but those are the basics and are common to all winches.

Metal winches are susceptible to corrosion, and deposits of dirt and salt tend to compromise the lubricating grease, disrupting the winch's motion. You can check a winch's motion by spinning the unloaded drum backwards. If it doesn't spin freely or has a rough sound, it should be disassembled and cleaned. Don't wait until your winches show signs of wear, they should get routine maintenance to prevent internal damage.

A word of caution—a winch's internal parts are small and easy to lose during disassembly. You should prepare your work area before taking the drum off a winch. Spread a cloth on the deck to contain runaway components, and make sure scuppers are plugged. Before disassembly, pay close attention to the order and position in which parts come off. If a manual is available, lay it out next to the work area. If you don't have a manual,

get one. Many marine equipment manufacturers have downloadable owners' manuals available on their Web sites.

Start by removing the top. Depending on the type of winch, you may need to unscrew a single screw, several screws, the whole top, or a retaining clip. Carefully remove the top, since some self-tailing winches are under spring tension and may pop up when the top comes off. Some winches have metal, C-shaped inserts called collets beneath the top. Slide those out, and then bring the self-tailing assembly out, noting its position on the winch before removal. Once these components, which are located at the top of the winch, are removed, you can lift out the exposed drum.

Under the drum is the spindle, with its gears above and bearings around the periphery. Note a plastic key that holds the bearings into position on the shaft that rests on a rounded platform holding the gears. Also note the gear shafts around the platform. The gears should be moveable and, if removal is necessary, lift the shafts up and out to free the gears.

Once the parts are exposed, clean them with gasoline or kerosene and check for damaged gear teeth, misshapen bearings, surface corrosion, and dented or chipped pawls. Any damaged components must be replaced to assure optimal winch performance. After cleaning and inspection, apply oil to the pawls and springs, and grease the gears and bearings sparingly with marine grease. Reassembling the winch should be painless as long as you check your drop cloth for spare parts before securing the top!

Navigation lights

Inspect the navigation lights as part of the hull. Running lights are situated forward. Wiring extends forward from the main circuit breaker, usually at or near the navigation desk, within the deck. There are bundles of wires, so a short or break can occur anywhere along that path. Flip the nav lights' breaker and check that both lights go on.

Check the light covers—red to port, green to starboard—for debris, cracks or faulty seals. Any gap that allows water inside can short out the light and corrode points of connection. If either of the running lights fails to operate, remove the covers and check the bulbs. Burned out bulbs are usually easy to spot, but not always. A malfunctioning bulb may look perfectly normal, so test the bulb itself with an ohmmeter. If the reading shows a low number of ohms, the bulb is OK. Very high numbers indicate large resistance, and internal damage; the bulb is toast. You should also inspect the light socket. If you find corrosion, turn off the current at the breaker and scrape the corroded terminals clean with a knife. Insert a new bulb and test again. If the light still fails to operate, test the terminals with a voltmeter. If no current registers, trace the electrical wiring back to the circuit breaker, testing every connection along the way. At the breaker, test the wire connections to ensure the breaker switch is operational. If the breaker switch itself is at fault, it must be replaced. Follow the same steps to examine the stern light.

The compass

Check the compass while in the cockpit. Long the most important piece of equipment on ships, the compass is composed of four parallel strip magnets positioned beneath the compass card and enclosed within a transparent waterproof bowl filled with a clear liquid. Some compasses are outfitted with gimbals to ensure that the card remains stable no matter the motion of the boat. The compass is best located in front of the helmsman's primary position and should be at least two feet from any iron or steel structures, or any equipment that may possess a magnetic field, including engine instruments, radios, navigational instrument wiring and lights.

Check for electrical or magnetic influences by turning off all circuits and comparing the compass reading with a hand-bearing compass held away from the cockpit sole. If the readings don't match, there's probably an influence from the engine, fuel or water tanks, wiring or electrical gear nearby. To isolate the influence, turn on electrical circuits one at a time and watch the compass card, taking note of anything that moves the card. If possible, the influential wiring should be repositioned away from the compass, and if disturbing influences are found to affect the compass, it should be compensated. Another way to check the compass is to direct the boat on a known, fixed course on your chart. This could be toward a set of ranges, a course directed down a channel, or a course plotted toward a buoy or other marker. When the boat is steady on this course, observe the compass course. Any bearing other than the known heading indicates the need for compass compensation.

Compasses are manufactured with two sets of tuning magnets that provide their own weak magnetic fields to cancel out unwanted disruptive magnetism. The compass also has a set of rods, or compensators, on each side that connect to the compensation magnets. There may be inserts that cover the ends of the rods—these are the port, starboard, fore and aft compensators. Gently loosen the compass from its secured position in the pedestal, but do not rotate it. Check the cockpit and area beneath the compass for any metallic objects, electronic gear, or wiring that may cause deviation. Make sure that all gear in the immediate area is stowed as it would be at sea.

Tuning the compass

The first step in the tuning procedure is to run the boat directly, or within a few degrees of, due north. Select a range or charted course, plot a course toward a stationary target, and follow a hand-bearing compass away from electromagnetic influences. You may also maintain a GPS course, being sure to differentiate between true and magnetic headings—charted courses are either true or magnetic, so check the chart. Hand-bearing compasses are magnetic, and GPS courses are usually magnetic, unless otherwise designated. Once on a steady course, observe the compass, compare with the known course, and compensate out the difference if one exists. Adjust

the port and starboard compensation rods until the compass gives the correct heading.

On the return course, hold steady within a few degrees of south, and if the compass does not read the correct heading, it's misaligned. Rotate the compass itself to null out half of the error, and then repeat the procedure on the north heading by adjusting the compensation bars. This should enable the compass to read correctly on both headings. Next, determine an east course to follow and assume a steady bearing within a few degrees of east. Compensate the compass as required using the fore and aft compensators. Reverse course, bearing true within a few degrees of west. At this point it would be unusual to find a difference but, if one exists, remove half of that difference by rotating the compass itself, then repeat the procedure for east. Once the compass reads correctly in all directions secure it firmly into place.

Check that the fluid bathing the compass components has not leaked or turned yellow. Discoloration of the fluid or the compass card is due to direct exposure to sunlight, so you should use a cover to shield the compass when it's not in use. If there is discoloration, bubbling or low fluid level, the compass should be drained and filled with fresh fluid by a professional compass technician. A compass light is typically installed within the compass itself or on the binnacle. It may have its own circuit breaker or be connected to another circuit. The light should allow you to read the compass at night, but not be so bright as to compromise night vision. Be sure the compass light is illuminated when the switch is on—if not, check the bulb and trace the electrical circuit back to the panel. This light is important, as steering is done at night by the compass course because it is in real time; an autopilot display is delayed.

Teak decks

Inlaid teak decking should be checked for cracks in the wood or gaps in the black caulking between wood slats. Spray these areas with water and watch carefully for leaking down below. It may be necessary to remove aged caulking and apply new to secure the deck properly. Teak sawdust can serve as filler to repair cracks or deep scrapes in the wood. Once the sawdust is mixed with wood filler and laid into the cracks, it takes on the appearance of the original teak. Teak that has more substantial damage will need to be replaced.

Most teak decking consists of ⅜-inch thick slats, and you'll want the replacement slats to match the size and curve of the originals. Place sheets of paper over the repair area and trace the shapes of slats you need. Transfer these tracings onto replacement teak and cut new slats. Next, position the new slats and drill up from below deck to match the hole positions. On deck, drill countersink holes to allow for proper seating of the screw head. The countersinks will be filled with precut teak plugs, so make sure the holes are drilled to a size that will accommodate the plugs. Modern teak decking is positioned and secured with epoxy adhesive instead of screws.

This is a better method, as it eliminates all those holes in the deck that can leak, sooner or later.

Caulking compound can be purchased at marine woodworking shops or marine hardware stores. Apply the bedding and position the slats. The slats are easily secured with one person on deck with the bolts and another below to control backing, washers and nuts. Fill the gaps between the slats with bedding and allow it to dry. Take care with this sloppy material—it's easy to track it onto the wood.

Blemishes

Most rubs, scrapes, minor cracking and breakouts to gelcoat (a polyester resin with pigment and filler added) are only cosmetic, but in preparation for a long cruise they should be repaired to prevent exposure of the underlying fiberglass. For minor repairs, wipe the damaged area with acetone to remove any wax and then clean thoroughly to remove shards of gelcoat, fiberglass, dirt or debris. Spider-cracks must be enlarged to provide an area large enough for the gelcoat to bond properly. Repair of gelcoat blemishes requires the use of gelcoat putty, and some gelcoat brands require that wax be added to keep air off while they dry.

Matching the gelcoat color to the boat is the first step in the repair process. It may be possible (and preferable) to obtain premixed gelcoat from the manufacturer, but getting a good color match becomes difficult as the boat ages and the color of the original gelcoat fades.

Gelcoat repair:
1. Enlarge spider-cracks as necessary
2. Clean damaged area of debris and wipe with acetone
3. Match gelcoat colors, then mix gelcoat with catalyst
4. Thicken as needed with talc
5. Apply gelcoat and work into defect
6. Allow adequate drying time
7. Sand, buff and wax (deck or hull) or sand and apply barrier coat (hull below waterline)

You may also mix dispersion colors into neutral gelcoat yourself—beware, it doesn't take much—or contact a boat-builder or fiberglass boat repair company to mix them for you. Gelcoat used in brush or spray application is too loose to stay in its applied position except in thin coats. This consistency is suitable for small or very thin repair areas, but for larger or deeper repairs the gelcoat must be thickened by slowly mixing filler—talc is the filler of choice—into the less viscous gelcoat.

The second step in the repair process is to mix the gelcoat with a catalyst. It's important to incorporate the catalyst completely, because with insufficient mixing a portion of the gelcoat will cure very slowly, or not at all.

Next, apply the gelcoat to the damaged area and work it in thoroughly. Remember that gelcoat shrinks as it dries, so it's best to apply enough putty to fill the defect with extra gelcoat that can be sanded off once it dries. Another method is to apply just enough gelcoat to fill the damaged area, then, once it dries and shrinks, apply more. Whichever method

you choose, after the gelcoat has dried and been sanded, it should be polished to impart the luster that marks a successful repair job.

INTERIORS

Once you've examined the outer decks and hull, move below to continue the inspection. Begin with the bulkheads, which are the hull's principal support structures. Examine all bulkheads for broken material, loose connections with the hull, water stains down low indicating leakage, or any other abnormalities. Bulkheads are held in place in a number of ways. They may be situated between integral slots in the hull or between wood slats placed on either side. There may be some movement evident between the hull and a bulkhead, since the hull flexes in a seaway, but bulkheads should not be able to move from their designed locations.

All molded sections of fiberglass should be in perfect condition. Any cracks or fractures are indications of great hull torque, shock loading, grounding or collision.

Headliners

The overheads (ceiling panels or headliners) should be checked for signs of leakage, usually detectable by the appearance of yellow or brown stains in the ceiling material. Leaks are quite common, but detecting their source can be a challenge. If you think you've found a leak, remove the panels and spray the top decks with water. The source of the leak is often found several feet away from the stain due to the curvature of the decks. Deck leaks almost always stem from equipment bolted to the top decks.

To gain access to the leak, you'll need to remove the overhead. It's usually composed of sections that have been secured with screws and separated by wood slats held in place with small screws or Velcro. Once you've removed the sections beneath the leak, locate the nuts and backing plates of the leaky fitting. Unscrew the nuts and the bolts, and remove the gear from the deck, looking for any underlying damage. Make sure

there is adequate backing for a secure hold—inadequate backing often allows for excess movement that loosens the bolts and allows water to enter. Substantial washers or metal plates should be used to provide support for all deck appurtenances. Apply waterproof sealant under the gear and into the deck holes and securely tighten the nuts and bolts against the backing plates, then spray the decks with water to be sure the leak is repaired.

Mold and mildew may be present where water has soaked through and caused an area to remain damp. Inspect the lockers and other areas where the

PHOTO 2-3
This mildewed area received a thorough cleaning with a bleach solution. The underlying wood was not structurally damaged.

hull is visible for stains, discoloration, mold, or insects. Treat mold with one part bleach diluted in 16 parts water.

Framing

Internal framing (IGU or Internal Grid Units) gives longitudinal and horizontal support to the hull and is found beneath the floorboards and in bilge areas. Look for fractures between frame segments or between the frame and hull.

Minor gelcoat stress cracking on structural elements is common due to normal flexing of the hull, and doesn't necessarily indicate that the structural integrity of the vessel has been compromised. Cracks or larger fractures of the framing should be repaired with appropriate material, depending on the yacht's construction.

In fiberglass boats, the damaged IGU area should be cleaned of debris and any damaged fiberglass should be removed with a grinder. Lay mat and fiberglass on with resin to reinforce the weakened area. Don't be afraid to fortify this area, since it may be a point of particular stress. Apply gelcoat to seal the new fiberglass, but, because the IGU is covered by floorboards, it's not important that the gelcoat match exactly or that it be applied as smoothly as a gelcoat repair on deck.

Bilges

Now lift the floorboards and inspect the bilges. They should be clean and dry, except for the very lowest areas that may not trip the bilge pumps. Remove any debris such as pencils, plastic bags, sawdust, wood fragments and paper labels from canned goods, which can clog the pumps just when you need them most. Mildew or algae can grow in stagnant bilge areas and cause a smelly, unhealthy environment. Take this opportunity to thoroughly clean the bilge of any growth to make the area fresh and sanitary. Chlorinated cleaners work best, but wear rubber gloves and make sure you have proper ventilation.

Also pull up the floorboards in the forward compartments and inspect for water damage, mildew or evidence of collision. Transducers for the sonar, knot meter and speedometer are usually located beneath the sole within the hull. Check for signs of leakage, corrosion, or wiring defects.

Leakage into forward compartments sometimes comes from anchor wells when taking seawater over the decks. I've been concerned with hull breaches at sea when a large amount of water appeared in V-berth areas from the anchor well.

Bilge pumps

Check all bilge pumps next by flipping on the breakers. You may also activate the pumps manually by manipulating their float switches, but don't just watch or listen to a pump, as that gives no assurance that it's actually driving water, or that the hose is patent to the external port. Pour water into the bilge and then activate the pumps one at a time, observing the exit port in the hull as bilge water leaves the boat—only then can you be sure the system works.

Remember to test all bilge pumps, even those often found in the engine room. Pour more water in the bilge and test the manual pump(s) as well, considering it satisfactory only when the water leaves the boat. Remember, in case of a serious leak, the manual pumps, a bucket for hand-bailing, a separate hand pump, and even the engine water intake hose are much more efficient at removing water than most standard electric bilge pumps.

Submersed electric bilge pumps are usually diaphragm pumps driven by electric motors. Most problems with electric motors involve the brushes, which must be clean, able to move freely, and have enough spring tension to assure contact with the commutator, which is comprised of a series of metal bars. The brushes should not be worn too low—they should be at least as long as they are wide. Worn brushes should be replaced. Pull out the old brushes and remove all carbon debris from the commutator and brush housings. Secure the replacement brushes, making sure they slide in freely, then wrap 600-grit sandpaper beneath the brushes around the commutator and spin the armature to lightly sand the ends of the brushes. Continue until the brushes are shiny and bed securely with the commutator.

If the commutator is dirty, it may not make proper contact with the brushes and will need cleaning. Using 600-grit sandpaper, gently sand each segment of the commutator bar. You can also test the commutator windings with an ohmmeter by touching one probe to a commutator segment and the other probe to the opposite segment. The reading should be slightly above 0.0 ohm. Low ohms indicate a short between commutator windings. High ohms indicate a burned-out winding, in which case there may be evidence of scorch marks. In either case, it's probably best to replace the motor rather than attempt to unravel the problem within the windings.

Any pump motor that fails to activate must be checked for electrical disruption. Trace the flow of current backward from the pump to the circuit breaker to locate the problem. If you don't find any problems there, examine the pump motor including brushes, commutator and windings.

Regarding the pumps themselves, centrifugal pumps have a central inlet and water is forced to the pump periphery by spinning rotors. From there the water is pushed out of the pump into the discharge hose. You're probably familiar with the engine seawater pump and the impeller that propels water toward the periphery and out toward the discharge hose.

These pumps must be primed, i.e. fluid has to be supplied to the pump in order for it to work. Either the pump must be mounted below water level or a retaining check valve in the inlet hose must be installed to prevent water from escaping when the pump is off.

A centrifugal pump whose motor runs without pumping water has most likely lost its prime. You'll need to remove the discharge hose and pour water into the pump. Worn impeller blades will cause an ineffective seal between the blades and the pump housing so that the pump's power will diminish, then fail totally. Remove the top of the housing to reach the defective pump impeller and replace it with a new one.

Centrifugal pumps have difficulty pumping against excessive line, or head, pressure. Plugs or kinks in the discharge line, a long discharge hose, or high positioning of the discharge port may weaken the pump's power causing it to become inefficient or run without moving fluid. If this happens, check the discharge hose and, if no obstructions or kinks are found, disconnect it from the outer discharge port to see if the pump operates better. If it does, the rise is too high and you'll need to replace the pump with a more powerful one or simply not use it if boat heeling has made the discharge port too high.

Diaphragm pumps are designed with the central pump reservoir fed by an inlet valve. Water leaves the pump through an outlet valve beneath the movable diaphragm. As the diaphragm is lifted, either manually, like that in a manual bilge pump, or by a motor-driven piston, it creates a vacuum that draws fluid into the pump. Then the diaphragm descends and forces the water through the outlet valve.

No priming is necessary for diaphragm pumps, but their shortcoming is obvious—if the valves become fouled with debris, the pump will fail.

Except for valve issues, diaphragm pumps are very dependable so they're used more frequently in the fresh water system than in the bilge. If there's a diaphragm pump in the bilge and the motor operates but doesn't pump water,

check that the strainer isn't plugged, a hose kinked or the pump inlet obstructed. Check that the inlet line has no leak allowing air into the pump and destroying its prime. Check the drain port for obstructions. It may be necessary to disassemble the pump to verify that the diaphragm is intact, the drive belt or coupling is operational, and the connecting rods are intact.

Disassembly of a bilge pump isn't difficult, but you'll need to disconnect the pump from its position and hoses. Remove the screws that secure the outer covering and inspect the drive unit and diaphragm, which cover the valves on either side. Replace a torn diaphragm by removing the ring that holds it in place—peel off the diaphragm, noting its exact position in the pump. The valves are removable as a unit and the trick to replacing them is to note the unit's positioning prior to removal and making certain it's replaced the same way.

Keel bolts

While below deck, carefully inspect the keel bolts, bearing in mind that losing the keel creates a survival-type emergency. Take a wrench to every bolt to make sure it's secure. Check for laxity along with flaking, rust, corrosion or bending. If there is any question as to the strength of the keel bolts, be sure to have your concerns addressed—even if it takes a haul-out to be sure. Most instances of keel bolt concern involve corrosion and flaking. Scrape the bolts down to metal, test them for a tight fit, and apply fresh paint as a sealant.

UNDERBODY

Any barnacles or growth covering the understructures may conceal damage and will also hinder boat performance. This should be noted on the checklist. Any boat leaving port for a long sail should have a clean bottom and propeller.

Keels

The keel, centerboard or daggerboard, is best inspected on the hard or after a haul-out. Before an extended cruise or ocean crossing, a thorough inspection of the bottom is essential, and a haul-out is warranted. The keel-hull junction must be checked carefully, as keel damage is frequently found here.

Note the condition of the keel. Groundings or collision with debris in the water usually leave marks somewhere on the keel, especially on the leading edge, at the hull junction or the wings. Groundings with impact on the keel front push the upper, aft portion of the keel upward into the hull, and damage can also be detected there. Note any gouges in these areas and repair them.

Repair of hull or keel gouges is not difficult. Start by thoroughly cleaning the area and remove any jagged protrusions. Next, mix epoxy resin with hardener, stirring completely so that the color is uniform, then mix with filler to the consistency of mashed potatoes. Apply filler to the prepared gouges, conforming to the keel shape as much as possible. After a sufficient drying period, which varies according to temperature and humidity, sand the repair area smooth. Apply a bottom barrier coat to seal the area properly, and then apply bottom paint to prevent growth.

Look for scrapes or gouges, especially at the leading edges, from collision or reef damage. Inspect the hull for more significant defects caused by water infiltration, blisters and delamination.

Blisters

Hull blisters typically involve superficial water infiltration. The paint itself bulges, but there is usually no penetration of the barrier coat into the fiberglass. It's a good idea to scrape away the blistered paint and examine the gelcoat and fiberglass for signs of delamination—water damage to the gelcoat and fiberglass. Water entering the fiberglass and coring inside the gelcoat's protective surface will cause weakening of the hull. To find areas of osmotic delamination, boat surveyors rap the hull with a rubber-tipped hammer, listening for a dull thudding sound much different than the sound heard when the hammer strikes a normal section of hull. Areas adjacent to the delamination may contain raised and flaking paint, while cracks or pores may be seen through the gelcoat.

Immediate repair of delamination is necessary since the problem will only worsen. Explore the area by drilling small holes into the fiberglass to determine whether water has infiltrated the core. If not, the repair is fairly simple. The outer layers of skin will need to be ground away to allow the interior to dry.

Once the delaminated area is dry, repair involves patching the area with fiberglass resin.

Apply wax to the damaged area as well as surrounding surfaces to prevent spills from damaging the gelcoat. Then drill one hole at the bottom of the delaminated area as access for the resin, and one at the top to vent air out. In smaller repairs, these two holes are often sufficient but more may be required to repair damaged areas that are large or oddly shaped. For larger defects, after a determination of the delaminated circumference has been made, drill the holes then fix a hose to the bottom hole with glue or by tapping the hole and screwing a pipe into it. Mix enough resin and hardener thoroughly, and then pour it through the hose into the delaminated void. As the resin fills the void, air escapes through the upper vent until the hole is filled.

A simple delamination repair involves:

1. Applying wax to the surrounding area
2. Drilling a hole beneath the defective area in which to inject resin
3. Drilling at least one hole above the defect to vent
4. Mixing resin and hardener thoroughly
5. For small repairs, using a large syringe to inject resin into the bottom hole or, for larger repairs, pouring resin through a hose connected to a pipe that's been tapped into the lower hole
6. Injecting resin until it oozes from the upper hole(s)

Severe delamination

If the delaminated area is deep or the hull has other defects, simply injecting resin won't be a sufficient treatment. In those situations, the repair will involve grinding away the outer skin to reach the undamaged areas of laminate. Take care when grinding fiberglass—always use goggles to protect your eyes and wear a mask to prevent inhalation of dust particles. It may also be wise to shield your skin since some people develop a rash from airborne fiberglass dust.

Sometimes while grinding, you'll find an opening between laminates into which you can pour the resin and seal the area. Cut a layer or two of mat and lay it into the repair area. Once it's dry, alternate layers (up to four at a time) of mat and roving. Allow these to cure before adding more, then grind smooth before setting the final layers. After the final layers have dried, smooth the defect by mixing resin and talc to the consistency of mashed potatoes and applying the resin with a plastic putty knife. Once the resin has dried, sand it smooth with 100-grit sandpaper.

Finally, if the area is above the waterline, apply gelcoat, allow it to dry, sand it smooth and buff to a shine. If the repair is done below the waterline, there's no need to apply gelcoat—just coat the area with five layers of barrier protective, then bottom paint it.

Core repairs

I mentioned earlier that you must determine whether there is water present in

For more serious repairs or hull defects, follow these steps:

1. Grind away damaged or ragged fiberglass to reach fresh, dry areas beneath. Thoroughly clean the area of dust and debris
2. Cut sections of fiberglass mat and roving to fill the defect void
3. Mix resin with hardener
4. Coat a layer of mat with resin, and position it into the defect
5. Coat fiberglass roving and place it over the mat
6. Add roving and mat layers (a maximum of four layers at a time) and allow to dry
7. Repeat until the defect is almost completely filled
8. Mix resin, thicken to mashed-potato consistency, and apply to defect with plastic putty knife
9. Allow resin to dry, then sand smooth and apply gelcoat if above waterline, barrier coat if beneath

an area of delaminated fiberglass. The above repair outlined a situation without water infiltration, but if water is detected, the core material is likely degraded and the repair will be more complicated.

Deck hardware, and the bolts that attach it, are usually the entry points of water from the top decks. Water can also enter the hull through leaky ports, areas of collision damage, and via through-hull fittings that have been damaged or lost watertight integrity. Once water has infiltrated the gelcoat, it eventually makes its way to the core material and the delaminated area continues to grow. In cold climates, the freeze and thaw of

water will accelerate the process. In the worst cases the entire deck may need replacement, but I have found that most areas of delamination are fairly localized and repair is feasible.

For repairs of the hull, it's preferable to work from inside the boat. By approaching from the interior, you leave the outer layers of laminate and gelcoat intact, thereby avoiding the need to meticulously smooth and match the gelcoat. The following process is used to repair areas of the hull if the core material is saturated with water, has become weak or mushy, and no longer retains its proper integrity and strength. This repair could also apply to the deck, with the exception of the areas that have a nonskid surface. If a nonskid surface is not molded-in, it may be removed to allow for repairs of the underlying deck. But molded-in nonskid presents additional challenges that will be addressed shortly.

The skin and affected areas of laminate, either inside or outside, must be removed to expose the damaged core material. If the material is wet but maintains its integrity, it must be dried before the laminate is replaced. You may let the material air dry, or you can use a fan or hair dryer. Acetone may be applied to aid in water removal, but the fumes are toxic and flammable. Sometimes it's easiest to simply replace all the soggy core material. Despite the fact that you'll probably end up removing some undamaged material, fitting replacement material is easiest if you square the corners of the work area and remove material in square-foot sections.

Using the deck as an example, work from the interior and remove the headliner, settees, shelves and anything else that lies in the way. Protect the sole and nearby furnishings with drop cloths. Select the replacement core material and cut it to size. Place resin-soaked mat on one side, which will be the exterior part of the repair (that is, the side that faces you), and layer resin-soaked fiberglass over the mat. When this has dried past the tacky stage, put soaked matting on the opposite side of the core material, brush resin to the defect, fit the wet side core/mat into place on the overhead,

and place wooden shoring against the repair to secure its position.

When dry, more layers may be added to give the area additional strength. When all applications of resin have dried, use a grinder around the perimeter of the replacement to form a depression two inches wide on both the new and old fiberglass, where they join. Place strips of resin-soaked fiberglass into these depressions (called rabbets) to securely fasten the new material to the original. Once the repairs have been made, you may replace the gear and headliner.

Replacing nonskid

If you must perform repairs from the exterior, you should be careful to maintain the nonskid surfaces. If the surface is removable, the job will be easier—just remove the nonskid, make the repairs and replace the surface. If the nonskid is factory molded, it's best to make a new mold of the surface.

To do this, clean a section of undamaged nonskid and, when dry, apply a coat of wax, being careful to completely coat the area of the mold. Tape the area to match the size of nonskid necessary for replacement. Using matching gelcoat, mix with hardener, apply to the waxed nonskid and allow to dry. Then apply resin-soaked matting and several layers of fiberglass. Once this dries, simply remove it from the deck, and behold your mold!

To summarize:

1. Clean a section of undamaged nonskid

2. Apply wax

To repair delamination or hull damage involving the inner core, the procedure is as follows:

1. Remove headliner and expose damaged core by grinding away damaged fiberglass
2. Dry or remove the core
3. Cut out replacement core material to fit the defect
4. Place resin-soaked mat on one side of the core material, and fiberglass roving over the mat. This will form the exposed part of the replacement
5. Allow materials to dry just past the tacky stage
6. Brush resin onto the defect
7. Place soaked matting on the other side of the replacement core, and fit the replacement into the defect
8. Shore into place and allow to dry
9. Add more layers of mat/roving to fill the void
10. When dry, grind rabbets into the perimeter of the replacement
11. Place strips of resin-soaked roving into the rabbets and allow to dry

3. Tape area to match size of damaged nonskid

4. Mix gelcoat with hardener and apply to the waxed nonskid

5. Build up with fiberglass mat

6. Allow sufficient drying time, and pull the mold from the nonskid

The new section of deck is built the same way, beginning with the waxing step of making the mold. Remove all air bubbles from the gelcoat and laminates, then proceed as with a repair made from the interior but without the necessity of shoring, since gravity will hold the replacement section in place. After the mat/core/mat and fiberglass have set and dried, apply resin to the laminate and decking, and then lay the nonskid into position.

Transducers

Transducers are usually found near the front of the keel. Locate them, making sure the depth finder and sonar are clear of bottom growth and not painted over. The knot-log paddlewheel should be nearby. It is often jammed with growth that prevents normal spinning. An accurate speedometer and knot-log are fundamental to navigation, so be sure the paddlewheel spins freely. Have an assistant observe the readouts for depth and speed after cleaning the transducers. Simply spin the paddlewheel to simulate passage through the water.

At this point it's not a bad idea to compare the depth sounder reading to that of a lead line dropped to the bottom. Observe for variation in the readings, knowing that the lead line will always be correct. It may be that the depth sounder indicates depth below the keel versus depth below the transducer. Either way is fine—just be aware of how the depth sounder translates to the actual depth.

Any failure to register at the display is due to either instrument error, improper connection with transducers, or electrical malfunction. If the transducers are found to be functional below the waterline, they can be eliminated as the culprits. Check the electrical wire connections with transducers beneath the sole, noting loose connections, water or corrosion that could interfere with transmission. Make sure the breaker for the instruments, the DC power and the instruments are all turned on. There should be readouts on the display indicating that power is present. If the instrument does not turn on, trace the current from the display back to the circuit panel to find the source of electrical interruption. If the instrument is getting current but still failing to operate, then it is faulty. You may perform additional electrical tests using the multimeter as described in Chapter 7, or simply repair or replace the instrument.

Through-hulls

Before departure, I create a diagram of the hull with the positions of all through-hulls, and post it near the nav station so that everyone knows the locations of all through-hulls and seacocks. I also put the locations of all fire extinguishers on this diagram. It's also wise to tie a wooden bung to each through-hull fitting before sailing.

Moving aft on your inspection of the bottom, examine the skeg, rudder, propeller shaft, propeller (these are usually plural in multihulls), cutless bearing and sacrificial zinc anode.

Rudders

The rudderpost should be solid, with minimal give. Observe the lower rudder bearing for excessive play or movement of the post. From inside the hull, check that there is no leakage near the rudder tube—any wear of the lower rudder bearing can lead to leakage of water up the post shaft. If this occurs, you'll need to replace the lower rudder bearing, and this requires that an exact match be located. Rudder bearings are metallic rings that snap into position, from underneath the boat, into a groove around the post. It's possible to replace them while the boat is in the water using scuba gear, but having the boat hauled makes the job much easier—and the inspection easier as well.

Once the old bearing is removed, usually with a screwdriver wedged underneath the ring to pop the bearing from the groove, the replacement bearing is opened up and slipped into the groove. This should remove all play from the rudderpost and stop water seepage into the hull. If excess rudderpost movement persists, the upper bearing (located beneath the floorboards of the cockpit) should also be replaced. This bearing is usually made of fiberglass or other synthetic material and held in position with six to eight bolts. Just remove these bolts, place the new bearing into position, and tighten the bolts.

An internal structural unit, called the rubber web, is fixed firmly to the rudderpost. The rudder is constructed around the web into a solid unit.

Rudders are subject to physical damage, usually along the leading edge or bottom. Common problems include growth of algae or barnacles, delamination with possible leakage into the rudder interior, and separation of the inner webbing structure. Separation from the rudderpost is a possible consequence of collision damage, excessive shock loading, or leakage of water into the rudder from holing, delamination, or leaking pintle screw holes. Examine the rudder top, at its junction with the post. This is called the lap zone, and is the site of water leakage as the rudder structure separates from the post. You can search for internal signs of deterioration by drilling a hole into the rudder adjacent to this position. Any evidence of rust or moist, crumbly fiberglass indicates internal damage. After inspection, the hole is filled with epoxy resin and bottom painted.

All growth is readily evident and easily removed. Any damage must be assessed according to severity. Minor abrasions that don't disrupt the outer integrity aren't important, although they call for sanding and bottom paint because any penetration of the gelcoat, or even unseen outer damage, can lead to delamination. Water can enter the rudder and cause damage to the interior structural components.

The rudder should demonstrate no give whatsoever on the post—note that this differs from rudderpost movement into the rudder tube. This is movement of the rudder itself around the post. Any movement between the post and the rudder signifies some degree of damage within the rudder. This, along with delamination or other damage, indicates that the rudder and post must be removed from the boat and taken onshore for closer inspection and repair. You can often detect water sloshing inside a rudder that has been holed or delaminated. You can also check for water inside the rudder by drilling a small hole into the bottom of the rudder.

Should penetrating damage or delamination be found, first verify that the rudder and post are soundly attached as a unit. If so, you'll need to repair the damaged areas and this usually involves cleaning out the damage with a grinder. Clear away all loose material, just as you would when repairing a delaminated hull, until you arrive at clean, functional fiberglass. Be sure that all water is drained from the rudder before continuing with the repair. If you find a loss of integrity in the rudder/rudderpost union and suspect the internal structure is weakened, then repair of the external damage will not suffice. The rudder will have to be opened up and the internal framing elements repaired. This is a more serious undertaking and probably should be done by a professional, or you could consider replacing the rudder. Either way, you must never sail with a rudder that is unstable on the post.

I mentioned the possibility of rudder damage from shock loading and now would like to offer further explanation. A storm tactic you might be familiar with is running before a storm or "scud-

ding." As the boat travels in the direction of the storm, waves can build to an extent that they contain enormous power. Should a wave impact the rudder of a boat whose stern is lifted, a direct blow can jam the rudder hard over, causing tremendous damage. If the rudder and post integrity is compromised, then the rudder will be able to turn on the post as I've discussed. This damage can also occur to a boat lying to a sea anchor with too much rode out for the conditions. Slack in the line can allow the boat to be driven back by a wave, wedging the rudder hard over against the rudder stops and bending the post.

Propellers

Next we will check the propeller(s), the prop shaft, the strut or skeg, cutless bearing and sacrificial zinc anodes.

Lines that wrap around the propeller shaft are often responsible for a great deal of damage. Crab pots, fishing nets and lines hanging overboard are the usual suspects—they can become tightly wrapped and do serious damage to the propeller, shaft, strut, cutless bearing and stern tube. Galvanic action will also eat at a propeller not protected by a zinc anode. Over time in salt water, a protected propeller might succumb to the ravages of galvanic corrosion. This decreases the propeller's efficiency and can even cause the metal to crumble.

Determine the severity of the erosion and decide whether the integrity of the propeller is in question. Only the most extreme damage would make it unsuitable for sailing, but I replaced my own propeller once for this very reason. Bent propeller blades can cause shaft vibration that leads to cutless bearing problems. It's possible to realign bent blades, but you must remove the propeller from the shaft and visit a machine shop.

Propellers fit onto tapered shafts, with a key and retaining nut followed by a second nut or cotter pin. Many shafts also accommodate a zinc anode aft of the rudder. Remove the propeller by loosening the nut and pulling back on the propeller to bring it off the shaft. If the propeller is stubborn, you may need to use a prop puller. In lieu of a prop puller, you can place a piece of wood behind the prop body and strike it smartly with a mallet, then wiggle the prop until it comes loose. If that fails, the prop body can be heated with a propane torch applied evenly around the body, so that the metal expands and finally gives with the mallet blows. Take note of the metal key fitting into opposing slots in the shaft and the propeller body. When refitting a prop, determine how far up the shaft the hub seats so that the key fits perfectly. Grease the shaft and position the propeller, then replace the key and secure the retaining nut with another nut or cotter pin before securing the propeller. Replace the zinc if indicated.

If the boat is equipped with a feathering or folding prop, make sure the blades deploy readily by hand or when engaged by the engine at low rpm. Problems are usually due to algae or barnacles, which must be cleared away. If the blades are fitted with gears that mesh with a central gear on the shaft, these may be impaired by galvanic corrosion, excess grease within the housing or damaged gears within the unit. Remove the propeller from the shaft, open the cone assembly and observe the inner workings. Remove excessive, hard-packed grease, then inspect the gears at the base of each blade along with the central gear. Remove any burrs on the gears with a small file. Reassemble the unit, testing each blade individually, then lubricate if indicated by the manufacturer and refit the propeller onto the shaft.

Shafts

Proceed to the shaft, strut and stern tube, first checking for play in the propeller shaft. There should be none at all—anything more than $\frac{1}{16}$-inch of movement per inch of shaft diameter is excessive. Check the strut for cracks caused by a line that may have wrapped around the prop shaft.

That kind of damage requires not only fiberglass repair, but also raises the possibility of problems forward along the drive train. Excess shaft play calls for replacement of the cutless bearing and careful examination of the stuffing box, transmission and engine mounts, which are subject to damage from a misaligned shaft. These must be observed from inside the hull.

Cutless bearings

The cutless bearing consists of a metal or fiberglass tube containing a rubber or plastic insert through which the shaft turns. The rubber insert is ribbed so that water is allowed to enter and lubricate the bearing, which is usually fixed to the bearing case with set screws. The cutless bearing controls the prop shaft as it emerges through a strut, skeg or directly from the stern tube, and is subject to damage when the shaft is forced out of alignment. The shaft should emerge from the cutless bearing in such a way that it turns without causing vibration, with no play between the shaft and the bearing.

In order to remove the cutless bearing from the propeller shaft, one end of the shaft must be freed to allow the bearing to slip off. On shafts leaving the stern tube directly to the propeller, the propeller is removed, and the shaft also must be removed. This usually necessitates rudder removal as well, unless the shaft can be squeezed backward past the rudder. The stuffing box must also be removed to allow access to the bearing. For those fortunate boat owners with strut or skeg mounts, the bearing is located within those structures and can be dislodged directly, and only the propeller has to be removed.

After loosening any set screws, it's possible to remove the bearing by inserting a pipe up the shaft to make contact with the bearing. You can tap the pipe with a hammer to loosen the bearing without damaging the surrounding structure. Another method is to insert a threaded rod through the bearing and its housing (strut or skeg). At the inner end, insert a large washer and nut. Over the threaded rod on the outer end, insert a length of pipe just large enough to cover the rod but not to enter the shaft. Place a large washer over the rod that covers the end of the pipe, and place a nut on the rod end. Tightening this nut will draw the bearing out as the inner nut is drawn outward.

Once the bearing is removed, grease a replacement and slip it into position with gentle taps of a hammer. There should be a secure fit over the shaft, but not so tight that the shaft is difficult to turn or the bearing housing distorted. Tighten the set screws into the depressions in the bearing cases, and secure with Loctite thread adhesive.

Zincs

A zinc anode should be attached to the propeller shaft and if it appears small or moth-eaten, it should be replaced. The anode is held on the shaft with a set screw into a depression on the post. Locate the old screw (you may need to remove growth or corrosion), remove it, and take the old anode off. Replace with the same size anode, simply tightening the screw to secure it in place on the shaft.

If all the underwater structures have been examined, the hull and adjoining structures portion of the inspection is complete. Every defect noted on the checklist should be repaired before leaving the dock.

Spares for this chapter:
▪ Resin
▪ Resin catalyst
▪ Fiberglass cloth
▪ Roving
▪ Tape
▪ Winch repair kits

CHAPTER 3

THE RIG

RUNNING RIGGING

We will begin our inspection of the rig with the running rigging first and climb the spars later. Lines that show wear or chafe may be of little concern in light, everyday sailing, but will need to be replaced if they're expected to hold up under heavier loads. Inspect the entire length of all halyards, sheets, downhauls, and topping lifts, noting areas of damage or wear on the checklist provided in Appendix C. Chafe in the center of a line like the topping lift, which rarely moves and may wear on the masthead sheave, indicates that it should simply be replaced. If the line is usable, keep it for lighter duty on something other than running rigging. Lines showing wear at one end only may be end-for-ended and kept in service, or you can cut away the chafed length and whip or burn the end to stop it from unraveling.

Damaged shackles at the working end of lines should be replaced because they can let go. The shackles can be secured with a bowline or anchor bend, but an eye splice will always be stronger. There may be damage or chafing of the eye splices themselves, along with worn

knots in the line. These should be cut off, the end whipped or burned, then respliced or tied. Note that some shackles have small lengths of trip line. These trip lines love to snag on the bow pulpit or furling gear as the sail is hoisted, allowing the sail to fly free and the halyard to be hoisted alone. Make sure that your trip lines are small and free of rings that can snag. I've come to the point of removing them entirely, and here's why.

In the late 1980s, shortly after *Jaws* was released into theaters, I was on a delivery from New York Harbor to Charlotte Amalie, St. Thomas. One morning, about 80 miles south of Bermuda, as we attempted to hoist the spinnaker, the shackle lanyard snagged and opened up. The shackle and halyard were pulled way up out of reach, and we watched as the kite settled gently into the ocean, and then under the boat. The boat owner and crew had no interest in going into the water to retrieve the sail. So, after making sure they were keeping the boat pointed into the wind, I tied a line to my harness and jumped in. The sail had snarled around the winged keel and propeller, and it took me about twenty-five minutes to free it and haul it aboard.

With *Jaws* fresh in my memory, every minute spent in that water seemed like more time for a shark to draw a bead on me! Of course no sharks ever appeared, but that wayward shackle with its trip line caused an event I won't forget.

It's always good to have a spare jib and spinnaker halyard available. They're easier to run at the dock and, in case a primary breaks at sea, a spare becomes invaluable. This could even be considered a safety measure, should something break during a blow. If you don't stock spare halyards, be sure to run a feeder line from the mast base, around a masthead sheave and back down to the deck. Secure it in an unobtrusive spot so it won't tangle with other halyards. Should a halyard part, this line is available to reeve a replacement without climbing to the masthead.

Running a feeder line

To run a feeder line, hoist one person to the masthead and station someone on deck. Pull the primary halyard down all the way to the bitter end. The person aloft ties the feeder line to the primary, and the deck mate hauls the primary in until the feeder emerges from the mast. That person then cuts the feeder's other end, so that two ends are now available. If a halyard breaks, sew one end of the feeder line to the replacement halyard, fake the halyard on deck to remove kinks, and hoist the line and halyard with the other end of the feeder. Continue hoisting until the halyard has ascended the mast, passed over the sheave, and returned to the deck and out the

mast base to a lead block. Once you remove the feeder line, the new halyard is ready for service.

Line controls

Cheek blocks, mast base lead blocks, deck organizers, turning blocks, fairleads and all other deck-mounted hardware should be inspected for functional ability and sound attachment to the deck. Sheaves should be flushed with water periodically or after any prolonged contact with seawater.

Mainsheet

The mainsheet control system is comprised of the traveler, its hardware, the traveler car and the sheet itself. The traveler is the foundation of the system. Figure 3-1 shows a 4:1 purchase mainsheet traveler system and the component parts.

The main traveler is often exposed to heavy use, so you'll want to make sure it's securely attached to the deck. Begin a repair of a loose track by accessing the backing and nuts below decks. You'll need to remove the headliner, or the wooden panel that often covers the underside of the main traveler, and its screws. Remove the bolts and the traveler to inspect the deck underneath. Clean the deck area of any smudges or debris, apply sealing compound to prevent water infiltration, and replace the traveler. Squirt sealer into the screw holes, then seat the bolts through stout backing plates and tighten from below. Be sure the track is solid before replacing the headliner.

End stoppers (end controls), or blocks that also serve as stoppers, are located at either end of the traveler. End stoppers are often the site of failure if the main is back-winded or an accidental jibe occurs and the traveler slams to the other side. Having rarely seen such heavy use, the fittings may be corroded or weakened by the elements. It's an accident just waiting to happen, so be certain that these stoppers are solid. End stoppers have a variety of configurations, but all are secured to the traveler with stainless steel screws or rivets. Secure loose stoppers (or blocks) before trusting them offshore. If you find that some are loose, either tighten the screws or remove the damaged rivets and replace them with similar rivets or machine screws.

The traveler car is a complex gadget that moves from side to side when under load of a trimmed mainsheet. Most traveler cars use ball bearings for ease of motion, but movement is hindered when bearings are missing or dirt and corrosion hinder their normal motion. Clean the car and the traveler itself with fresh water and pressurized air; then spray with Teflon. If the car still fails to move freely, you'll need to examine the bearings. Refer to the owner's manual before removing the car from the traveler. There are many different makes of traveler and you run the risk of losing the ball bearings if disassembly is done improperly. Replacement bearings are available from the manufacturer or marine hardware stores.

The cam cleat is an integral part of the traveler car that allows the mainsheet to be cleated into position. If not functioning properly, cam cleats can come loose from the car and become incapable of holding the sheet in a trimmed position. The car is controlled on either side by lines to blocks, which provide mechanical advantage to control positioning. There may be a sheave on either side of the car and line stoppers (cam cleats) on each side of the traveler to control the car's position, or there may be line stoppers on deck, in front of the traveler, through which lines from either side of the traveler pass. These stoppers tend to cause leaks because the lines are under

FIGURE 3-1

The 4:1 purchase basic mainsail traveler unit.
A) Traveler car   D) Traveler track
B) Double block   E) Cam cleat
C) Terminal controls

Courtesy of Harken

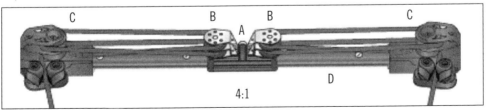

load and stoppers are often poorly backed under the deck. Make sure the stoppers are securely mounted to the deck with an adequate backing and that the sheaves spin freely.

If the stoppers fail to hold the traveler lines in position under load, they may simply be worn out and in need of replacement or they may be sized incorrectly. Line stoppers are designed to work within a limited range of line sizes; measure the size of the traveler line and replace inappropriate stoppers with suitable ones.

Finally, inspect the blocks and line that constitute the mainsheet system attached to the traveler car. Mechanical advantage should be at least 4:1, and needs to be greater as the mainsail increases in square footage. Figure 3-2 illustrates a 6:1 mainsheet system with a triple block with becket that attaches to the boom bail, and a second triple block with becket and cam cleat.

FIGURE 3-2

A 6:1 mainsheet system with triple block with becket (A), and triple block with becket and cam cleat (B).   *Courtesy of Harken*

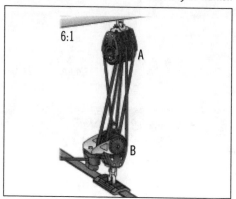

The blocks should work smoothly and the cleat must be able to hold the sheet securely in position under great loads. Check the sheet itself, as any line exposed to the elements is prone to weakening and failure, especially if it appears faded, has a dry, brittle feel, and shows evidence of broken fibers or chafe. A line in that condition is not trustworthy and should be replaced with a new line of similar size. Pay attention to how the old line is removed and retrace the procedure exactly when installing its replacement. Install the new line fairly so that it functions without twists.

I have found that corrosion and weakening of rivets holding the mainsheet bail to the boom is most common in tropical climates. Make it a point to remove corroded rivets, clean the holes thoroughly, and replace with new rivets or machine screws into newly tapped holes. Take care when placing screws into the boom, since the ends often snag and damage lines running through the area. When dealing with the spar, you must use machine screws of the right length, with blunted ends.

Jib leads

Inspect the jib fairleads. While most boats on a cruise or offshore passage are not in racing mode, most sailors like to go fast when they can. Remember, speed under sail is a benefit to fuel efficiency, and it's a good idea to determine how to move the leads fore and aft once you're underway. You can gain speed by appropriately moving the jib leads as the sheet is manipulated, keeping the sail drawing properly top to bottom. Most cruising sailboats have jib leads that move when a pin, lever or knob is lifted from holes in the track, and the lead car is physically pushed into position. The tracks are prone to jamming due to corrosion or the accumulation of salt crystals and dirt. In some cases the lead blocks are corroded into one position but are easily freed with a bit of cleaning and lubrication with penetrating oil. Lead tracks can bend too, impairing lead car movement. Maximizing your boat's performance is well worth a few minutes of effort, so clean all tracks and spray with Teflon.

Figure 3-3 shows a more advanced jib lead system that enables the car to be moved forward by pulling on a line that runs along the track to a block forward. The system works better with at least a 2:1 purchase, so use double blocks as a minimum. It's a simple system, but it makes trimming the jib easier and more accurate. This is also a safer way to adjust the lead position, since no one has

to go forward. Examine each component of the system: lead track, lead car (or block), forward double block with becket, and line. Each should be securely in place and in proper working order. The line is subject to degradation and chafe, so inspect it closely.

Note the overall lay of the deck, identifying locations available for the attachment of snatch blocks, spinnaker guys, tweakers, barber haulers and the boom preventer. These locations may be on a suitable toe rail, eyebolts in the deck, cleats, or anywhere that provides a solid point of attachment.

SAILS

Your inspection of the running rigging at deck level is complete, so proceed to the sails themselves by hauling your entire inventory out of the boat and onto a clean surface. Pull each sail from its bag and examine the headboard, leech, foot, luff, seams, slugs or slides and hanks. Also check any windows for tears, broken

FIGURE 3-3

Genoa track with adjustable lead system.

Courtesy of Harken

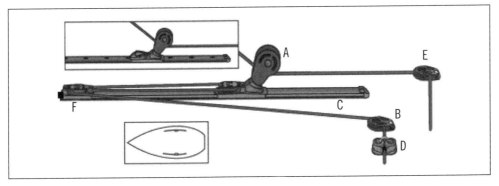

battens and damaged cringles. Common sites for tears on the mainsail are low on the luff where the gooseneck catches a reefed sail, along the foot if excess outhaul is applied, the fore and aft sections of battens, and along the areas contacting the spreaders.

Foot and leech cords should show no chafe or damage and they should maintain their positions well. A flapping leech or foot is not healthy for the sail and impairs air flow. If the cords refuse to hold securely, a new system should be sewn onto the sail, and that's really a job for a sailmaker.

Sail battens are subject to great abuse from storage, luffing sails, contact with spreaders, snagging with a topping lift, running backstays or lazy jacks, or from bending during flaking on the boom. You shouldn't try to repair broken battens; they should be replaced. The leech end of batten pockets can tear, loosen, or open up entirely, allowing the batten to fly in the air to leeward and land gracefully in the water.

Telltales are the best guide to sail trim, so be sure they're properly placed on the main and jibs. Remember that shear causes the wind at the top of the sails to come from a different direction (usually aft) and at a different velocity than the wind at deck level. Telltales are the primary method for detecting this difference in wind direction, allowing you to monitor sail twist to account for shear.

Extreme outhaul tension, especially when associated with hefty halyard, backstay or cunningham trim, can cause long, sail-wrecking tears along the foot of the main. I've only seen this happen while racing in a lot of wind and high seas, but it's worth mentioning here. It's also a good idea to protect the mainsail adjacent to the spreaders, since a great deal of chafing can occur there. If downwind trim allows the sail to contact a spreader, add a layer of sail material to prevent chafe. If the boat will be used for extended cruising and subjected to the elements for long periods of time, the sail material should be stronger than that used for inland sailing. Triple stitching of the main is a safety feature, and three reef points should be available on the main.

Sail cringles and bull rings are designed to be very strong, so tears in this area indicate that the sail material has weakened. Other tears may be present, indicating that a sail has reached the end of its life expectancy. In these cases, the cloth will appear dull and dry, with areas of thin or torn fabric. Don't try to salvage sails in this condition; they should be retired and made into tote bags.

Jib clews are the sites of wear and tear where they snag on spreaders, lights, and the spinnaker track. This area should also be reinforced to sustain heavy loads.

Jibs are subject to chafe and tearing just aft of the tacks as they rub on lifelines and stanchions. At sea, you can prevent this by using Yankee cut jibs. Spinnakers can tear just about anywhere from snagging while being hoisted, doused, or jibed. Tears in spinnakers tend to be dramatic, as they can split wide open along a seam in big air. We recently lost our ½ ounce asymmetrical in the Annapolis to Bermuda race when it ripped along the leech from foot to head.

Repairs

Repairs of sail tears depend on the location and the extent of the damage. Most repairs of punctures or tears at sea involve covering both sides of the affected area with adhesive Dacron tape. Tape doesn't adhere to wet, salty, or dirty material, so begin by rinsing any salt or dirt from the affected area, and drying. To repair small holes, punctures, or tears of about six inches or less, cut two patches of repair tape large enough to cover the defect, and overlap the area by at least two inches on all sides. Positioning the two sides of the tear exactly opposite one another is vital, as the sail will have wrinkles and an improper patch job if the edges are not in perfect alignment. Ask a crewmate to assist by holding the area while the patch is positioned. Place the first patch over the defect, and mark its perimeter with a pencil. Then remove the plastic backing from one patch and put it onto the sail, in the marked area. Next, turn the sail over and repeat the procedure to position the second patch. Once both patches are on, rub them firmly for a secure repair.

Large holes or tears are more challenging to repair. If the tear is straight along the sail without jagged edges, sail tape placed on both sides, as above, can work. The area of tape overlap should be at least three inches on all sides for added strength. For jagged tears, it's best to replace the torn section of sail with a piece of new sail fabric.

Most tears run parallel to stitching. Bring the sides of the tear into position, and insert pins if needed. Remove the paper backer from one side of double stick tape, and adhere it around the defect edges on one side of the sail. Align the tape either parallel or perpendicular to the cloth weave direction. Now begin removing the defect area by cutting the sail *inside* the tape area. Use either scissors or a hot knife to obtain sharp sail edges.

Cut repair cloth, from fabric that matches the original, with the threads in the same direction as in the section removed. This replacement cloth should fit over the defect and extend to the outside edge of the tape.

Once the new fabric is cut, lay it over the defect, and remove the backing paper from one of the tape strips. Press the sail against that strip, and continue until all edges are adhered and the repair material is perfectly flat against the sail. The repair section is now sewn into position at the outside edge as described below:

Select white, Dacron/polyester thread for the repair. Always use a triangular-shaped rather than round sewing needle; the hole it makes is less likely to tear. Hand stitch by using a zigzag pattern, which spreads the "pull" out and stretches as needed. Push the needle through the new fabric, move it forward along the repair by 1 mm, and push it through the original sail. Pull the thread taut at each step, but not so tight as to crimp the sail material. Continue this along the whole side of the repair.

Now stitch backward in the opposite direction, into the needle holes just made, to complete the zigzag pattern. Each stitch is pulled taut as before. Terminate the stitching by tying the two ends of thread together, and melt them to form a more permanent closure. Use the same pattern along all sides until the repair is completed. If the repair is in a high-chafe area, cover the stitching with sail repair tape.

Part of any sailor's offshore gear is a sail repair kit, with extra sail cloth to match the sails. Fully stocked kits are available at marine hardware stores and are highly recommended for those intending to spend considerable time at sea. The kit should include a sailor's palm (which is also good for protecting your hands in other situations), a variety of straight and curved sewing needles, polyester twine, waxed nylon thread and sail repair tape. In a pinch, sail repair tape or even duct tape works to stop tears from growing, but the rip should be repaired as soon as conditions permit. Be aware that some sailmakers dislike working on sails repaired temporarily with duct tape.

While still on shore, sails with torn seams or larger rips should be taken to a sail loft for repair. I recommend taking flawed sails to a qualified sailmaker while the boat is in port, and explaining exactly what repairs you need and what the sails are used for. Have your sails in the best possible condition before sailing to prevent problems while at sea. All seams must be very strong and should be stitched by a knowledgeable and experienced professional.

Don't overlook the quality of your sail inventory before sailing offshore, especially if you intend to cruise. Your sails drive the vessel and are important to offshore passagemaking. It's also a good idea to have the current sails measured in order to have an accurate guide if you need to make changes in dimensions or cut.

Notes on reefing

Take care when reefing the main to prevent gooseneck holes in the sail. When the reefing cringle is placed over the gooseneck, the gooseneck's prongs often pierce the area of sail beneath the cringle. One way to prevent this is to use reefing straps. Place a strong strap, with rings sewn onto both ends, through the cringle so that one ring is available for reefing on each side of the sail. When the sail is lowered in preparation, a ring is placed over the gooseneck instead of the sail cringle so the prongs can't hole the sail. Any holing requires that both sides of the sail be patched; adding extra thickness to that area doesn't hurt.

Check the mainsail's reef points and determine the reefing method. Know how to perform the operation easily, since you'll often need to do it in the dark. Many modern boats have reef lines running aft into the cockpit, called single-line reefing, which is a luxury and safety feature during heavy weather. Figure 3-4 shows a reefing system that prevents the need to go forward. Reefing lines are run from the front boom, up to the cringle, back down and through the boom aft. From the aft boom end, each line extends to the corresponding cringle on the leech, and then back down to be secured

Since all the reefing is done from the cockpit, this single-line reefing system is more convenient and safer for short-handed crews.

Courtesy of Harken

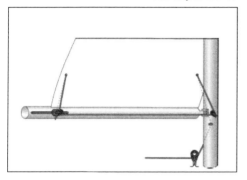

through an eye on the boom. The line at the fore-boom fitting leads down to a mast lead block, and then back to the cockpit and a line clutch. The figure demonstrates a single line for the first reef point, but a second and third line should also be rigged for deeper reefing.

The main problem with single-line reefing is excessive friction as the line negotiates the various turns it encounters, especially through cringles or bull rings. Installing single blocks at those locations solves this problem.

Make sure the reefing lines are run properly and that they're undamaged by chafe or exposure. Note that chafing on reef lines inside the boom can only be detected by direct examination. I once had a reef line part on an ocean passage, during a blow on a blustery, moonless night. The noise when that line popped and the confusion of the luffing mainsail were pretty surprising. That situation taught me to check reef lines inside the boom by pulling them through to expose all of the line.

Pay particular attention to the forward boom end cap. These frequently have sharp edges; when the reef lines are pulled through the boom and downward toward the mast lead blocks, they're chafed against this sharp edge of metal. When reefing, do not lower the halyard all the way to the final position; leave it at least a foot above the boom so that when the reef line is tensioned, it does not pull the forward cringle (or block) to the boom. That will help prevent the reef line from chafing against the forward boom end fitting.

Hoist the main and reef it down from the first reef point to the last. Haul in on the lines hard, to test whether they'll break when called on. Also pay attention to the aft end; be sure the sail leech is pulled aft during reefing to prevent excess draft in the sail.

Sail inventory

If coordinating your sail inventory, it's wise to consult with a sailmaker who has experience with cruising sails. Many sailmakers focus on racing, so their expertise may not lie in making the types of sails you need. Racing sails are different from cruising sails, so your sailmaker should understand and practice handstitching of fittings, such as sail slides, jib hanks and reef points, instead of the pressing or machine-sewing that is used for racing sails.

Your sailmaker should also be someone you feel comfortable working with because he or she will be your consultant

PHOTO 3-1
Reefing friction is markedly improved by installing blocks at the reefing cringles/ bull rings.

Material

Dacron remains the best fabric for most offshore cruising sails. It is extremely durable, relatively easy to cut and sew, and maintains its shape for years with proper care. Dacron can be folded on the boom without damaging the fabric, whereas laminated sails must either be removed from the boom or furled. Older sails may need to be recut, since Dacron stretches 1 to 2 percent with age. This stretching can cause more draft in the sail, making it fuller and more powerful, with more weather helm and diminished pointing ability.

If the sailmaker is making a new sail, it should be cut to allow for this stretch. Offshore sails should be triple-stitched with UV-resistant thread. The seams should be placed widely apart to allow room for restitching during repairs. A zigzag pattern gives the stitching greater surface area and has more integrity if you fold the edges over before stitching.

High-tension sail areas such as the head, clew, tack and reef cringles should be triple-stitched using several layers of fabric. These areas are usually "fingered," with several pieces of fabric emanating from the area instead of a straight cut. This configuration handles sail loads better. These areas are prone to chafe and should have leather chafe-guards sewn in.

during the whole outfitting process, and afterward for questions and suggestions. Your sailmaker should measure the boat to ensure that the sails will be of proper size and dimension. Ideally, a sea trial on your boat is included in order to better understand boat characteristics that will determine the sails' cut and scheme. Be sure to explain your plans for the boat, your sailing style and cruising grounds. With this information, a sketch of the boat and its current sails is created, along with any alterations and new sails. You'll want to get a copy of this profile drawing and keep it for future reference.

Mainsail

The mainsail is the most important sail on the boat and should be constructed with durability and functionality in mind. The mainsail is configured as either a regular (traditional) or furling sail. Regular mains are hoisted each time they're used, and lowered and flaked on the boom. Furling mains are stowed by furling either within the boom or mast, or sometimes outside of the mast.

Regular mainsails are more efficient than their furling counterparts. They have battens that help to control shape and allow for more roach, which adds size to the top of the sail where more wind is usually available. Since most sailing is done in 15 knots of breeze or less, it makes sense to have a roached main to improve performance. Standard battens are relatively inexpensive, allow for this additional sail area, and also for easy folding of the sail when off the boom. Fully battened mainsails maintain their shape even better, resist luffing, and are easier to flake on the boom than those with standard battens. However, full-batten mainsails are more expensive and they must have the battens removed for folding when taken off the boat.

Sail slides hand-sewn with webbing, or a loose-footed main are preferable to a boltrope along the foot. The foot with a boltrope that slides into the boom is subject to chafe, prone to tearing and difficult to remove from the boom. Intermediate reefing holes should be hand-sewn, high-quality rings, not pressed grommets.

The main disadvantages of full-battens are their tendencies to chafe along the front end of the batten and to bind against the mast track during hoisting and lowering. Installing a fitting called an end receptacle at the luff end of the batten will help diminish these problems.

I have always been leery of furling mainsails on offshore vessels, and am cautious about reducing sail for fear the furling mechanism could fail, but new technology has made furling more dependable. Although furling mains are easier to handle, they are smaller and less powerful than traditional mains, and must be standard cut (as opposed to having additional roach at the top).

The furling mast and boom are larger and heavier than standard equipment, so they offer more windage and weight aloft, and are noisier in a breeze. It's usually not possible to add a storm trysail track to the furling mast. The sails can only have minimal reinforcement at the corners and intermediate reefing cringles to allow for efficient furling. They don't have reefing points, so if the furler fails there is no reefing possible.

Jibs

There should be at least two jibs on board—the working jib and the storm jib. In lieu of a storm jib, and actually preferable, is the storm staysail. Offshore jibs should be constructed in the same way as their mainsail counterparts. Most boats are equipped with roller-furled working jibs, and sometimes furling secondary or storm jibs as well.

The headsail should be constructed to maintain strength, offer UV protection, and keep its shape when furled. Most working jibs are 120 to 140 percent of the sail plan's foretriangle on sloops and 100 to 110 percent on cutter-rigged boats. Again, these dimensions should be arrived at after consulting with a sailmaker, who is aware of the purpose and characteristics of your boat.

The working jib should be effective in a wide range of winds, from a light breeze of 6 to 8 knots to just over 35 knots. Its versatility and effectiveness can be optimized with a padded luff, which reduces draft as the sail is furled. Without this padding, the sail tends to have deeper draft and headstay sag when furled, creating more heeling, leeway and difficulty in balancing the sail plan.

An ideal forward storm sail is fully hanked and fitted to an inner forestay. This allows the primary jib to be removed completely or furled tightly, with the furling drum fixed into position to prevent unfurling during storm conditions. The storm jib or storm staysail is usually about 25 percent of the foretriangle, equivalent in size to the trysail or triple-reefed main, constructed of 8- to 10-ounce Dacron, with hand-sewn hardware. The clew should be cut high to clear waves, and must clear the mast when hove-to.

An option for boats that cannot have an inner forestay is a storm jib that is hoisted over the furled jib. While workable, this means that the working jib is not removed, which adds weight aloft and reduces stability as waves build. It can also be difficult to hoist over the furled jib. I'll discuss storm trysails in Chapter 10.

Light air sails

Offshore sailboats should have a light air sail in their inventory. Use of this sail allows for sailing in breezes of 4 to 8 knots instead of having to rely on the engine. Fuel savings are significant and the sailing is often a wonderful steady progress in light air and small-wave conditions. Traditional spinnakers, asymmetrical spinnakers, gennakers and the drifter-reacher are options for light air conditions.

Symmetrical spinnakers that are mandatory equipment on racing boats are rarely seen on other offshore boats. They are powerful sails that require a spinnaker pole with topping lift, downhaul, and after guys for control. They must be jibed, not tacked, and are most easily doused with a snuffer. Trim is constantly maintained aboard a racing boat, requiring more crew than on cruising yachts.

Spinnaker sheets are forward of the forestay, led aft port and starboard outside of the shrouds, to screecher blocks at the quarters. From those blocks, they are taken to the cockpit winches for easy control. Spinnakers must be hoisted on their own halyard, which is set at the masthead to prevent chafe as it moves along with the sail position.

Asymmetrical, or cruising, spinnakers are more popular on non-racing offshore boats, and are used commonly on racers as well. They tack to the stem or sprit and don't require a pole, although a sprit pole allows for convenient adjustment of the tack position. The tack is attached to a line that runs through a block for adjustment of the tack height. The tack is pulled down with the wind forward of the beam, and progressively let out as the wind moves aft. Sheets are run like those of symmetrical spinnakers. The sail is most often jibed by dousing with the snuffer, and then hoisted on the other side after the jibe is complete.

The drifter-reacher is a fuller, light-weight version of a large genoa, but cut flatter than a spinnaker. It is very versatile and can be used on virtually all points of sail. It needs no special hardware, no snuffer, and is a good option for sailors who don't want to deal with spinnakers.

Sail controls

Vangs

Traditional boom vangs (Figure 3-5) consist of an arrangement such as a fiddle block on the boom with another fiddle block with a cam and becket at the mast base. This usually provides at least 6:1 purchase, making control easy.

Modern rod or power vangs are built with a spring mechanism to push the

FIGURE 3-5
This vang system provides a 6:1 mechanical advantage and leads to both sides of the cockpit for improved accessibility.

Courtesy of Harken

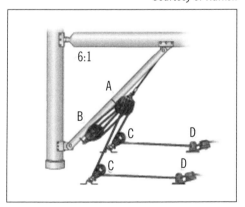

boom upward, thus acting as a topping lift, and can be hauled down to provide downward force on the boom to control boom bounce and close the leech off to the wind. Examination of traditional vangs is just a matter of eyeballing each component to check the line for chafe and the block for corrosion, damage, or wear that could prevent it from holding the vang sheet taut.

Rod vangs should be tested to ensure that they support the boom and can also exert downward force. They are typically composed of anodized aluminum and are very hardy. They may be disassembled for maintenance and are preferable when outfitting since they can support the boom.

The weakest point of most boom vangs is the attachment point at either end. The bails can become loose or the fiddle blocks weakened, so pay special attention to these points. Inspect the boom vang's connection with the mast, as well as the attachment point on the boom. Considering the loads often borne by the vang, it must be securely joined at both ends. Vangs are secured at either end in a number of ways, usually with a clevis pin. Check the pin for bending and make sure that a cotter pin holds it in place. Any corrosion or physical damage to the vang's fiddle blocks must be corrected—this involves replacing the weakened component.

Headsail furler

We'll check the main luff groove later when going up the mast, but for now, inspect the forestay luff slide since this must hold the sail onto the stay in all weather conditions. The jib must be easy to hoist and lower; it should slide right down the luff groove when no wind pressure is present. The slide is often contaminated with salt, fine dust particles and spider webs. Use a moist cloth to clean the groove, paying particular attention to the luff of the jib, as any abnormality in the luff can disrupt its movement in the luff groove.

The roller reefing mechanism should be examined closely. I say reefing because it has largely replaced the older, true furling system. True furling systems employ a wire halyard in the sail that is hoisted. A furling drum attaches to the sail tack, and is secured to an eye on deck. The sail is furled around its halyard wire as the drum is turned with a furling line. Since this system is difficult to use in high winds, most riggers have gone to the roller reefing systems. Roller reefing (still usually referred to as "furling") uses an aluminum extrusion slotted to house the jib luff. The extrusion may either attach to the head stay, or become the head stay. Either way, the jib is hoisted through and held in place by the extrusion. The halyard attaches to a swivel that rotates around the head foil.

Check Figure 3-6 to see that the extrusion fits into a furling drum, which attaches to the deck. The furling line in the drum spins the extrusion, which furls the jib along its entire luff from foot to head. At the masthead, the extrusion terminates at the upper furling apparatus. Note the top and bottom fittings that secure the sail and the halyard, respectively, along with the terminal for the forestay.

FIGURE 3-6

Lower apparatus and components of the Schaefer roller furling system.

Courtesy of Schaefer Marine

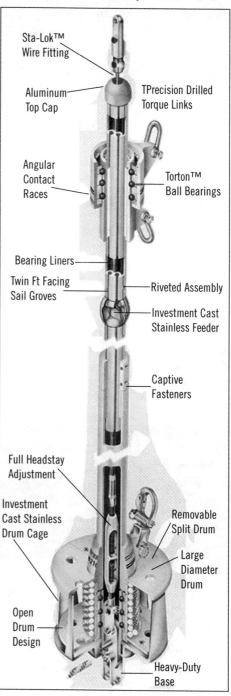

Sta-Lok™ Wire Fitting

Aluminum Top Cap

TPrecision Drilled Torque Links

Angular Contact Races

Torton™ Ball Bearings

Bearing Liners

Twin Ft Facing Sail Groves

Riveted Assembly

Investment Cast Stainless Feeder

Captive Fasteners

Full Headstay Adjustment

Investment Cast Stainless Drum Cage

Removable Split Drum

Large Diameter Drum

Open Drum Design

Heavy-Duty Base

Since the reefing drum, extrusion and swivel integrate with or become the head stay, failure is catastrophic and can lead to a dismasting. According to one rigger, the main cause of roller reefing failure stems from motion of the forestay. There is pressure from both fore-and-aft and sideways directions, and if the top and bottom of the system are not toggled to allow for these motions, undue stress is placed on the attachment points at both ends.

At the stem, the drum may be attached to a turnbuckle that usually extends to a swivel. If the swivel allows motion in only one direction, a point of considerable weakness exists. There must be a toggle to allow motion in a direction perpendicular to the swivel. Likewise, the top swivel should have freedom of movement in both directions. That is, there should be motion allowed in the fore-and-aft direction by a clevis pin attachment to the masthead, and a toggle attachment to the swivel in the lateral direction.

Examine the furling/reefing system in detail, with a mind toward any deficiencies that can lead to failure. Even knowing that inadequacies in the rigging of roller reefing can lead to failure, I have on occasion delivered yachts so ill-equipped. This was only after careful inspection for any sign of impending failure and with the knowledge that I would not be sailing the boat for long. As insurance against rig failure, it becomes prudent in this situation to shackle a spare jib or spinnaker halyard to the stem and haul it in tight. Rest assured that I informed the owners of

those boats that they needed to re-rig their reefing systems.

Furling drum

Moving on to the furling drums, make sure that they spin easily on their bearings. Corrosion is an enemy of metal bearings and they should be lubricated and sealed to avoid contact with water. Bearings are subject to stress and can actually be deformed by sails furled under heavy wind pressure. Drums that are difficult to turn have most likely become corroded, lost bearings or become salt-caked and deformed. Drums in this state require service, but only after consulting the owner's manual.

Examine the furling line for degradation and chafe. Trace the line through its leads back to the cockpit to make sure that it leads fair.

Before leaving the stem at deck level, inspect the forestay, which may or may not be enclosed within the furling gear. The forestay stem fitting is crucial to a standing rig, so it deserves a careful examination for loose bolts, cracking or corrosion. There must be very strong backing to hold the structure in place against the pull of the spar and the backstay. It should also have freedom of movement in the fore-and-aft and lateral directions to prevent rig fatigue.

Observation of the upper foil, swivel and halyard is done when you go up the mast, but here's what to look for: Check the shackle attaching the jib to the swivel. Check the point on the swivel where the halyard is shackled, and observe the toggling of the roller to the mast box. You'll need a mate to unfurl the jib and then roll it back up while you watch the upper mechanism.

One common problem is when both the upper and lower halves of the swivel turn when the furling line is hauled in. The top half, attached to the halyard, should not spin because that motion causes the halyard to wrap around the forestay. If this happens, the sail will not furl properly, the halyard is subject to chafe, and there is excess pressure applied to the swivel.

The halyard runs neither parallel to the forestay nor toward it. It must ascend at an angle away from the forestay (back toward the mast) and sometimes this requires the use of a fairlead block. Sometimes halyard wrap is caused by the swivel position. If the swivel is too low, the length of halyard exposed increases the chance of halyard wrap. The solution is to add a pendant, from the sail head to the bottom of the swivel, allowing the swivel to position higher and expose less of the halyard.

Your goal is for the mechanism to furl easily enough to come in without a winch and with only one person hauling on the line in light to moderate wind conditions. There will be times when reefing must be done fast, so your furler has to work freely. You should avoid placing significant torque on the segments of extrusion when the jib is rolled in against a heavy load. Never haul in the reefing line against significant sheet tension; ease the sheet enough to make furling easy. Examine the extrusion's entire length for segments that are misaligned. When the jib is rolled in, the sheet should be eased to avoid any excessive torque on the extrusion.

Hoisting sails

Become familiar with the procedures for deploying every sail in the inventory, be they hanked-on, roller furled, hoisted up the luff groove directly by the halyard, in-mast mainsail furling, electrically driven winches, stayless hoisting or club-footed sails. There's a wide variety of sails and different methods of handling them. Examining each sail for seaworthiness is one consideration, knowing how they all work is another.

STANDING RIGGING

Check all components of the standing rigging carefully because if there is one system that will fail according to the strength of its weakest link, this is it. Inspect all turnbuckles, cotter pins, clevis pins, mast tangs, spreaders, and attachments to the masthead and deck. The rigging should be cleaned before inspection because debris can disguise small defects.

Look for signs of disrepair such as rust, weakened wire, pitting, kinks or bends, corrosion, frayed strands of wire (meat hooks are particularly nasty on bare skin), and abnormal positioning of components like damaged mast tangs and bent clevis pins. You are searching for general areas of structural weakness and for components that are close to failure—such as bent pins. Anything that threatens the seaworthiness of the yacht must be replaced before subjecting the rig to the shock loads of ocean wind and waves.

In addition to a visual examination, you may also employ magnifiers, a penetrating dye test, X-ray imaging and ultrasound. I find it inconvenient to haul a radiograph machine aloft, so a careful visual inspection, sometimes supplemented with a dye test, suffices for me.

Dye test

The penetrating dye test is best done with the hardware disassembled, so that the dye can penetrate easily. I find the test to be most effective on rigging hardware (turnbuckles, toggles, tangs and end fittings) and rod rigging rather than wire rigging, as explained below. An inexpensive (though not as trustworthy) way to perform dye testing is to apply a mixture of red or blue food coloring with 3-In-One oil to the test areas. The mixture will seep into cracks and make them more apparent. A better system is supplied in kits, such as the Magnaflux Spotcheck Dye Penetrant Kit, which provides complete instructions as well as every component needed for testing. Included is a cleaning solution for the test components along with a developer that accentuates a positive test.

The procedure begins with disassembly and cleaning of the hardware. When the components are dry, spray them with the kit's red penetrating dye and allow to dry for up to thirty minutes, depending on the temperature and humidity. When dry, remove the dye with a rag, and then carefully wipe the area again with a rag moistened with cleaner from the kit. If you're attempting to test stranded wire, this is particularly difficult, as it's impossible to "get the red out."

The goal is to completely remove the red color from all surfaces then lightly spray with the powdery-white developer. Wherever the dye penetrates, a red line will appear to accentuate the damage. If you find a defect in any rigging component, including rod rigging, replace it.

Don't be fooled by the fact that a component may have recently been worked on. In fact, that's a red flag to examine the area more closely. I remember a delivery from Tortola where I discovered a tang attached upside down on a mast that had been serviced by the yard several days earlier. The tang came out of the mast at about a 50-degree angle and was obviously rigged incorrectly, even though the yard was satisfied with the job.

Chainplates

Making sure the rigging is securely attached to the boat, examine the chainplates for the shrouds and stays. This may be impossible if the chainplates below are difficult to view, but if they're accessible you should check for weakening or corrosion. If there are cracks in the deck around a chainplate, you should inspect the attachments below deck. If you find corrosion, the integrity of the entire standing rigging is doubtful. It's not uncommon for yacht surveyors to condemn chainplates and require their replacement before they consider the boat insurable. This is because some "stainless steel" is anything but, and corrosion can do severe damage to chainplates as well as anything else metallic.

Replacing the chainplate requires first disassembling it from the shrouds. Bring a halyard over to the beam and secure it to a cleat or pad eye to support the rig as you remove the shrouds and unscrew the bolts that hold the chainplate in position. Any cracking or damage to the deck should be repaired after the chainplate is removed. Refer to Chapter 2 for deck repair suggestions. Once the chainplate is off and the deck is in satisfactory condition, mount the replacement chainplate with new bolts, sealant, new backing plate and nuts. Everything needs to be replaced once corrosion has begun to set in.

Stays and shrouds

One x 19 stainless steel wire is best suited for shrouds and stays. Compared to rod rigging, it's more flexible, lasts longer under similar usage (although with modern rod materials this is in question), and is easier to install. In addition, stainless steel wire gives early indication if wear and fatigue begin to cause weakening; as exhibited in the braids of wire separating or unwinding.

The braided nature of wire allows for corrosive infiltration of water, especially at the junction with end fittings. Rod rigging is more common on racing boats, although it's more expensive, more difficult to replace, a challenge to store on board at sea, and can fail without warning.

Corrosion, especially when rigging is exposed to the sea and not rinsed routinely, is a constant concern. Eyes at wire terminals are formed around thimbles by securing the wire with Nicropress sleeves, cable clamps, swages, or one of the newer terminal systems like Norseman, Sta-Lok, or CastLok.

The Nicropress unit consists of a copper sleeve that encloses the wires after being looped around a thimble. The sleeve is then crimped to secure the eye. Cable clamps consist of two parts: the saddle and the U-bolt. The saddle lies against the standing portion of wire after it has formed the loop around a thimble. The U-bolt then fits into openings in the saddle and is tightened to secure the loop. Be sure to use three cable clamps and tighten them securely.

The swage system can also be used to provide eyes at the ends of standing rigging. The eye is manufactured at the end of a hollow tube that fits over the end of the wire. It is machine-squeezed onto the wire under such pressure that it conforms to the wire and becomes a secure fit. These look nice, but it can be difficult to determine how strong the union really is since the joint is covered.

Norseman, Sta-Lok, and CastLok terminals all separate the outer individual strands of wire from the wire's inner core. A socket slides over the wire end, with threads facing the end. An inner component is then placed at the end of the inner core of the wire, with the outer wires overlapping. A terminal component, with the eye manufactured-in and threads to match the socket, slides over the inner cone and screws into the socket. When these are screwed together tightly, the terminal squeezes the outer wires down onto the inner cone to form a strong end fitting. These systems have an advantage in that they may be disassembled and inspected to ensure a strong fitting.

No matter whether you use wire or rods as standing rigging, a boat offshore should always have one length of replacement wire aboard in case of failure. This wire should be as long as the longest stay on the boat. One end should have the eye in place with the other end left bare, but wrapped in protective tape. In the past I've carried a supply of cable clamps and thimbles in case of rig failure, but I am now considering switching to the Norseman system. Either way, make sure you have a plan and the gear necessary to place an eye at the end of your wire when at sea.

I recently replaced my boom topping lift with Technora line. Technora is a synthetic material that is light yet exceedingly strong. This has now become my replacement for damaged stays or shrouds, allowing me to remove the cumbersome length of wire from the boat.

Don't forget that if you've stocked spare wire, you may need to cut it, so another piece of indispensable offshore gear is a pair of hefty bolt cutters—a hacksaw just isn't the tool to cut rigging. In the event of dismasting, the cutters also may be crucial to remove a portion of the rig that threatens to hole the hull.

The boom

The boom should be your next point of examination. Case in point: At around 0430 one windswept early morning a few years back, we were sailing off Prince Edward Island in the Bay of St. Lawrence and I had just settled into my bunk after the midnight watch. I was roused by calls from the deck for help. After stumbling up the companionway, I saw the boom swinging crazily. It took me a while to get my bearings, but finally I realized that the boom was completely loose forward, flailing at the mast freely while tethered aft by the mainsheet. Each wave and roll caused the boom to careen off the mast with a crash, then continue its arc, returning to clank off the mast again on its return trip.

I cranked on the vang to diminish the motion, then brought the yacht into the wind and began fisting down the main. After a while, the sail was piled on the starboard side of the boom and the dangerous escapades of the spar were controlled. The bolt was later found in a winch handle pocket on the mast, but the nut probably went swimming. This should have been checked more carefully before we left the dock, but some lessons are destined to be learned the hard way—I never miss anything like that now, believe me.

The boom is attached to the mast by a large pin or bolt fitted through the boom end cap and through the mast fitting; the bolt/pin should fit precisely through its hole in the end cap. There should be washers on either side of the boom fitting and a bolt securely holding the boom in place. Once you've determined that the bolt is not bent, check all parts for corrosion, and make absolutely sure the nut is securely tightened. It's wise to have a cotter pin on this crucial connection between mast and boom fittings.

Check the mast and boom fittings for cracks, breaks and loose rivets, and replace any damaged parts. If corrosion was the problem, be sure to place a nonconductive interstice between the fitting and the boom or mast. Given the saltiness of the environment, corrosion is a nemesis of your fixtures. Aluminum is not particularly corrosive, but most metal hardware on spars and even fasteners (rivets, setscrews, etc.) is far more noble. Even the aluminum or aluminum alloy rivets holding hardware to the boom or mast are prone to corrosion if they're in contact with metals, like stainless steel or bronze, that are farther up on the galvanic scale. Note that anything affixed to an aluminum spar (mast or boom) made of a metal other than aluminum should be insulated from the spar with a nonconductive substance like wood, nylon or plastic. You can also apply zinc chromate paste between the fixture and spar to protect against galvanic action, much like sacrificial zinc anodes.

Any boom attachment found to be loose or corroded needs to be removed, cleaned with acetone, and replaced with a thought to corrosion prevention. Of particular interest are the bails for the vang and mainsheet. Both are subject to heavy loads, and, if weakened by corrosion, are apt to let loose.

Next examine the aft boom cap, or fitting, with its sheaves and positions for line attachments. Check that the sheaves, often plastic, have not been damaged from reefing lines jumping out

and being tightened against the sides of the sheaves. The sheave pin also may be bent, so replace it if necessary. Repair damaged sheaves by taking them out with the center pin, keeping in mind that you may need to remove the boom end cap. Watch for telltale twigs or grass poking out from the boom end—sure signs of bird nesting activity that should be cleaned out before it blows all over the cockpit while you're sailing.

The mast

Begin your examination of the mast directly at the base. Establish how the mast is stepped first, and examine the point where the spar is made fast, whether that's on deck or down below. The mast base is a prime area for corrosion, no matter where it's stepped—on deck the mast is exposed to salt water, and below the bilge is often a damp environment with little air circulation.

Check the mast base bolts for looseness or corrosion. If they're loose, you'll need to remove, clean and tighten them. All corroded bolts should be removed and cleaned, but at any sign of weakness they should be replaced, as the mast base connection must be strong. Any damage to the deck surrounding the mast will weaken it, leading to mast movement, strain on the standing rigging and possible collapse.

Inspect wiring that exits from the mast base and ensure that wires are clean and show no signs of wear, that no bare wires are exposed, and that connections are sound, with wires leading to the circuit breakers. In the case of deck-stepped masts, the wires emerge either into a box mounted to the overhead, or below in the bilge area, where the compression post rests.

The mast boot secures the mast at the deck to prevent water leakage below. The boot is prone to damage from physical abuse of lines and feet, and from UV damage to the material itself. I have stopped leaking past the mast boot by applying silicone beneath the boot and then securing a hose clamp at the top to improve the seal, but a cracked or torn boot should simply be replaced. At most chandleries you can find mast boot tape, a self-sealing product that waterproofs the boot and resists UV damage, but ever-reliable duct tape is effective for short-term control of leaks at the mast base.

The mast should be firmly positioned, with no side-to-side or fore-and-aft movement where it passes through the deck. If you notice movement, remove the boot and check the mast partners, or chocks, that wedge the mast into position. Replace any missing or damaged chocks, and reposition those that may have shifted during re-stepping of the mast or excessive motion of the spar. Position the mast correctly so the motion is controlled—if the stays and shrouds remain in place during the repair, the mast should be correctly positioned.

I first check the mast for proper lateral positioning after determining that the shrouds and stays are seaworthy. The easiest way is to use the main halyard and measure the distance from the masthead to the same point on the beam port and starboard, and then compare the two measurements.

Different measurements indicate that the spar is not aligned vertically and an adjustment is necessary to properly present the sails to the wind. Remember that the upper shrouds control the top section of the mast and the lowers control the middle. Adjust the uppers first to bring the mast top into alignment.

For example, if there is a four-inch difference in the measurements, shorten the long side by two inches and lengthen the short side by two inches by adjusting the shroud turnbuckles. In other words, halve the distance of the measurement difference and apply it to the upper shrouds to center the mast. After the adjustment, repeat the measuring process to assure the stick is straight. When you're satisfied that everything is balanced, replace the cotter pins into the turnbuckles and cover them with sail tape.

If you have a tuning gauge—an instrument that determines the degree of tightness of the shrouds—use it before starting the shroud adjustments. If a tuning gauge is not available, "measure" the shrouds by hand to get an idea of how taut they are. Remove the retaining cotter pins from the turnbuckles at the shroud bases, and then secure one portion of the turnbuckle with a wrench while using a screwdriver to loosen the shroud on the side that the spar curves. For example, if the mid-mast bends to starboard by about three inches, loosen the shroud on the starboard side.

It's important to count the number of turns you make as the turnbuckle is loosened. If you make two turns of the turnbuckle on the starboard side, then tighten the port turnbuckle two turns. Check the mast groove alignment to find how much two turns straightened the mast. Continue with this method, loosening one side and tightening the other, until the mast is perfectly straight. Now simply replace the cotter pins, slap some sail tape over the turnbuckle to hide the pins and call the job done. Remember, tightening of the lowers produces less fore-and-aft and lateral bend in the mast, resulting in a fuller mainsail. But don't over-tighten the shrouds; adjust them only enough to straighten the spar, unless a fuller main is desired. Fine-tune the adjustments while sailing, as you observe the degree of laxity in the leeward shrouds.

A lot of action takes place at the mast base. Lines from the mast often exit at the base and pass through turning blocks, where they're directed aft toward line organizers near the cockpit. These will be absent if the lines are not led aft. Check the blocks' attachments to the deck and examine the sheaves; they should turn freely and lead the lines fairly, usually toward deck organizers or line clutches.

Now move your assessment of the mast from the base to the boom. Be aware that wherever a mast has been welded, the aluminum spar is weakened due to the heat of the welding process. Inspect any welded area of the mast for stress cracking or elongation of an opening for a tang fitting or cutout. The corners of cutouts should be rounded—not squared—because cutouts (rectangular holes in the mast) with squared corners are prone to cracking from the corners.

Examine these cutouts carefully for small cracks extending from the corners. If there's enough room, they can be repaired by screwing or riveting an aluminum patch over the crack and affixing it solidly on both sides. For an on-the-water fix, tighten a large hose clamp around the mast directly over the cracked area—it won't look pretty, but it will effectively bolster the spar and prevent elongation of the crack.

A crack may also be controlled by drilling the starter hole for a self-tapping screw at the end of the crack, then inserting the screw into the hole. The crack will stop once it encounters the screw.

Going aloft

You'll need to ascend the mast for examination of structures aloft. A bosun's chair is used for this job and there are a number of readymade chairs and harnesses made specifically for climbing the mast.

When seated in the chair, you should fit snugly and comfortably. Whenever ascending the mast, you'll need to take some tools for making minor repairs and adjustments. I like to take a sailing knife, sail tape, an adjustable wrench, electrical tester, pliers, flat head and Phillips screwdrivers, Teflon spray, a line for lowering should you need anything else from below, and a camera, since the view is usually worth capturing.

It's my experience that yacht owners appreciate photos of their yachts from the masthead and I provide them on deliveries whenever possible. At sea, though, it's often only from the first spreaders. You may take any other items that you can carry, but be sure that they're all safely "stowed"—that you know where they are and can reach them easily. No one on deck should stand directly below the person aloft since falling items can be deadly.

I usually use a jib halyard as my hoist and, as a precaution, tie the halyard to a ring on the chair in addition to attaching it to the shackle. I also attach another jib or spinnaker halyard to the chair and have a mate keep it snug as I'm hoisted. The primary hoist halyard should be taken to a substantial deck winch, with the end properly tailed and the halyard clutch closed. There's no problem using the main halyard as a hoist, but I find it more convenient to use a jib, since there are other halyards in front of the mast to use as a safety line. Do not use the topping lift since it's usually smaller.

Spreaders

Proceeding up the mast, check every mast appendage as you go, beginning with the lower spreaders since this area of the mast is seen as a weak link in the spar. The middle section of the mast, especially at the spreaders, is subject to excess sideways movement with loose shrouds, bending with high backstay or runner tension, and pressure on the spreaders from the mainsail when eased for downwind sailing. If the mast breaks, it's usually near the lower spreaders or shroud tangs. For this reason, it's wise to have a planned jury-rig should the mast break in this area, with the upper portions of the

stick gone, leaving only the mast from the base to just above the lower shrouds.

The spreaders are attached rigidly, usually with pins that hold them into the spreader base, or socket, which is riveted or welded into the mast. They aren't designed to withstand a great deal of motion, which stresses the spreader bases where they're attached to the spar. Excess motion may cause the rivets to loosen or pull out and a portion of the spar, usually at the back of the socket, to bend inward.

Spreaders are often aerodynamically designed, like an airfoil, to provide strength in the fore-and-aft directions, but not vertically. Spreaders are often a bit higher at the tips than they are at the mast connection. The tips should never be lower. Any evidence that the spreader body is bent is reason for replacement, since the spreader will be substantially weakened.

Remember, if a spreader goes, the mast is not far behind unless you tack immediately to relieve the pressure on that side and rig a halyard to the beam to take the load. Replacement spreaders should come from the original manufacturer, since they must match the layout of the boat and the spreader bases just as the originals did. Check the outboard end of the spreaders, where grooves or openings for the shrouds are found, and check the tips for cracks. It's wise to cap the spreader tips to protect the jib during tacks and upwind trimming.

Lights

Just past the lower spreaders you should find the steaming light, deck light and spreader lights. Check them for cracked or missing covers that may have been damaged by slack halyards or by the jib or its sheets during tacks. Light covers must be secure to prevent water from corroding the electrical connections inside. Have someone turn the lights on and check that they work. If a light fails to go on, check the bulb first and, if intact, remove the bulb to check the socket for signs of corrosion. If corroded, have the light switch turned off below then scrape the contact points with a knife blade, replace the bulb and test it again.

If the bulb still fails to operate, check the socket with an electrical tester. If juice is flowing, check the bulb with the ohmmeter. If the reading is high, replace the bulb. If there's no electrical current, check the connections at the mast base, then follow the wire back to the breaker panel and the circuit breaker itself. By far the most frequent causes of mast light failure are burned out bulbs, corrosion at the light socket, and wiring problems at the mast base where wires have parted at their connections or corroded. Occasionally, wires are crushed if the mast has been recently re-stepped and the wires were trapped as the spar came down.

Radar

Now check the radar scanner if one is fixed to the mast on a pedestal. Make sure it's bolted firmly to the platform, with unobstructed drainage for rainwater. Most mast-mounted radomes have a scanner guard—a stainless steel ring that girds and protects the scanner. How the scanner platform is secured to the mast varies per make and model of scanner, but whatever the method, inspect the attachment now, and make sure all fasteners are tight.

A cable extends up through the mast and connects to the scanner. Check the cable for chafe.

Inspect the spinnaker topping lift as it emerges from the mast. If there's a cutout, check for cracking at its corners. The topping lift should be over the sheave, which should spin freely. If a baby stay is rigged, check its tang and the upper eye of the stay.

Rig fatigue

Most experienced yachtsmen agree that rig failure can usually be traced to wear on the spar or its components. This is known as fatigue cycles, wherein damage is caused by repeated strain over time. This is usually due to poor articulation between components, causing excess friction or restricting motion entirely. Prime examples of the fatigue cycle occur at the shroud fittings on the mast—usually the pin and eye and the stem ball. The pin and eye is actually a toggle arrangement, bolted or riveted to the spar on one end, engaging the shroud with a clevis pin at the other. The toggle and clevis pin combination is an acceptable way to diminish the fatiguing effects of motion.

Stem ball systems resemble our own shoulder joints. A ball at the terminal shroud fitting is captured within the socket of the mast fitting that, in theory, affords the shroud adequate freedom of movement. But when the shroud is snugged into position, enough pull is applied to the ball that considerable friction occurs within the socket, creating fatigue over time.

As the inspection proceeds up the mast, pay attention to these methods of receiving shrouds and stays, with an idea of what to look for in the way of fatigue. Inspect all mast tangs, welded terminals, storm trysail track, spinnaker track (if present) and additional spreaders, noting problems or making repairs along the way.

As you continue up to the masthead, have the person grinding the winch stop at a point where you're comfortable, and be sure that the halyard is properly stopped at the clutch and the bitter end of the halyard cleated. Now check the upper shroud tangs and make sure that they are in correct vertical alignment and receive the shrouds fairly. Check that welds in the area have not cracked.

Head box

Next focus on the head box—the structure that fits over the masthead into a cutout—and is either welded or bolted into position. There's a lot going on at the head box, reflected by the presence of sheaves for various halyards, positions to fix radio antennae, various instruments such as the Windex and wind speed/direction indicators, possibly a lightning rod, static dissipater and lights of different configurations. Welded attachment points for backstay, forestay and cap shroud tangs

make this an important spot in your inspection.

Observe the sheaves and the halyards that pass over them, making sure no halyard has jumped its sheave. Check for salt crystallization that can impair movement of the sheaves. If such impediment is found, take the sheaves out for proper cleaning by removing the capping plate of the head box, or by loosening cotter pins holding the sheave axles in place, and driving the pin out with a center punch and hammer.

Removing the cap plate sounds easy but the screws are often tight and corroded, making them difficult to break loose, so use a box wrench that won't slip off when you apply pressure. You may also need to use a penetrating spray lubricant. Once the cap is off, be very careful in lifting out the sheave. Sheaves are easy to drop down the mast, so pass a looped line over them before loosening. Clean the sheaves with soap and water and be sure the pins aren't bent. Lubricate with Teflon spray or penetrating oil, and set the sheave back into position.

Check for solid connections of all masthead gear. Turn on all lights and examine as you did the deck and steaming lights. If an anemometer is installed, spin the rotors and have a partner below watch the readouts. Observe that the component rotates freely according to wind direction, and that the cups spin properly. Spider webs are a common hindrance to this gear or the Windex, but there are more unusual obstructions to instrumentation, as in Photo 3-2.

PHOTO 3-2
Home sweet home. The reading light is on in the penthouse suite.

Now's the time to inspect the forestay and foil of the roller reefing system. Be as thorough as possible once you're hoisted—anything that can't be fixed on the spot should be listed for repair before leaving the dock. If you need a spare halyard feeder line, this is a good time to rig it, since you're aloft and there's help on deck.

Once you're ready to descend, alert the crew and free yourself from any entanglements with the uppers. The crew should then uncleat the halyard, open the clutch, and, with at least three wraps still around the winch, feed the line smoothly as you descend.

As you're lowered down the mast, check the mainsail track along the way. If it's soiled with salt crystals or spider webs clean it with a damp rag. This is also a good time to spray the entire length of track with Teflon.

Wood spars

I've discussed anodized aluminum spars to this point because they're so predominant in sailboats headed offshore. Ease of maintenance has made them the overwhelming favorite of yachtsmen over labor-intensive wood spars that can be heavily damaged by rot. Water is apt to find an entry point anywhere on the spar where the wood is punctured.

To repair a wood mast, remove any loose gear along with all rotted wood. Cut an area, similar to a mortise, into the spar and deepen any existing screw holes in order to better secure the gear. Next, fill the mortise and screw holes with epoxy. As the epoxy hardens, clean the screws with acetone. Then place the hardware in position, insert the screws and secure into place.

Mast bases, especially those that are keel-stepped in the bilge area, are prime sites for rot. Inspect the mast base carefully for signs of degradation and be certain that it is securely fastened. At the masthead, water seeks openings through head boxes and will damage the top of a wooden mast. Some older designs have only caps to protect the masthead, and all attachments are made below that level—not a bad idea when you think about it. As always, check every attachment for evidence of rot and loosening.

Canvas

We conclude this part of the inspection with the yacht canvas, including dodger, bimini, lee cloths, sail covers, stack pack, trampoline and canopies. A multihull's trampoline is an integral part of the deck and should be inspected as such. Any damage to the material requires patching or replacement. Trampolines are usually secured with line laced through the edges, alternating with adjacent fittings on the deck, like shoelaces. Inspect the trampoline and the "lacing"

in these areas. Weakness usually develops at the turns of the line, and may be difficult to detect.

Inspect sail covers to determine how well they protect the underlying sail. Torn or rotted sail covers may indicate problems, since the sail may have been unduly exposed to the elements. Check the dodger and bimini for weakness or tears, and tighten the straps to prevent the end clips from banging on the deck. Inspect the underlying stainless steel skeleton for solid attachments, strength and stability. Make sure you know how to lower these structures in preparation for heavy winds since they create windage and can easily become flotsam. You should be able to remove the canvas quickly while leaving and securing the stainless steel structure to the deck.

Stack packs are attached to the boom and are usually outfitted with lazy jacks or another guidance system for the mainsail. Exposure to the elements causes wear, so all lines must be periodically replaced. If fiberglass rods are integrated into the pack, check the ends for punctures of the canvas at the points of pressure.

Any tears in the stack pack fabric should be patched, and any lines associated with the damage should be replaced. Note also that topping lifts near the mast tend to make a lot of noise when the wind pipes up, and can keep you awake at night. Tightening these lines usually won't stop the slatting—in order to do that, you'll need to snug the lines away from the mast using bungee cords.

Mainsail guidance systems are invaluable, especially on larger boats where the boom is high enough to cause difficulty in bringing the main down and flaking it. But I'm opposed to any system that requires lines to be extended through holes in the sail itself. These inevitably cause localized wear and can get in the way when reefing. If you use this type of system, remove the lines from the mainsail and either go without the aid of mainsail guidance or install something new. Check the attachment points of the mainsail guidance system lines for tears or stretched fabric. Make sure the topping lifts are intact and show no defects, especially at the end knots or eyes.

Once all items in this section have been inspected, complete the checklist and make notes before proceeding.

A rigging spare parts list should include:
▪ Sail slides
▪ Hanks, if appropriate
▪ Grommet kit
▪ Turnbuckles
▪ Toggles
▪ Cotter pins
▪ Clevis pins
▪ Shackles
▪ Chain or straps to lengthen standing rigging
▪ Cable clamps, Nicopress unit, Sta-Lok or other system for fabricating terminal eyes
▪ One length of rigging wire equal in length to the longest stay on board
▪ Wire cutters sturdy enough to cut all rigging on board
▪ Electrician's snake wire (reefing line replacement)

CHAPTER 4

GROUND TACKLE

Ground tackle is not especially important to a boat while it's at sea. In fact, I always remove anchors from the bow so they can't be swept away or, worse, loosened from the stem head and left to dangle over the side. I stow them low in the anchor well, and they don't come out again until landfall is near.

However, any boat inspection will include a thorough examination of the boat's anchoring gear. You should also consider whether the anchor and rode sizes are appropriate for your destination as well as points along the way that may become havens during bad weather. I've encouraged boat owners to upgrade their primary ground tackle before heading offshore and have, on occasion, borrowed anchors with better rodes in case the existing ground tackle proved inadequate. A cruising vessel should always have ground tackle that can handle virtually any anchoring situation. There is no peace quite so rewarding, at midnight when the wind pipes up, as that gained by confidence in your ground tackle.

HARDWARE

Inspection of the ground tackle should include all hardware items used with the anchors and rodes. Thimbles, shackles and swivels connect anchors to anchor lines and are crucial components of the overall system. This hardware is often the weak link in anchor systems, so be alert to problems with this gear. Ground tackle hardware must be at least as strong as the anchor line to which it's attached. Problems can arise if the components are made of different metals, accelerating corrosion. Neglect is the other common problem.

I often find it necessary to replace shackles due to pitting of the metal caused by heavy corrosion. The pin is also subject to great physical wear during anchoring and should be secured with stainless steel wire to prevent turning and disengagement. It's also wise to apply waterproof grease or silicone to the threads of shackle pins to protect them from corrosion.

Check eye splices in the anchor line for evidence of chafe, physical damage, or rust. Nylon line that's stained by rust from a thimble may be weakened and you may need to splice in a new eye. Thimbles are usually constructed of galvanized metal or stainless steel, but some may be composed of a bronze alloy or plastic. Watch for corrosion if the thimble is composed of metal that differs from the swivel or shackle to which it connects.

You'll want to make sure that the thimble is securely placed within the eye of the splice. If the thimble isn't properly seated, it may slip out when the line becomes taut or twists, leading to accelerated chafe of the anchor line. Mismatched eyes and thimbles or chafing of the eye can lead to incorrect seating of the thimble. If the line around the eye is chafed, a new eye should be spliced around the thimble.

The motions of swivels can be hindered by corrosion and physical damage from line pressure. If a swivel has seized up, it may be possible to free it by applying penetrating lubricant and twisting the two ends in opposite directions. If the swivel frees, remove debris from the components with gentle wet sanding. If the swivel remains frozen or the working surfaces are pitted and damaged, you're better off replacing it. If you find any weakness in anchor hardware, I recommend replacement.

ANCHORS

Anchors are sturdy pieces of equipment and can withstand incredible loads. To date I have never seen an anchor so damaged or corroded that I thought it unsuitable for use, but you should still examine the flukes and shanks for bending or cracking that has exposed the metal to corrosion and rust. It's a mistake to assume any component is going to work as it should—it's important that your inspection remain thorough.

There will always be great debate as to the best anchor for any given boat, but it usually comes down to the skipper's personal preference as well as what type of environment the boat typically sails in. When selecting an anchor, you also need to consider its size and holding power. A vessel previously used for cruising and gunkholing in the Chesapeake Bay may have anchors too small for offshore destinations with deeper anchorages or more questionable holding ground. Anchor manufacturers publish tables correlating boat size and windage to the

Horizontal Loads Table			
Wind speed (knots) vs. Boat length (feet)			
	15 kts	30 kts	42 kts	60 kts
---	---	---	---	---
20ft	90 lbs	360	720	1,440
25ft	125	490	980	1,960
30ft	175	700	1,400	2,800
35ft	225	900	1,800	3,600
40ft	300	1,200	2,400	4,800
50ft	400	1,600	3,200	6,400
60ft	500	2,000	4,000	8,000
70ft	675	2,700	5,400	10,800

TABLE 4-1
Use the "Horizontal Loads Table" above to determine the holding power requirements for different wind speeds. NOTE: This table assumes boats of average beam and windage. If your boat has above average beam or windage, refer to loads for the next larger size boat. *Courtesy of Fortress Anchors.*

Wind speed (knots) vs. Boat length (meters)				
	15 kts	**30 kts**	**42 kts**	**60 kts**
6m	41 kgs	163	327	653
8m	57	222	445	889
9m	79	318	635	1,270
11m	102	408	816	1,633
12m	136	544	1,089	2,177
15m	181	726	1,452	2,903
18m	227	907	1,814	3,629
21m	306	1,225	2,449	4,899

appropriate anchor. These guidelines should be considered the minimum sizes of anchors and rodes in boats intended to cruise offshore.

Rodes

The possibility of being anchored in high winds, deep water or in swell raises the standards of the anchor lines. It's never a mistake to be one size over the suggested diameter or length of line.

There are three types of anchor rodes: nylon, chain and a combination of nylon with chain at the anchor end. Nylon is particularly suited to anchor rodes because of its great strength and ability to stretch. The holding power of nylon anchor lines is enhanced by the addition of chain between the nylon and the anchor. The chain's weight creates a more horizontal pull on the anchor, allowing the shaft and flukes to remain in alignment with the bottom. In addition, chain is better able to withstand the abrasive effects of the bottom, should the boat drag the line over rock, debris or coral.

Use a short length of chain and three-strand nylon line. The nylon is very elastic and greatly reduces shock loads on your boat and its anchoring hardware. If you regularly anchor in 25 feet (7.6 meters) of water or less, use 6 feet (2 meters) of chain. For greater depths, use 6 feet for every 25 feet of water depth, i.e. use 24 feet (7 meters) of chain if you regularly anchor in 100 feet (30 meters) of water.

The chain must be of galvanized metal and attached to the thimble and eye splice of the rode with its own shackle. All pins should be stainless steel wired. The chain is attached to the anchor ring by a swivel and shackle. All-chain rode is seen most often on large heavy boats and those that anchor in rock or deep anchorages. Chain doesn't stretch like nylon and can cause shock loads to the boat in high winds or seas. Chain will also add weight to the bow—another consideration for the sailor concerned with making good way.

A snubber (Figure 4-1), composed of a length of nylon anchor line with a line compensator, is secured to the primary chain line by a hook or rolling hitch, led back through chocks at the bow and tied to a strong cleat, samson post, the mast, or the windlass. Use the windlass as a

FIGURE 4-1

The anchor snubber is essential when using all-chain rodes. The nylon snubber line and line compensator alleviates shock loading to the anchor chain.

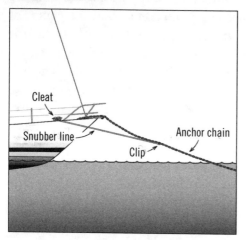

give serious thought to deploying another anchor.

Chain at the working end should be from 15 feet, ¼-inch diameter galvanized for 25- to 35-footers, 20 feet of ⁵⁄₁₆-inch for boats to 48 feet, and at least 20 feet of ⅜-inch for those up to 60 feet. All-chain rodes are much heavier than chain-nylon combos, so they require shorter lengths of rode.

Before completing your inspection of the anchor lines, don't forget to check the bitter end. If it isn't secure, even the best anchor won't hold! The attachment usually involves another eye splice, thimble, and shackle. These components should be examined closely and the shackle must be secured to something very sturdy that cannot break away—usually an eyebolt in the anchor well, but anything extremely solid will work. Note that everything in the anchor well is frequently exposed to seawater, so corrosion is common. Make it a habit to rinse all gear in the anchor well with fresh water after each exposure to seawater. When seawater dries, salt crystals are left behind to form a fine filmy coating—especially on ground tackle.

last resort—it's an expensive piece of equipment bolted to the deck. The other locations pose less risk of damage. Shock loads are transmitted to the snubber, which will stretch to alleviate the load on the boat.

An anchor rode with proper length and diameter will offer the most secure hold, and most anchor manufacturers or marine hardware stores have charts to assist your calculations. Nylon rode for a 25- to 35-foot boat should be at least ½-inch in diameter and 200 feet long. Boats to 48 feet need at least 250 feet of ⅝-inch rode. The nylon for boats to 60 feet in length should be ¾-inch or more and at least 300 feet long. Table 4-1 demonstrates that as the wind speed doubles, the holding requirement quadruples. Most working anchors should be dependable in up to 40 knots of wind, but, in conditions even approaching that, I'd

Rollers

Examine the bow roller and make sure it's sturdy and that it spins. It must be able to withstand the pressure of the anchor line as it pulls up an anchor dug deeply into the bottom—a load that increases markedly when a wave swell lifts the bow. Check the bolts holding the bow roller in place. On boats equipped with a windlass, the bow rollers should be configured to guide the anchor line directly to the windlass gypsy. This ensures a fair engagement of the line onto the gypsy and prevents the rode from scraping the deck.

The bow rollers' axles are particularly prone to corrosion due to their exposure to sun, salt water and dust. Check that the rollers spin freely when the anchor line is hauled up. A bow roller that doesn't spin will disintegrate with one hoisting of a chain anchor. Make sure the roller is not seized into a stationary position by salt accumulation and corrosion. Replacement wheels are available at marine stores and should be the same size, in terms of diameter, width, and size of the central opening, so that they fit precisely. Remove the old wheels by unscrewing the nut that secures the axle bolt. Apply a small amount of grease to the bolt and place the new wheel into position. Be sure to tighten the nut; remember that nylon nuts offer the most secure hold. After inspecting the anchors, their connecting hardware and anchor lines, turn your attention to the windlass.

WINDLASSES

Consider past maintenance, its mounting to the deck or in the anchor well, the electrical circuitry and the hydraulics of the windlass. No matter the specs, all windlasses are exposed to similar conditions and share many common internal components. Windlasses are located in an area of the boat prone to saltwater spray and are often mounted on deck where they receive heavy UV exposure. They're also subject to damage from tremendous shock loads, and will bounce around a lot. Inspect the windlass for external corrosion. If external damage is discovered, it is likely that internal damage has also occurred. If you find salt water in the gearbox, drain it and apply lubricant. Windlasses should be shielded from the sun and periodically flushed with fresh water. Inspect the gearbox annually.

The internal components of most windlasses are lubricated with grease or oil but, if a windlass sits idle, the lubricant can settle and harden, leading to rusting or seizure. Windlasses should be turned over periodically to ensure that they're evenly lubricated.

The windlass should be secured to a very rigid component of the deck or anchor well, and the site of attachment must be capable of sustaining the same loads as the windlass itself. This attachment is often damaged by snubbing loads applied to the windlass by the (usually all-chain) anchor rode or by use of the windlass to draw the boat up to the anchor site and break it loose from the bottom. Check that the windlass base is secure, the windlass is positioned correctly relative to the anchor rode, and that bolts and underpinnings are undamaged.

With continued use, any cracking of the deck will worsen and allow water beneath the windlass where it can damage the electrical wiring. Any such damage would require that the windlass be removed and the deck repaired. In that instance, it would be wise to add reinforcement beneath the windlass.

Repairing windlass deck damage: On a delivery boat just out of charter in the Caribbean—where sailors may not maintain boat hardware as its owner would—I found the windlass mounted to the deck adjacent to the anchor well. Excess loading had cracked the deck below the windlass and my fix was to glass-in a section of Wolmanized 2 x 6 wood plank beneath the windlass, spanning the anchor well. Any rigid material would work, but Wolmanized wood is a good choice because it's waterproof and easy to work with. The ends of the plank were cut at an angle to match that of the hull, then securely glassed to the sides of the hull, distributing the load and reinforcing the deck. Prior to glassing in the wood, the sections of hull adjacent to the plank ends were sanded and cleaned with acetone to improve adherence with the fiberglass. During the repair, the plank was supported by shoring from the floor until the fiberglass set.

Such a repair begins with laying mat on the underside of the wood, eight inches from the end and extending toward the hull/wood junction, and down the hull another eight inches. Continue on the sides and top of the wood, so that both ends are completely covered with mat that extends onto the hull.

Coat the fiberglass cloth with epoxy resin, then place strips over the mat and onto the hull. Allow to dry. Continue the process, one mat and one cloth, until five layers of mat and cloth have been laid down, each layer extending a bit further to make a smooth finish. Once the final layer is dry, sand the ends and sides, then finish with a coat of marine paint.

I forced the crack in the deck open from beneath and injected epoxy resin into the gap. Relaxing the upward force allowed the deck sections to settle back into position, leaving the crack virtually invisible. I repositioned the windlass, reseated it on a gasket, and secured it in place with new stainless steel bolts through the deck, plank, and an aluminum backing plate.

Manual windlasses

There are three types of windlasses: manual, electric and hydraulic. Manual windlasses are able to hoist heavy anchors by using the same mechanical advantage as winches. They convert the back-and-forth motion of the lever handle into unidirectional spin of the drum or gypsy. The ratchet action allows the anchor line to move in only one direction, so it can't run backwards. Most manual windlasses, like line winches, are dual speed in operation.

Inspect a manual windlass for corrosion; then release the anchor so the line runs out a few feet. Insert the handle and crank the windlass to retrieve the anchor. The action should be smooth, with the line moving only in a forward direction. Failure of a manual windlass indicates internal trouble. Corrosion can cause a windlass to seize, especially if it's been left idle and never cleaned of salt. Exterior corrosion is a frequent indicator of interior corrosion, and if the windlass fails to operate it should be dismantled and examined.

Unscrew the retaining bolts and remove the rope drum and gypsy. Check the interior for broken shafts or gears, and check that all shafts fit securely into bushings in the housing. Carefully remove the main shaft and its gears. Check all gears for broken or abraded teeth, check the shafts for irregularities, and see that the gears fit onto their shafts without play. Replace all broken or corroded gears, shafts, bushings or chain pawls.

Electric windlasses

Manual windlasses are typically found on small- to medium-sized boats with light anchors. Many intermediate to larger craft are fitted with windlasses driven by electric motors. Electric windlasses have the same gearing and are available in horizontal or vertical models, just like manual windlasses, but they differ primarily in the addition of the motor and the wiring circuitry that accompanies it.

Electric motors are not self-cooling and are not designed to function for long periods of time, especially under load. Your boat should always be motored toward the anchor, with the windlass taking in only slack rode. Pulling the boat to the anchor with the windlass not only causes undue strain on its junction with the deck, but can trip the circuit breaker, burn out the motor and lead to seizure of the armature inside the motor's field coil.

The electrical connections to the windlass are vital to its operation. The wiring must be properly installed, with adequately sized cables to prevent excessive voltage drop. In addition to the normal battery selector and isolation switch, wiring should include a circuit breaker or fuse located near the battery to provide overload protection. Cables leave the positive and negative bus bars and proceed toward the windlass, usually entering a solenoid that interrupts the current until activated by a remote or foot pedal. I recommend that this circuit from the foot pedal or remote have its own isolation switch, which is kept "off" whenever the windlass is not in use, preventing inadvertent activation. It can be mounted on the pedestal (with the risk of its electromagnetic field causing compass deviation) or at the main circuit breaker panel.

Our inspection of the windlass' electrical system begins with the windlass itself. Check for corrosion or damage to wires as they enter the windlass. Trace the wires and focus on each connection, making sure the wiring is fixed in place along its entire route, with no wires dangling where they could be snagged. Somewhere near the windlass you'll find an enclosed junction box where connections are made. Even though this structure is sealed, condensation can produce moisture inside. Electrical connections are prone to corrosion, so any loose or corroded connections should be cleaned, tightened, and sprayed with protective sealant. Ensure that any gear stowed near the wiring or junction box poses no danger. Be sure that the current is off while any repair or maintenance is done and don't ever handle wires that may be hot.

Our inspection of the windlass system is simply to ensure that it works—not that it's pretty. Begin by starting the engine—this should be standard procedure whenever using the windlass. Check the battery selection switch, placing it in the "on" position, and if a separate circuit breaker is used, be sure it's closed. If a toggle switch controls the foot pedal or remote, switch it on as well. Our test of the windlass needs only demonstrate that the motor works on demand. If the windlass is unidirectional—up only—either remove the rode from the gypsy and run the windlass, or lower the anchor 10 feet or so and run the windlass to bring the anchor back up. On bidirectional windlasses, assess the operation of the windlass in both directions.

Failure of an electric windlass to operate is usually the result of an electrical problem. Since wiring at the anchor end is subject to more corrosion and physical damage, it's wise to start your search there. Test the current at the foot switches first. Move to the solenoid and follow the wiring toward the battery isolation switch.

When you find the component that's not receiving current, the problem can be isolated upstream. Test each point to determine which one is receiving current but not passing it along. That's the component that must be replaced. If the circuit breaker trips whenever the battery switch is turned on, there's a short in the circuit. Once again, check the wiring from fore to aft looking for damaged switches, bare wires, disconnected wires, or wires in contact with metal components. Also check that the anchor isn't pulled too tightly against the bow roller, exerting excess line pressure on the windlass. Failure to detect any cause of the problem leads to the likelihood that the windlass motor is burned out. In that case, open the windlass and inspect the internal gearing mechanisms as well as the motor's field windings, commutator, armature windings and brushes. Tests with an ohmmeter may reveal a short circuit or areas of increased resistance, usually from internal corrosion. You may find components caked with corrosion, worn by usage, filled with carbon deposits, or covered with burn marks. Once you isolate the damaged component, consult a windlass manufacturer to discuss whether the system should be repaired or replaced.

Hydraulic windlasses

Hydraulic winch systems consist of a pump that creates high pressure in lines containing hydraulic fluid, which supply a hydraulic motor in the windlass and give it power. Reversing the direction of hydraulic fluid flow reverses the direction of the windlass action. Like the others, hydraulic windlasses are subject to corrosion, UV damage, and mechanical shock loading that can break shafts or gears. They can also be damaged by leaking hydraulic lines, dirt or other foreign material within pumps or motors, and condensation leading to internal corrosion.

By far the most common cause of hydraulic failure is leakage of fluid.

Your inspection should include a thorough check of hydraulic lines, motors and pumps for the telltale presence of leaked fluid. Leaks may be repaired by simply tightening the couplings or, if necessary, replacing a line or pump. After the leak has been repaired, replace the hydraulic fluid to bring it back to full pressure. Inspect all electrical circuitry, internal shafts, gears, and pawls.

Any problems with the ground tackle should be noted on the checklist.

Ground tackle
▪ Anchors
▪ Thimbles
▪ Shackles
▪ Swivels
▪ Rodes
▪ Bitter ends
▪ Snubber
▪ Anchor rollers
▪ Windlass
▪ Chafing gear
▪ Other

CHAPTER 5

STEERING SYSTEM

The steering system has a number of complex components operating under extreme pressure, and if weaknesses go undetected, there's a likelihood of failure. Given how important steerage is at sea, it surprises me how often yachtsmen forget this system or simply take it for granted. Your earlier inspection of the hull demonstrated the type of rudder on your boat. Given the differences between rudders and how they're mounted, it's worth taking a moment to discuss them.

RUDDERS

Rudders on small boats are often mounted to the transom on a hinged arrangement. The hinge attached to the boat is the gudgeon and the pin attached to the rudder is the pintle. Rudders placed below the hull, usually on larger boats, may be mounted to a skeg, an elongated keel, or directly at the rudderpost. On modern sailboats you'll usually find them at the rudderpost.

How the rudder is controlled is another variable. Smaller boats and many racers tend to have tiller steering, but wheel steering is seen on most other boats. The method used to convert wheel motion into rudder motion—be it worm gear, rack and pinion gearing, cables, or hydraulics—may differ, but regardless of the means, the wheel's turning shaft transfers motion in one direction or the other to a fitting on the rudder below. Hydraulic steering, where the wheel's motion turns a hydraulic pump, is used primarily in very large vessels. The pump directs hydraulic fluid under high pressure to a piston attached to the rudderpost fitting (rudderhead fitting).

Rudders consist of an inner framework, called the web, which is attached to the rudderpost. The framing is usually stainless steel that lends strength and support to the rudder constructed around it. Wooden rudders are seen occasionally, but most rudders are built of cored fiberglass and are prone to delamination and physical damage, just like fiberglass hulls. Inspect the rudder for signs of obvious damage. Anything that allows water to enter the rudder will cause corrosion of the framework and eventually lead to disengagement of the web from the rudder housing, re-

PHOTO 5-1
Delamination in this rudder has damaged the internal webbing, and the rudder moves around the rudderpost.

sulting in rudder failure as seen in Photo 5-1.

Note that outward signs of damage are not always obvious in cases of delamination. A substantial blow to the rudder can damage the inner layers of resin and permit osmotic entry of moisture. During inspection, always turn the rudder against a fixed rudderpost. In other words, while a mate holds the wheel or tiller, attempt to turn the rudder against the immovable rudderpost. There should be no movement whatsoever— any movement of the rudder around the post demonstrates weakening of the internal web and indicates that the rudder should be repaired or replaced.

Barnacles or algal growth should be removed from the rudder and hull to promote a smooth and hydrodynamic profile. The rudderpost needs to be perfectly straight. Check the post as the wheel or tiller turns the rudder. Grounding will result in bending and other damage to hollow rudderposts. Solid rudderposts are much sturdier and very difficult to bend.

Observe the gudgeon and pintles of transom-mounted rudders. Maneuver the rudder against the hinge mechanism, watching for any play. Screws that hold the gudgeons and pintles in place are easily loosened by wear. To secure them, grind or cut the surrounding area down to healthy wood, then repair the area with epoxy, and drill for a new screw when the epoxy is dry. (West System epoxy manufactured by Gougeon Brothers is highly recommended for repair of rotted or damaged wood.) When inserting the new screw, squirt a small amount of epoxy into the drilled hole and screw in the new, acetone-cleaned bolt before the epoxy dries. The epoxy will provide a strong bond to the new screw.

Grinding out the worn screw hole and filling with epoxy is also a good method for repairing loose pintle fasteners on fiberglass rudders. When the epoxy is dry, drill a pilot hole (just as with wooden rudder repair), fill with more epoxy and insert a screw. Be sure to check the fiberglass rudder, because loose gudgeon and pintle screws may lead to water leakage into the rudder itself. If you hear water sloshing inside of the rudder, or if the rudder seems heavier than normal, drill a small hole in the bottom to drain.

Internal damage

Most rudder failures, i.e. rudders breaking or being dropped from the posts, are due to the insidious leaking of water between the post and blade. Since fiberglass and stainless steel expand and contract at different rates, keeping that steel-fiberglass bond watertight is difficult.

Water inside the rudder causes delamination of the fiberglass and corrosion of the stainless steel elements of the rudderpost and webbing. Delamination can cause weakening and loss of fiberglass portions, and corrosion of the rudderpost can lead to total loss of the whole structure.

The so-called "lap zone" of the rudderpost is the top of the rudder, where the post enters the rudder. This is where most corrosion takes place. The corrosion is worst just inside the rudder, often where the post is welded to the internal webbing system. Over time, the rudderpost's stainless tube or shaft can corrode to the point of breakage and total failure, with loss of the rudder.

Stray electrical current can also have its corrosive effects on rudderposts. If corrosion of the propeller or the shaft zinc is evident, close examination of the post is warranted. This can be controlled by installation of a galvanic isolator, bonded to the rudderpost, stock, or both.

The wisest course for monitoring the lap zone is to periodically grind away the fiberglass atop the rudder blade to expose the post in that area, then refill with epoxy to seal it.

Check the lower rudder bearing by observing the amount of play in the post. Movement should be very slight, if it exists at all. Excess movement calls for a replacement bearing as described in Chapter 2. The rest of the steering mechanism must be checked from inside the boat, but be warned that the quarters are usually cramped, so bring a flashlight, and watch your head.

Bearing tube

The rudderpost enters the hull through the bearing tube, which continues upward to the deck or ends in a stuffing box, while the rudderpost alone continues vertically. The upper bearing is much larger than the lower, since it bolts onto the deck and often supports the weight of the spade rudder. It supports the upper rudderpost motion and should be replaced if play becomes excessive. To replace the upper bearing (usually secured with four to six bolts), simply unscrew it from its attachment to the hull. Position the new bearing over the screw holes and bolt it securely into place.

Inspect the bearing tube carefully as it enters the hull. Any cracking here may lead to insidious yet serious leaking. Repair of any cracked bearing tube is mandatory.

Rough-sand the hull surrounding the crack, extending out about six inches, and wash it with acetone. Use fiberglass cloth in combination with mat but, before applying mat and resin, be sure that no water drips from the tube, as any dampness will impair the curing process.

Cut the cloth and mat into small sections that are easily laid onto the curved surfaces (strips 2- to 3-inches wide by 6-inches long work well). Saturate the mat with resin and lay the cloth over the mat, being careful to overlap the edges, keeping it as smooth as possible. If you want extra reinforcement, put on another layer—first the mat followed by the cloth. The fiberglass and matting of all successive layers must be longer than the underlying layers to guarantee a smooth repair with no abrupt edges. Once the repair has dried, sand the area to a smooth finish. You can apply gelcoat, or a marine finish such as Pettit paint.

STEERING

Tiller steering employs the simplest design and involves fewer moving parts than wheel steering. The tiller is simply bolted onto the rudder at its upper end, usually with metal straps secured to both sides of the tiller arm and the rudder. Inspect these fasteners for integrity and a secure fit. The tiller arm should pivot up and down at its rudder attachment.

Rack and pinion steering features an axle from the steering wheel that ends in a pinion gear. When this gear turns, it rotates a shaft extending down the pedestal by its meshing with a rack gear atop the shaft. Below, the shaft is fitted with an arm that connects to a similar arm extending from the rudder head.

Worm gearing is usually seen in large boats. The steering wheel shaft is not directed down the pedestal, but extends more directly to the rudder head

by a series of U-joints in various configurations.

By far the most common system in use today is cable, or chain-and-wire, steering. A sprocket inside the pedestal is connected to the steering wheel. A chain engages teeth in the sprocket, and extends downward on both sides. The ends of the chain connect with cables (Photo 5-2), which run through sheaves at the pedestal base and turn aft toward the rudderpost.

The cable may be guided by more sheaves, directing them to either a radial drive or quadrant. The cables encircle the quadrant or radial unit and their terminals are made fast there with an eye and cable clamps. When the wheel turns, motion is transferred via the chain and cables to the rudderpost fitting—radial drive or quadrant—that in turn rotates the rudderpost.

PHOTO 5-2
Chain from the wheel spricket as it joins with the cable. Note the frayed cable wires within the eye terminal. This cable is dangerously weakened and must be replaced.

In a boat with hydraulic steering, you'll see copper pipes extending from the pedestal. These should connect to a bypass valve and then extend to the hydraulic piston assembly. A tiller arm extends from the piston assembly to another arm on the rudderpost, where it attaches to turn the rudder.

Once you've identified the type of steering system your boat has, you should inspect its components accordingly. Turning the wheel should elicit motion of the turning shaft in the pedestal, no matter what system is in use. Any failure here—such as hesitancy, difficulty, or a lack of turning— is a signal to open the pedestal for inspection.

Gaining access inside the pedestal is done in different ways on different boats. Access panels are usually found on either the front or rear section of the pedestal, but sometimes the compass and top panel must be removed, and occasionally access is only possible from underneath.

Before removing the compass, place strips of masking tape at the noon, 3, 6 and 9 o'clock positions, and slit the tape along the joint with a razor blade. This will allow you to replace the compass in the correct alignment.

Once inside, inspect everything while you have the opportunity. First, check the brake pads for wear. Tighten the brake down and watch the brake pads engage. Oil the threads with Teflon lubricant. Observe the wheel bearings as the wheel spins, and apply Teflon or winch grease into the holes on the bearing housings.

Cable steering

Troubleshooting chain/cable systems usually starts at the quadrant or radial drive unit, where the cables are easily viewed. Check the cable terminals where they connect with the drive unit for kinks, laxity, chafe or corrosion. Metal shavings indicate cable chafe or damaged sheaves. The cables must run fairly, without contacting any other part of the boat, its components or each other.

Frays in the cable wires, often called "meat hooks," signify worn cable. A quick way to locate meat hooks is to put on leather gloves and run tissue paper over the length of the cable. Any damaged wire should be replaced. Cables usually change direction at least once in their run from the pedestal, and sheaves can be the source of problems. If they loosen, cables can jump off the sheaves, or, if corroded, they can seize and prevent motion.

Gears are fastened to shafts with pins and sometimes a locking key. Check these pins and keys for wear or shearing. You should also check that the gears mesh properly, are greased, and show no signs of stripped teeth. It may be necessary to replace some components (worn gears or pins, a sheared key or ball bearings) if they're damaged or corroded. A rule of thumb while examining this system is that whenever metal shavings are detected, something is wrong.

As you can imagine, there are about as many cabling systems as there are boats, so all you can do during your inspection is check what's there and assess it for soundness.

Examine the sprocket for bent or missing teeth, making sure the chain is clean and well lubricated. Steering chains are rugged and rarely fail, but they can come off the wheel sprocket, become corroded, or disconnect from the cables.

As a matter of routine maintenance, the steering apparatus should be inspected annually, and before any offshore adventure. Chains should be kept lubricated with 30-weight motor oil. Use gasoline to remove dried lubricant and apply fresh oil. If you're unable to clean the chain thoroughly within the pedestal, disconnect one end from its cable, and pull it over the sprocket and out of the pedestal. The cables in the binnacle should be checked for frayed wire or defective terminals. The cables terminate in an eye and thimble, and any time a cable is wrapped severely this way, the strands are placed under strain making failures apt to occur.

Engine controls

Inside the pedestal bowl, take a look at the engine throttle and shifting mechanism. Check the engine control shaft bearings and apply 30-weight oil if necessary. Given their popularity, you're also likely to find push-pull cables. Check the cable ends and all of their connection pins. The connections should be tight, with pins properly placed. Cables extending down the pedestal should run fairly, with no sharp angles. Any stiff or corroded cables should be replaced now to avoid failure at an inopportune time. Cables should

be sprayed with Teflon lubricant to prevent corrosion. Finish the job at the engine by checking the cable terminals there.

Rudderpost fittings

While most steering defects occur because of problems found somewhere between the rudderpost fitting and the pedestal, the most serious issues often involve the rudderpost fitting itself. Tremendous loads are generated when the boat is driven hard upwind or is slammed in rough conditions, and any weakness is surely compounded under these conditions. The fitting is fixed to the rudderpost with setscrews, through bolts, usually with a key or clamp. If the wheel or autopilot fails to turn the rudder, be sure to check for slippage at the rudderpost fitting.

Make sure that the fitting is secure. If the post is hollow, the hole for the bolts can dilate and allow excess motion. In that case, just drill a larger hole and fit a larger bolt. Sometimes setscrews are simply placed into depressions, or dimples, in the post. These can give under pressure, allowing the setscrew to escape and the fitting to rotate around the rudderpost. The dimple should be drilled to give the screw more security within the post. If you notice a loose clamp, you can secure it by filing it down or tighten it by wrapping a thin piece of metal around the post beneath the clamp, noting that the metal must be compatible with the post to prevent corrosion.

Corrosion of the rudderpost fittings from water dripping through the deck is

PHOTO 5-3
This photo depicts a severely corroded and weakened rudderhead. This could only be detected by crawling into the restricted space of the steering compartment.

another cause for concern. Like the fitting in Photo 5-3, time and inattention can result in weakness leading to failure.

Inspect the rudder stops. These are projections from the rudderpost, quadrant or radial drive unit. They are designed to meet a solid structure at the farthest points of the rudder's turning radius. There are stoppers at the port and starboard extents of the steering range. Check that the stopper is in the right position to connect with the rudderpost fitting squarely, that it's large enough to prevent the rudder stop from becoming wedged against or underneath it, and that the rudder stop is mounted securely on the rudderpost or drive unit.

Steering failure at sea often involves the rudderpost fitting being slammed violently against the stopper and becoming wedged into a fixed position. For this reason, the wheel must be controlled at all times, especially against following seas or when backing. Losing control of the steering wheel in these situations may slam the rudder hard over with enough force to cause damage. Whenever the boat is at anchor or dock, the wheel should be locked into position to stop rudder movement if waves approach from astern and turn the rudder hard over.

SELF-STEERING

Next, consider the self-steering system, which will fall into one of two broad categories: electronic systems or wind vane steering.

Electronic autopilot systems have improved with technological advances. Modern versions can hold courses more effectively than earlier models, even downwind in following seas. Once the boat is placed on a desired heading, the sails trimmed, and the autopilot engaged, the programmed heading will be maintained even if the wind shifts. This will put the sails out of trim, but the heading will remain constant unless a very large wind shift occurs, in which case an off-course alarm will sound. Mechanical breakdown of the autopilot is often irreparable at sea, so many boats have two autopilots installed and ready to use—significant electrical drain being the biggest disadvantage.

Wind vanes

Figure 5-1 illustrates examples of wind vane systems. Wind vanes keep a boat on a desired course maintained by the angle of apparent wind as it hits the vane. The heading is always in relation to the *apparent* wind, meaning that if the true wind direction changes, the apparent changes, and the boat follows suit. The heading must be monitored closely with wind vane self-steering. If the wind direction changes, the boat is steered on a different heading as well. This makes little difference in a steady or oscillating breeze, but can be problematic if a large shift occurs.

Wind vane systems are generally capable of maintaining a heading in moderate to heavy breezes both upwind and downwind, but, since they require apparent wind to steer the vane, they have difficulty in light downwind conditions and while motoring. The main advantage to this system is that it requires no electrical power.

The vane itself resembles, and functions much like, a windmill. When the helmsman places the boat on its desired course, he engages a clutch mechanism that aligns the wind vane with the apparent wind angle. The wind pushes the vane from side to side as the boat changes direction relative to the wind. The wind

FIGURE 5-1

Examples of windvane steering systems. *Courtesy of Scanner International.*

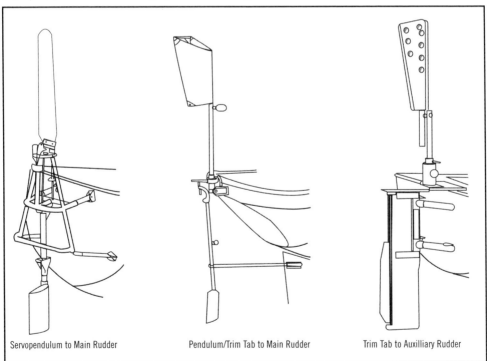

Servopendulum to Main Rudder   Pendulum/Trim Tab to Main Rudder   Trim Tab to Auxilliary Rudder

vane then uses one of two systems to correct the course in relation to the apparent wind—either trim tabs on an auxiliary rudder or a servo-pendulum unit connected to the main rudder. The wind vane must translate changes in the wind into enough energy and power to control the boat's course.

In the auxiliary rudder system, trim tabs are located on the trailing edge of an auxiliary rudder. When the wind causes the vane to shift, the trim tab is moved along with it. The water pressure that develops on one side of the trim tabs generates enough torque to turn the auxiliary rudder and cause a course correction. The servo-pendulum is somewhat more complicated. The wind vane is mounted atop a horizontal platform, which turns in conjunction with the vane shaft. The turning platform is connected to another shaft that can be linked to either the primary rudder or to a trim tab connected to the main rudder. When the wind vane rudder turns against the flow of water, the water pressure pushes it in the opposite direction. Lines attaching the servo-rudder to the boat's tiller or rudderpost then cause corrective steering by the boat's own rudder.

Begin your inspection of a wind vane system by determining which system is in use. Check the vane itself, inspecting its integrity and its connection to the shaft. Look over the vane assembly's attachment to the transom. The auxiliary rudder with its rugged rudderpost is a heavy mechanism, and custom brackets are often built to ensure stability and stoutness on the transom. The bolts and

backing plates should be larger than those of the servo-pendulum units. Since the rudder is mounted permanently, it is subject to damage, algal and barnacle growth, and corrosion, but the advantage of a fixed rudder is its ability to serve as an emergency rudder should the need arise.

No matter the system in place, you should inspect the installation. Make sure the wind vane is solidly installed with adequate bracing and strong stainless steel bolts secured into large backing plates. Beware of loose bolts that may have allowed water to enter the holes and do internal damage. Loose screws should be tightened. Any screw that can be wiggled should be loosened, its hole filled with bedding compound, and retightened. If a loose screw cannot be tightened, begin a repair as described for the rudder.

Check the clutch mechanism. When engaged, it should lock the vane to the auxiliary rudder or servo-pendulum unit. It's important that the clutch engage easily and operate smoothly. Any corrosion, salt or dirt accumulation, or other damage can cause friction and impair the translation of wind direction change to the units. It can't be overemphasized that the power generated by the vane itself is not enough to steer the boat. The impetus from the vane must be transmitted to either the trim tabs or servomechanism to actually correct the course. Make sure the mechanism is clean and well lubricated—it must be able to disengage quickly from the vane to allow for manual control of the wheel when necessary. Because it's mounted on the transom, the wind vane system is fully exposed to the elements. Salt and corrosion are enemies of the linkages involved and will render the mechanism balky and sluggish if not removed.

Check the servo linkage between the horizontal portion at the base of the vane and the vertical shaft extending down to the servo-rudder. Watch for salt buildup and corrosion. You may be able to salvage damaged parts with careful cleaning, but if weakened they should be replaced with parts from the manufacturer. Check the servo-auxiliary rudder and check the lines that connect it to the main rudder, or to a quadrant on the rudderpost. Be sure the lines lead fairly, without signs of chafe or weakening, and engage properly at both ends. Make sure there is no growth or damage to the trim tabs that would impair water flow. Look for delamination or cracking that may indicate separation of the rudder halves, or physical damage that may have come from following waves, collisions or damage at the docks.

Autopilots

Electronic self-steering has evolved greatly since its introduction. Units now have a greater capacity to hold a course in a rough seaway, use less electricity and have become far more dependable. The course is set at a controller located on the pedestal, down below, or both, and the boat's heading is monitored by a compass, which transmits heading information to a small computer. The computer, called the Central Processing Unit (CPU), controls a motor that turns the boat's rudder as compensation when the boat is off course. One goal of off-shore route planning is to choose courses with the wind abeam or aft of the beam whenever possible. This won't always happen, of course, but the self-steering system must be able to hold a true course in downwind conditions.

Autopilots come in a variety of configurations. Pedestal or cockpit-mounted versions typically don't have enough power to control a boat in ocean swells and wave action. They are also vulnerable to being drenched with seawater, which can soak the CPU or drive motor and knock the unit out of commission. Corrosion is also a concern whenever metallic parts are exposed to seawater. Autopilots that are mounted below deck have more powerful motors and are positioned in a secure, dry area, making them the type most commonly employed on offshore vessels.

Most drive motor units control an arm extending from the unit. The arm moves in and out, and is controlled either by gears within the unit or by hydraulics. The arm may be connected to the steering quadrant or radial drive unit, or may be connected to steering cables. Some drive motors control a geared shaft that meshes with a geared section of quadrant. Inspect the drive unit and become familiar with its linkage to the steering system. You must be knowledgeable about the setup in case failure occurs offshore. In the event that the drive motor fails, the regular steering may be impaired by the drag of the unit, so make sure you know how to disconnect the drive motor from the steering gear.

Inspection of the electronic self-steering begins at the control unit. The unit may be mounted in the cockpit, wheelhouse, or navigation station, or there may be multiple repeating units. Turn on power to the unit at the circuit panel, and be sure that its separate toggle switch is "on." If the control display does not illuminate, you'll need to determine the cause of the electrical problem. Use the voltmeter selection of a multimeter on the wires leading to the unit. If there's current flowing to the unit, it may be that wires to the control are corroded or disconnected, or the unit is not functional. You'll need to contact the manufacturer or a qualified repair center for assistance.

If you detect no current flowing to the unit, the problem lies upstream, so trace the wiring back toward the control panel. Become familiar with the controls available on the unit. It is imperative that you understand how to set a desired heading and how to put the unit in standby mode, so that the helmsman can take control of the wheel at a moment's notice. This is one of the crucial items to discuss with the crew in the "cockpit chat" before shoving off.

Now locate the autopilot's fluxgate compass. Check that the wires are connected properly and show no corrosion. Make very sure that no metal objects, other compasses or sources of magnetic interference are located within three feet of the autopilot compass. This is an easy rule to forget as gear and stores are brought on board and stowed for a voyage. Make sure that everyone involved knows where the compass is located and

stores metal gear appropriately. If the boat sails in a circle, refuses to obey the control unit's desired course line, or intermittently sails off on its own, it's probably due to interference with the autopilot compass from sources like radios, the engine alternator, an SSB transceiver, sonar, or radar. The engine alternator is often the culprit, so you may need to relocate the compass.

My first autopilot, a Robertson, had just been installed and we were preparing to leave Lake St. Clair, Michigan, for the Erie Barge Canal, the Hudson River, and beyond. The autopilot had been calibrated, tested and shown to work perfectly. Stores and gear were loaded and we prepared to leave. Entering the lake from the Clinton River, I engaged the Robertson and was surprised to find the boat turning in a circle and heading back toward the river and the lake. I put the autopilot on standby and steered us back to port to begin the search for whatever was disabling the autopilot. We eventually found a can of teak oil in the aft berth not far from the compass and, sure enough, when the can was removed the pilot worked perfectly and we were off.

Wires from the compass lead to the CPU, which is usually installed low in the boat, often beneath an aft quarter berth. Make sure that the unit is secured tightly to a bulkhead or other sturdy structure and that no gear could damage it in rough conditions. Check the wire connections for security and corrosion. There are numerous connections within the unit, and they must all be secure. There are also fuses inside, so check the fuses and be sure that replacements are on hand. If the control unit is getting power, but the pilot still doesn't work, the problem is most likely at the CPU. Check that it's receiving current from the control unit. There should be a toggle that turns power on to the unit. If the power is activated, program a change of course into the control unit and test for current in the wires coming from the CPU. If there's current, the problem is isolated to the drive unit. If there's no current, it's the CPU that's damaged. I'd consult with the manufacturer or a qualified repair facility at this point. As for repair of electrical autopilots at sea, replacement of the major components is the only practical option, so it's best to carry replacements for these cornerstones of your steering system.

Move on to an inspection of the drive unit. Down below, it's mounted aft near the rudderpost and usually controls steering with a connection to the quadrant or radial drive unit. It's best to mount the drive unit in the engine room where its sound is muted. Your main concern here is that it is sturdily mounted on a strong base. This is very important, as the drive unit produces considerable torque and must have a firm supportive base that can withstand the forces generated in turning the rudder.

If the unit is hydraulic, check the lines for leaks. With electric and hydraulic units, check the wiring. Be sure wires are secured as they run from the CPU to the drive unit and can't be damaged by stowed equipment. Check that the wire is securely connected to the drive unit and that no corrosion is evident. Since this area is prone to corrosion, the elec-

trical connections should be coated with grease or silicone for protection.

Inspect the drive assembly where it links with the steering mechanism. In my experience, the drive arm most often has a simple, single connection to the steering quadrant. The arm end fitting usually has an eye, through which a bolt or pin connects to a hole in the quadrant. Inspect the connection for security and corrosion, and make sure that the pin is secure. A slow response to a course change may be the fault of the drive unit. Check the current coming from the drive unit when it is instructed by the CPU to operate. If the current is low, there's a problem with the drive unit's electric motor.

If the drive unit connects to the steering cables, check them carefully. There may be cheek blocks added to the cable system, so be sure they are secure and that cables run squarely through the blocks. If the driver controls a geared shaft to the quadrant, correct driver positioning is critical to ensure that the gears mesh properly with those on the quadrant. Inspect the gears for dirt and debris making certain nothing impairs their functionality.

Any slow or sluggish course corrections may be related to the linkage, and the message "Drive Stop" will appear on the display. Check closely for binding of the drive arm, a bent drive arm, or loose connections between the drive arm and quadrant. Boat fenders or other objects may also be jammed against the drive arm, sensor arm, cables or quadrant.

You can customize how the autopilot functions—how quickly it responds when off course and how much the rudder is moved when the unit responds. On long passages, set the autopilot to a low setting for response to course alteration. This will conserve battery power since fewer adjustments will be required of the pilot. You should also dampen the rudder response so that the drive unit works less and requires less power. The best way to judge how the pilot performs is with a sea trial. Observe how the autopilot operates to maintain a course, and be satisfied only when the unit responds properly to maintain a heading while working in an energy-conserving manner.

Sailing in balance

There is another method of steering that uses no electrical energy, has no moving parts, and drives the boat while the steering gear and helmsman take a break from the action. The boat will drive herself if balanced correctly in the right wind and sea conditions. The wind, and particularly wave action, must be near the beam or forward, but not so high as a dead beat. A close reach is the ideal point of sail for our purposes. Waves from aft of the beam tend to hit the windward side of the hull before the leeward side, pushing the stern down and making it impossible for the boat to maintain course. With wind from the proper quadrant, we just need to balance the sail plan and provide enough power to keep the boat steadily making way against the wave action.

A balanced boat should be the goal no matter what steering system is used.

FIGURE 5-2

CE is determined for each sail by intersecting lines drawn through the angles. Overall CE of this vessel is also depicted.

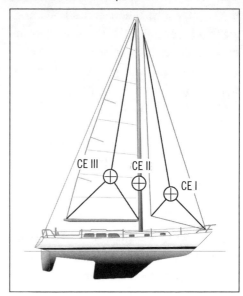

When the sail plan is balanced, the sails are correctly trimmed to provide drive, and very little rudder movement is required to stay on course. Minimizing rudder movement results in a decreased workload, lower energy usage, and a straighter, more efficient course through the water. To achieve balance, we are concerned with two opposing forces—the Center of Lateral Resistance (CLR) and the Center of Effort (CE). In Figure 5-2, the CE of the entire sail plan is shown to be comprised of the combined CEs of the fore and aft sails. In a ketch-rigged sailboat, the mizzen also would be factored in.

Extending lines from the midpoint of the triangular sides to the opposite angles of the sail determines the CE for a given sail. The point of intersection is

FIGURE 5-3

Weather helm is created when the CE moves aft or the CLR is shifted forward.

that sail's CE. This is true of both sails in the diagram. The combined boat CE is usually just aft of the mast, below the mainsail's vertical midpoint. The CE is defined as the center of all wind forces pushing to leeward. These forces are responsible for causing heel and creating the lift of our sails and keel, which propels the boat forward. Without a countering lateral force, the wind would push the boat sideways and capsize her. The CLR opposes the heeling forces of wind.

Boat designers attempt to locate the CE forces just aft of the CLR (Figure 5-3)to maintain slight weather helm in a properly trimmed sail plan.

The CLR is determined by the hull configuration, location of bottom appendages and ballast. In our efforts to balance the sail plan, it's convenient to consider the keel as the fore and aft pivot point of the hull.

In this scheme, as seen in Figures 5-3 and 5-4, when the CE moves aft, more forces push the stern to leeward and the bow heads up (weather helm). Should our sail increase the relative forward CE, the overall CE moves forward, and pushes the bow down (lee helm). Too much mainsail, an over-trimmed main, a too-high traveler, or a small jib can cause weather helm. Also, aft mast rake moves the sail plan aft and causes weather helm. Lee helm is the result of an over-canvassed bow, over-trimmed jib or spinnaker, or underpowered mainsail.

Alterations in the CLR also affect balance.

If moving the keel, or shifting the ballast or crew weight moves the CLR aft,

FIGURE 5-4

Lee helm results from movement of CE forward or CLR aft.

Forces that cause weather helm (Figure 5-3):	Forces that cause lee helm (Figure 5-4):
CE moves aft: • over-canvassed mainsail • mainsail over-sheeted or too high on traveler • under-canvassed, under-sheeted headsail, or fairlead too far aft. • mast stepped farther aft • mast raked aft CLR moves forward: • crew moved forward • ballast moved forward • lower swing keel • keel moved forward	CE moves forward • reefed mainsail • under-sheeted mainsail, too far down on traveler • over-canvassed headsail, spinnaker CLR moves aft • ballast, crew move aft • keel moved aft • raise swing keel

the effect is the same as moving CE forward—the boat heads down. The opposite is true if CLR moves forward (by losing the rudder, for example). The CLR becomes closer to the CE and the boat heads up. Any change in sail plan, mast rake, or ballast that causes the CE to move back, or the CLR to move forward, also creates weather helm.

A convenient way to remember CE versus CLR is: Whenever CE moves aft or CLR moves forward, weather helm results. When CE moves forward or CLR moves aft, lee helm is created.

Our goal is to have a couple of degrees of weather helm, indicating that the jib is working to provide drive through the water. The jib, of course, directs air past the mainsail, creating lift and forward impetus. With the sails trimmed to a balanced configuration, steering becomes simply a matter of holding the wheel steady. At this point, lock the wheel down to that heading and watch. If she holds her course, the sail

plan is in a state of equalization, and only a wind shift or change of course will knock the boat out of balance.

EMERGENCY STEERING

Locate the emergency tiller and take the time to remove it from storage and fit it onto the rudderpost. Be sure the fitting isn't damaged or corroded, and become familiar with how the tiller operates. Some emergency tillers are actually too long to work with the steering wheel in place. For these tillers, the wheel must be removed. After inspection, store the emergency tiller in the cockpit.

Since your mind is focused on the steering system, now's the time to visualize the stern of the boat, the pushpit and backstay arrangement to get an idea of how you might jury-rig a rudder if the primary is lost. Have a plan for how you'd build, install, and operate one, given the configuration of the boat's transom.

You can make your own system or purchase an SOS Emergency Rudder manufactured by Scanmar International. Scanmar's Monitor wind vanes also offer MRUD, which converts the servo-pendulum wind vane system into an emergency rudder.

Another idea is to build the components of an emergency rudder and store them on board. Depending on the design of the transom, you'll need a system that will support a rudder and new rudderpost. The post must be supported at the top and bottom, and must be free to rotate the attached rudder as required. This arrangement must be sufficiently strong to withstand the weight of the post, rudder, and steering mechanism attachment.

Giving thought to this rudder arrangement and prefabricating some of its components allows for a sturdier, more reliable rig, and considerably less offshore angst should the rudder break.

Conclude your inspection of the steering system by making sure that all deficiencies are noted on the checklist.

Spare parts list for the steering system:

- Rudderpost fitting
- Replacement parts kit for electronic autopilot
- Replacement parts kit for wind vane steering
- Plan for rudder replacement, with portions of the rig fabricated and ready for use

CHAPTER 6

AUXILIARY ENGINES

In this chapter, we'll discuss the inspection and evaluation of the boat's engine, transmission, propeller shaft, and stuffing box. There's a breed of traditionally minded mariners who prefer not to use auxiliary engines, but most offshore sailors today enjoy having dependable propulsion systems. With engine power, the boat can move without wind, charge its batteries to run electronics, keep refrigeration systems cold, remain manageable in gale conditions, and make landfall under power.

I've adopted a theory about sailing on the ocean: The faster you travel and the less time your boat is at sea, the fewer opportunities you have to encounter dangerous conditions. I have a hard time meandering at 2 knots when I could motor sail at 5 or 6, making steady progress toward landfall. But in deference to tradition, I'll admit to never having had the opportunity for extended, leisurely cruising. My ocean experiences have all involved deliveries, racing, or teaching offshore sailing classes, so the opportunity to truly sail by the will of the wind has never been mine. Given that circumstance, I'd probably be will-

ing to curtail my desire for steady progress, but would still insist on a reliable engine and drive train.

ROUTINE MAINTENANCE

We'll begin this inspection with an overview of the engine compartment. Check the engine for accumulations of oil or oily debris indicating gasket failure or loose, leaking or frayed hoses. Examine the bilge for the presence of water or oil, and the engine for carbon deposits or other obvious signs of trouble.

Familiarize yourself with the general layout of the engine. Learn the whereabouts of oil filters, the oil dipstick and filler port, fuel tank(s), and fuel line(s) and how to open and close valves between fuel tanks, primary and secondary fuel filters, the lift pump, primary fuel pump, injectors, injector pumps, air filter, starter motor, solenoid, alternator, raw water seacock, raw water filter, seawater pump, closed water system pump, header tank and antifreeze fill port, exhaust manifold, exhaust hose and exhaust port. Remember that examining the engine here in the calm atmosphere of port is very different from performing the inspection at sea.

Turn on the engine room light. If no light is installed, it's wise to run a couple wires to the circuit panel and install one. It helps so much to have a light source available when inspecting, monitoring and maintaining the engine. Holding a flashlight means you can only use one hand during repairs—an especially difficult maneuver on a rolling ocean—although a headlamp or bite light works well in this situation.

If you can't locate every fundamental engine component, refer to the owner's manual. You'll need to be very familiar with the engine in the event that it fails to start, loses power, races, or shuts down at sea. Familiarity with the engine makes troubleshooting that much easier. Routine engine maintenance and monitoring must be standard procedure at sea, so be certain that you can perform the following tasks:

- Check engine oil, add oil, and change the filter
- Closely monitor fuel usage, switch fuel tanks, or add fuel from jerry cans
- Check the closed water system coolant levels and add coolant
- Examine all hoses for cracks, breaks, or loose hose clamps, and replace any damaged hoses: All hoses connected to the engine must be approved for this usage. They should be fire retardant and flexible to absorb engine vibration. Each point of connection must be secured with two 316 stainless steel screw-type hose clamps
- Replace the primary and secondary fuel filters
- Bleed the fuel system
- Trace a blockage in the fuel line and clear the obstruction: Remove the fuel line from the primary fuel filter and blow backward toward the fuel tank, or insert a long wire to push the obstruction back into the tank
- Manage interrupted fuel flow due to an obstructed primary filter
- Examine, tighten, and replace an engine belt
- Monitor the alternator brackets, water pump, and refrigeration compressor and their belts, and tighten the belts
- Turn the engine off manually by shutting fuel flow off at the tank or at the fuel pump, or by interrupting airflow
- Start the engine manually if the solenoid fails by placing an insulated screwdriver across the solenoid positive-to-positive terminals or by jumping the starter with a hot wire
- Check the transmission fluid and refill as necessary
- Manually operate the gearshift in case of linkage failure; understand the linkages of gearshift and throttle and how to make repairs
- Manually operate the engine throttle in case of linkage failure
- Disconnect the raw water intake hose from the filter and use it to pump water from the boat in an emergency

- Clean out the raw water strainer
- Inspect and replace the raw water impeller
- Monitor and service the stuffing box

This list may seem daunting, but although you don't need to be a certified diesel mechanic to confidently sail offshore, it's important to know how to monitor and maintain the engine and perform these basic repairs at sea. As with all systems, a thorough inspection before sailing should minimize the mechanical expertise you'll need offshore.

Simple diagnostics

The best way to test the engine is to start it up and run it. Pay attention to how long the starter turns over before the engine fires. Does it continue to run or does it need more cranking? Unless the temperature is low, hesitation in starting could indicate sludgy fuel, inadequate fuel through the injectors, insufficient air supply, or inefficiency in building compression. When the engine starts, does a large puff of smoke come from the exhaust? If so, there may have been oil in the compression chambers or too much fuel. Observe the engine for abnormal noises and vibrations—all signal a problem.

There are many reasons for abnormal sounds, so the best deductive method is to follow the noise to its source. Loose parts are the usual suspects when metallic sounds occur around the engine. Vibrations are not welcome around diesels, since they usually indicate engine mount defects or problems in the drive train—damaged propeller, bent prop shaft, worn cutless bearing, or misaligned driveshaft to prop shaft coupling. A heavier vibration or rumbling could be a worn crankshaft or main bearings in the engine. A screeching sound is usually from loose or greasy belts.

Black smoke is the result of inefficiently burned fuel; either the injectors are allowing too much fuel or the air supply is not great enough to burn the fuel properly. White smoke signifies faulty injectors that admit insufficient fuel into the cylinders. Blue smoke is emitted when the engine burns oil. This is normal in a two-stroke diesel, but indicates cylinder wear in four-stroke engines. Pale blue smoke is considered normal exhaust in the four-stroke engine.

DIESEL ENGINES

You can compare a diesel engine to the human body—they're both composed of various systems that function independently as well as in close cooperation with other systems. When each one functions correctly, the whole organism thrives. A breakdown in any single organ leads to dysfunction of all interrelated systems. A brief discussion of the diesel engine's systems helps in understanding its upkeep and maintenance.

Diesels need clean fuel, an abundance of clean air, adequate cooling, lubrication and removal of heated exhaust gases. If diesel engines are properly monitored, they can run for thousands of hours with only basic maintenance, but will shut down quickly if not supported properly.

Diesel engines operate by compressing air within the combustion chamber. As it compresses, the air becomes superheated. At a precisely calibrated moment, the fuel injector sprays a small amount of atomized fuel into the combustion chamber. As the fuel particles meet the heated oxygen molecules, the fuel burns—but doesn't explode as in gasoline engines. This slower, more controlled burning of fuel allows the engine to provide a more measured, even supply of power. As the fuel burns, it forces the piston down within the cylinder, providing power to the driveshaft. After the power stroke, in a four-stroke engine, the piston returns toward the combustion chamber. The exhaust gases, unused fuel, vaporized water and unused air are expelled from the combustion chamber through the ejection port, which is controlled by the exhaust valve.

The inlet and exhaust valves of the compression chambers control precise operation of the diesel engine—from air compression and fuel injection, to the burning and power stroke of the piston, and the exhaust of waste. These valves, located and restrained within valve guides, connect to push rods, which are enclosed by valve springs. The camshaft powers a rocker arm that controls the up-and-down movement of the valve push rods. Although none of these components is visible without removing the manifold and injectors, it's important to know that smooth operation of the engine requires intricately timed performance of many precision-engineered parts.

Fuel

By far the most common cause of problems is fuel fouled with dirt, metal fragments, water, or algae sludge. Dust particles as small as 15 to 20 microns (one micron is one millionth of a meter) can damage the valves, pistons, cylinders, and injection pumps that must fit and work together precisely. Overheated water within the cylinders can turn to steam and force engine components to break, while cooler water can condense and form sludge in the oil sump. Algae slime will obstruct fuel lines, filters, pumps and injectors.

Monitor fuel for sediment, and the engine tank for sludge on the bottom or sides. If you discover any debris, empty and clean the tank before any solids enter the engine (polishing). Before using a portable tank, check inside to be sure that it's clean.

Make note of the fueling stations you visit. How busy are the pumps? Is the place well maintained? Are they in foreign countries where fuel standards may not be enforced? I run fuel through a Baja filter before it enters my fuel tanks. After pumping a gallon of fuel I inspect the filter for any debris. If there's sedimentation present, I'll look for another fueling station.

Filtering the fuel before it enters the engine should be a two-step process. The primary fuel filter removes water and larger particles of sediment. It will usually have a removable bowl at the bottom, where water and debris accumulate. You can purchase primary filters that sound an alarm when fuel flow is restricted by accumulated matter. The secondary fuel filter targets the smallest of dirt particles. The paper mesh in this filter is very fine, so larger particles or water can quickly obstruct the filter and stop fuel flow.

Whenever the engine begins to hesitate, become wary of restricted fuel flow; shut the engine down and examine the filter. Examine the primary filter, checking for deposits in the bowl and emptying if debris or water is present. Use the engine maintenance history to determine the need for fuel filter changes. If unknown, check the filter elements by unscrewing the retaining bolt that holds the top on the filter, pulling the filter element out and checking it for particulate matter. Small amounts of debris can be removed by flushing the filter with clean diesel fuel, but I recommend a wiser course before going to sea—install new filters. Retain the old, usable ones as spares.

If you disassemble the filters, remember that air introduced into the fuel system will have to be bled off. If you only open the primary fuel filter, replace any fuel that spilled out and you shouldn't have to bleed the engine. Trace the fuel line from the tank to the injector pump. Note the positions of filters, the lift pump, the fuel injection pump, lines to the injectors, and positions of the nuts to unscrew during the process of bleeding air from the fuel lines.

I mentioned being able to manually shut the engine down in the event that the push-button or knob controls in the cockpit fail. These controls both cause a cable (the knob by direct connection and the button via a solenoid to the cable) to operate a plunger in the fuel rack inside of the injection pump. When activated, the plunger is moved into position to shut off fuel flow, stopping the engine. Locate the cable coming from the cockpit, or the solenoid near the injection pump. Find the cable where it enters the injection pump so you can manually shut off fuel flow if necessary. Also check the fuel line coming from the fuel tank—many systems have a valve that can shut off the flow of fuel. You can also shut fuel off at the tank, but the engine will run until all fuel in the primary and secondary filters along with the fuel line is burned off.

Oil

Diesel engines require more lubrication than gasoline engines. Air is compressed to pressures in excess of 500 psi within the combustion chambers, and it's necessary that the components fit precisely to maintain this pressure. Parts must be well lubricated to maintain their surface condition or performance is hindered. The lubricating oil in diesel engines is subject to higher operating temperatures than in gasoline engines, so diesels burn through more oil and require close monitoring offshore.

The oil that lubricates the engine components is also responsible for removing heat that builds up during air compression. As the oil circulates it absorbs heat, cooling as it makes its way to the crankcase. Monitoring oil levels should be a daily task (actually, several times per day with continual usage) whenever the engine is used. Check the oil level with the dipstick. The level should measure at or just below the full line—but never above. Increased oil pressure will shut the engine off within minutes or lead to uncontrolled engine race. When topping off, add the oil slowly to avoid overfilling. You'll have to remove excess oil from the pan or oil filter if you overfill, and that's a slow process if you don't have an aspirator on board.

When checking oil on the dipstick, note its texture and color. Lubricating oil that has been exposed to high temperatures becomes thin and dark. Black oil is a sign that carbon, or soot, is being formed by oil that's been broken down by high temperatures. Check for a problem with the water-cooling system.

Black carbon is deposited on pistons, piston rings, valves and walls of the cylinders when fuel is incompletely burned in the combustion chamber, and this indicates a possible obstruction of airflow. The soot is normally removed by lubricating oil, which cleans it from the machinery and carries it to the crankcase. If the engine doesn't have enough oil, deposits will build up and eventually interfere with proper valve function leading to loss of compression and engine failure.

If the engine oil doesn't look new, replace it with oil recommended by the manufacturer. Always follow manufacturer recommendations on oil change intervals. You should replace the oil filter at the same time.

Any spilled oil needs to be contained within the engine compartment. The engine bilge should not commingle with the general ship bilge. Remember, it's against U.S. Coast Guard regulations for engine bilge oil to be pumped overboard. Spills in the engine room are cleaned by hand, and never pumped overboard.

Air

Another characteristic of diesel engines is their insatiable appetite for air. Only small quantities of fuel are admitted through the injectors with each combustion cycle because, to burn efficiently, as many of the fuel particles as possible must combine with oxygen molecules. Since air is only 23 percent oxygen, an abundance of air is admitted with the fuel to assure peak combustion efficiency. Diesel engineers design the engine to make air input as efficient as possible by using large air filters and passageways. A dirty, clogged filter will restrict air flow and choke the engine, resulting in black smoke from the exhaust, accelerated buildup of carbon deposits, drastically reduced engine performance and rapid onset of component damage.

Air must be adequately filtered before it enters the engine because any dirt entering the combustion chamber can damage the cylinder walls and piston rings. Dirty air has the same adverse effects as dirty fuel. Air filters in most marine diesels resemble those in automobile engines and include disposable paper filter elements that should be replaced at the first sign of wear or accumulation of dirt.

Some engines use oil-bath air filters to trap airborne particles of dirt in oil that covers the bottom of the casing. The air then passes through oil-soaked filters for further cleaning. The oil in these filters must be routinely changed and the screens flushed with diesel fuel or kerosene.

In a "runaway" engine, the diesel accelerates on its own, out of throttle control. This is due to oil overfilling the crankcase, causing the diesel engine to burn that oil instead of fuel. A quick way to disable the engine in this unnerving situation is to disrupt the airflow to the air intake manifold by stuffing a cotton shirt (preferably someone else's) into the air cleaner.

So far we've discussed only those engines that draw air in with the vacuum created by the down stroke of the piston within the cylinder. Since diesels generate power in proportion to the amount of air available to ignite the fuel, increasing the air entering the combustion chamber allows the engine to generate more power. This process is called turbocharging. On four-cycle engines, the turbocharger is a fan (located near the top of the engine and powered by the exhaust gases) that forces air into the air inlet. On two-cycle engines, an engine belt powers the turbocharger. With either system, air is used at a greater rate to burn more fuel and produce more power.

In the cockpit, there's usually an air vent leading to the engine room. With turbocharged engines, the outer vent connects to a hose that delivers cool air directly to the engine inlet manifold. Make certain no water can enter the en-

gine intake through the vent hose. This is usually accomplished by using an outside fitting that points downward.

Coolants

Although diesel engines perform best at high temperatures, the process of air compression and burning of fuel often creates more heat than is needed for optimal engine performance. Excess heat must be removed by an efficient cooling system such as raw water cooling or heat exchanger cooling.

In an engine cooled by raw water, seawater is pumped through a filter directly to the engine-cooling jacket in the engine block. Despite the simplicity of this cooling method, it does have its disadvantages. One is a high risk of debris reaching the cooling jacket. Sand, silt, leaves, salt, paper or plastic refuse can obstruct the conduits within the system and overheat the engine. Another concern is that the system creates a high risk for galvanic corrosion. It's vital that zinc anodes be installed and monitored frequently to prevent the erosion of vital engine parts.

Also, frozen water in the engine can crack the block and ruin the engine, so proper winterization is crucial.

The second method of cooling your engine—use of a heat exchanger—is employed in the majority of marine diesels. Raw water is used as coolant here (just as in the previous system) but it doesn't circulate directly within the block. Instead, it's pumped into the heat exchanger through pathways used only by the raw water—engine coolant runs through separate lines. Heat is transferred, or exchanged, from the closed engine system coolant to the raw water conduits within the exchanger, so it functions much like an automotive radiator. This method is more efficient than the raw water system and keeps the engine closer to its optimal operating temperature of approximately 185 degrees Fahrenheit.

A thermostat monitors coolant temperature so that when the engine temperature is low the thermostat closes and shunts coolant past the heat exchanger, allowing temperature to build. As the coolant heats beyond optimum levels, the thermostat opens and allows hot coolant to enter the heat exchanger to be cooled. From the heat exchange unit, the thermostat directs coolant to the expansion tank if the temperature gets too high. There, the higher temperatures and increased pressure of the cooling fluid can be maintained safely, preventing the coolant from boiling over. The expansion tank has a pressurized cap to accommodate increased pressure within the tank. There is also a refill cap near the tank for adding coolant.

No such temperature regulation is possible in the raw water system, so the engine usually operates at less than ideal temperatures and the available power is decreased. Since water never reaches the engine block when the heat exchange system is in use, the cooling system has no chance of being obstructed with debris. The closed engine cooling circuit is also protected from corrosion by the addition of antifreeze and corrosion-preventive additives.

Inspecting the cooling system: To inspect the cooling system, start by determining which method your boat engine uses. Begin at the raw water intake, common to both systems, and check that the seacock is open. Inspect the intake hose at the raw water filter. The filter canister usually has a clear plastic top through which you can easily spot debris. If matter is present, simply remove the top, pull out the filter component and clean it. From the filter, a hose leads to the raw water pump. The water pump is usually a centrifugal pump that uses a rotating component, the impeller, whose blades force water out of the pump through the discharge elbow. The clamps at either end of the hose should be tight and free of corrosion.

Next, the water enters the engine cooling jacket, picks up heat from the engine and exits the exhaust manifold. Inspect each component of this system, including the hoses and clamps (there should be two clamps at the end of each hose). Check hoses for blistering or cracking, and be sure the clamps are correctly positioned, tightly secured, and free of corrosion. Check the raw water pump drive belt—it should not be worn or loose. The pump has a faceplate held onto the pump body by four to six screws. To inspect the impeller, you'll need to remove the faceplate. The impeller consists of a hub with rubberized blades radiating outward and terminating in a bulb. The hub fits over the shaft of the water pump. Check the blades to ensure they flex easily and none are broken or have missing end pieces.

The hub should not spin on the shaft

freely. You should only be able to remove the impeller by prying it off the shaft with a screwdriver or by lifting it off with needle nose pliers. Some impellers are also secured with a screw or clip. If pieces of the impeller blades are missing, they may be found in the discharge of the pump, in the hose or in the heat exchanger. These pieces can obstruct the flow of water, so they must be located and removed.

Find the lowest hose connecting to the water pump (that's probably the intake). Remove it from the other end (probably the water filter) and blow through it forcefully. This usually expels shards of impeller fin from the pump. When all pieces have been located, you must fill the intake hose with water to prime the centrifugal water pump before it will operate.

Examine the hose from the discharge elbow of the pump to the heat exchanger, checking for abnormalities and corrosion. Note that there will be four hoses connected to the heat exchanger: the raw water pump entry and exit, a hose from the thermostat, and a hose to the expansion tank. Closely examine all hoses, especially the elbow from the heat exchanger to the raw water exhaust, for wear and tight connections. The expansion tank is normally located toward the rear of the engine. Trace the hose from the heat exchanger to the tank. Make sure it is filled with coolant.

The thermostat is located toward the front of the engine and is covered by a metal housing. It has a hose from the engine's closed system water pump, and another exiting to the heat exchanger.

You should check both hose connections, but there's no reason to dismantle the thermostat unless the engine has problems overheating. In that situation, the thermostat may not be opening properly to allow heated coolant to enter the heat exchanger.

Exhaust

The final stage of the engine cycle occurs after the piston has traveled upward, compressing the air, followed by fuel injection and ignition. The compressed gases are then forced out through the exhaust valve.

The exhaust system is required to:

- Conduct hot gases out of the boat as quickly as possible. (Any airflow restriction or backpressure must be minimized, so make sure the hoses have sufficient diameter and as few bends as possible.)
- Diminish engine noise with some type of muffling action.
- Cool gases so that they don't damage the hoses, and prevent hot water from being discharged into the ocean.

In engines with a raw water cooling system, and most of those equipped with heat exchangers, water is pumped from the cooling jacket or heat exchanger directly into the exhaust piping where it joins exhaust gases from the combustion chamber. The hot exhaust gases are cooled by evaporation of the water, and, as the temperature and pressure of the gases are lowered, engine noise also decreases.

Heat exchangers may also use the so-called dry exhaust method, in which no water is injected into the exhaust pipes. These pipes are considerably hotter than in the former system and must be insulated. As far as engine noise is concerned, exhausts using the dry method are equipped with mufflers, similar to those seen on automobiles. Examine the exhaust elbow as it exits either the exhaust manifold or heat exchanger. No engine component is abused more than the exhaust elbow as it conducts hot water and gases from the engine to the exhaust piping, and its failure rate is very high.

Because exhaust hoses have high incidence of breakdown, the hose should be composed of sturdy, black, thick-walled material. Inspect it for areas of chafe, es-

pecially if it rests on a sharp corner or bulkhead. Look for kinks or severe turns in the hose that could cause an increase in backpressure. Carefully examine its connection on both ends, since temperature extremes and corrosion are both threats, as in Photo 6-1.

The exhaust port is the final point in the system and should be located above the waterline so that the exhaust gases and water can be seen from on board the boat. Inspect the exhaust port for debris or other obstructions.

Engine mounts

It's important to inspect the engine beds. The engine mounts must allow for

PHOTO 6-1
This exhaust hose looked normal until I discovered the corrosion that ate away the elbow piece hose clamps.

a degree of engine movement due to vibration and torque, but must also keep the engine in alignment with the drive train. Anything that interrupts this integrity will cause damage.

Misalignment between the engine, transmission, and propeller shaft causes undue wear on the entire drive train, as well as the stuffing box, stern tube, and cutless bearing. Motion is normally minimized in two ways. First, the engine mounts provide a cushioning effect to absorb engine vibration and twisting caused by torque. Second, the driveshaft couplings allow for motion between the engine and propeller shaft.

Examine the engine mounts carefully. They are secured to the engine bed by large bolts and should be inspected for corrosion, bent bolts, or cracking of the engine bed. There should be no movement between the engine mounts and the bed—the mounts themselves allow for motion—but the connection between mounts and bed must be solid. Sudden resistance to the propeller shaft's motion, as when a line wraps around the propeller, can damage engine mounts. The engine torque working against the immobilized propeller causes a violent twist on the engine that can break the mount, bolt, or the engine bed. The bent

PHOTO 6-2
The bent bolts seen here were the result of a line wrapping around the propeller.

bolts in Photo 6-2 should be removed and replaced after the engine alignment has been properly assessed.

To repair a cracked or broken engine bed, first clear away any broken bedding or debris. The bed is typically made of fiberglass, so sand away the broken section and repair by layering epoxy-soaked fiberglass mat and roving. Apply in layers until the area is plumb with the surrounding bed area. Sand if necessary to make sure the area provides a level support structure and strong base for the engine. Engine mounts can soften with age or become compressed by the engine's weight, and if the mounts have lost integrity, they should be replaced. The rubber mount shown in Photo 6-3 has deteriorated, and the engine component is weakened from corrosion. Both should be replaced.

PHOTO 6-3
The rubber component of this engine mount is old and brittle. It no longer cushions the engine properly.

Throttle

Engine throttle cables reach the engine from the pedestal controls, and in the push-push system most throttles are coupled with transmission shift cables. Throttle cables at the engine fit into a bracket that aligns the cable with the midpoint of the throttle control lever. Cable terminals are usually connected with the engine control lever by a pin, which is in turn secured by a cotter pin. The metal ends of the cable control should be clean, free of corrosion, and lubricated with Teflon grease.

Alternator

The alternator is usually located forward on the engine where it can be connected

to the drive belt and, if installed properly, requires little monitoring. The drive belt should not be worn or loose. The tightness of the drive belt is controlled by adjusting the alternator on its bracket either toward the engine to loosen the belt or away from the engine to tighten it. The electric cables to the alternator should have solid connections and be free of corrosion. Make sure the mounting bracket is secure and all the cables lead fairly.

Tanks

The fuel tank should be mounted near the engine, riding low in the boat to keep the fuel cool and lend stability to the boat. The tank is usually mounted at about the same level as the engine.

Fuel tanks are typically made of aluminum or stainless steel, although fiberglass tanks are sometimes seen. Be sure that the tank is tightly secured and will not shift, even if the boat is rolled. Inspect the fuel line fitting, the hose clamps holding the fuel line on the fitting, vent fitting and hose, and the clamps securing the hose to the primary fuel filter.

If there are observation ports in the tank, check there for signs of leakage. Take a port off to examine the tank for algae growth, and open the sump beneath the tank to check for sediment. Drain any sludge from the tank until only clean diesel fuel remains. If there is no sump available, insert a long pipette through the observation port down to the bottom. Cover the top of the pipette with your thumb and withdraw the pipette. If the fuel sample contains sediment, it's wise to empty the tank, clean it thoroughly, and refill with fresh diesel fuel.

It's quite common for fuel gauges to malfunction—either they don't work at all or they give inaccurate readings—so I've learned not to trust an electronic fuel gauge until it has been proven to work. One way to get a rough estimate is to observe the fuel gauge reading, then open the observation port and measure the depth of fuel in the tank. Using simple math, calculate the fraction of tank fullness and translate that into gallons.

For example, if a 60-gallon tank is ⅔ full, it contains:

$$60 \times ⅔ = 120 \div 3 = 40 \text{ gallons}$$

You should be able to monitor the remaining fuel without using the fuel gauge. If there are multiple fuel tanks, become familiar with the valves and make sure you know which way to turn the valves to open or close the fuel flow from each tank.

Instruments

There are a number of gauges with readouts (i.e. gauges displaying oil pressure, battery charge, and water temperature; an engine-hours meter; and a tachometer) in the cockpit or navigation area. With the engine running, observe each instrument to make sure it functions. The temperature gauge and its sensing bulb are constructed as a single unit and must be replaced as such. A malfunctioning tachometer is usually the fault of its cable.

Most modern marine engines are fitted with electronic instrumentation consisting of a sensor unit at the engine wired to a readout, warning light, or alarm. The receptor unit receives current from the ignition switch. The current travels from there to the engine sensor, which also acts as a switch. If there is a malfunction in what the sensor is designed to monitor, oil pressure for example, the switch will close and complete the circuit with the receptor unit. The current then activates the readout, alarm, or light bulb to alert you to the malfunction. To test for a problem with the instrument, trace the current's flow from the ignition switch to the gauge, then to the sending unit to determine where the current is interrupted or to what point current flows but does not activate that component.

If the sensor will not activate (it's shorted out) or will not shut off at all (it's open-circuited), turn off the ignition switch and remove the wires from the sensor unit. Test the sensor with an ohmmeter. Ohmmeter and voltmeter functions are discussed in Chapter 7. Connect the ohmmeter between the sensor unit's positive terminal and a ground source. The ohmmeter should read infinite ohms (total resistance) in normal operating conditions. A faulty sensor unit must be replaced—it cannot be repaired.

Starter

If the boat is equipped with a starter solenoid, inspect the wiring for corrosion or loose fittings. If the engine starts, the solenoid is working. Be aware that, at sea, if the engine fails to start, the solenoid may be at fault. In that instance, you can bypass the solenoid by making a connection, using a screwdriver insulated with rubber grips, between the incoming wire and the wire that leaves the solenoid to supply the starter. Alternatively, the wires can be connected directly to the starter to bypass the solenoid entirely, but these are only temporary fixes.

The starter should be located near the front of the engine, on the side closest to the battery. Check the wire connections and look for signs of corrosion of the motor. If the starter looks clean from the outside and turns the engine over, there's no reason to inspect it further. But if the starter fails to respond to the ignition

switch, and the solenoid works, the starter motor itself must be inspected. If the electrical connections are solid, you can use a voltmeter to determine whether current is reaching the starter. If so, it's best not to attempt a repair; just replace the unit.

Whenever a problem is detected in the engine, or replacement parts are brought aboard, I'd recommend installing the replacements and keeping the working originals as spares. This is beneficial in a number of ways—any defective parts are replaced; you learn the intricacies of making that repair under controlled circumstances at safe harbor rather than figuring it out on a tossing sea; and you have a spare part that has already proven itself in service.

This concludes the engine inspection portion of this chapter, and now we'll move on to the transmission.

TRANSMISSIONS

Most transmissions are either two-shaft or hydraulic. It's easy to differentiate between the two by a simple external examination. If the transmission has its own oil pump, oil filter, and rigid lines from the pump to the transmission, it's a hydraulic transmission.

Gearboxes are housings containing a series of gears arranged so that, when engaged by a clutch, the shaft is engaged and transfers torque in a forward or reverse direction. The arrangement of shafts, gears and clutches may differ between transmissions, but the basic principle is similar. The gearshift lever controls clutch action. In a two-shaft gear transmission, the gearshift controls the clutches directly, but a hydraulic transmission uses pressurized oil to direct movement of the clutches.

You should use a dipstick to check the oil level in the transmission housing. There is usually an O-ring on the dipstick to prevent leakage of transmission fluid from the opening. Transmission fluid is either a specific fluid recommended by the owner's manual or WD30 engine oil. The fluid should be clear. Dark fluid is an indication of hydraulic transmission overheating. These systems usually have an oil cooler to moderate the heated oil. Dark oil indicates that the oil cooler is not working, the transmission has been taxed too severely, or a cooler should be installed. Water or dirt can enter a hydraulic transmission through a leaky oil cooler that uses raw water as the coolant. Transmission fluid that's been contaminated by water has a milky, viscous appearance. Check for leaks in the oil cooler and make sure that the zinc anode does not need replacement.

Next, focus on the mode of gearbox control. The control station (pedestal) has connections for both gear selection and the engine throttle, and they must be worked in tandem when shifting gears. You'll also find a control station connection for the engine cut-off cable. Be aware that if there is more than one control station, i.e. in the pilothouse and cockpit, there will be cables from both locations.

From the control station, several systems are used to control the engine and transmission. These systems are: the cable system, the cable-over-pulley system, and the push-pull cable system.

The push-pull cable system is becoming the most popular method seen on boats today because control of the engine throttle and transmission shifting is accomplished with one movement of the control unit. By this I mean that, from driving forward at speed, when the lever is brought back, the engine throttles down. At the neutral point, the engine is at a low rpm and the forward clutch is disengaged. As the lever continues back the reverse clutch is engaged while the engine is still at a low rpm. Pulling the control lever back farther increases the engine output with the transmission in reverse.

Trace the cables as they run down from the control station. The control lever connects to two chains that in turn connect with cables. As the lever moves forward, one chain is elevated while the other is depressed. One cable connects to the engine throttle, the other to the transmission control lever. The cable system resembles the throttle control cable on a lawnmower, and the cable-over-pulley method features wire cables, often enclosed within a metal sheathing, directed along pulleys.

Trace each link in the control system to become familiar with its particular scheme and how it functions. Be aware that there are far more problems in shifting mechanisms than in transmissions, so don't take this part of the inspection lightly—as I once did.

I was heading for a slip with a stiff wind from astern in a Hunter 28.5, a new boat that had only recently been commissioned. To that point she'd been flawless, and I neglected to perform a thorough inspection, assuming it was unnecessary in a new boat. Big mistake. I backed off the throttle as we neared the outer piers and then shifted into reverse. I was concerned at not feeling the normal change in propeller direction, and with the wind pushing from aft and the dock getting closer, I pulled back on the control even more to increase power in reverse. The power increased all right—in forward—and we slammed into the steel breakwall. There was a deep gash in the bow (Photo 6-4) but no injuries except to my ego.

As it turned out, the reversing push-pull cable had become unscrewed from the gear lever, while the cable controlling engine power remained perfectly connected and operational. I have since adopted a different method of docking—before beginning docking, I throttle down and engage the reverse gear, just to make sure it's there. This way I know the engine throttle and gearbox are under my control before approaching the dock.

Continue the inspection by ensuring all cables make their way down to the engine fairly, and are not impinged upon or forced out of their normal routes. Look for cuts or breaks in cable

PHOTO 6-4
This bow was damaged when the vessel rammed into the sea wall following failure of the shift linkage. Sometimes we must learn from our misfortunes.

coverings and be sure the end terminals are sound. Corrosion is a factor with steel cables, so check them closely. The cables are often fitted to metal rods, so look for any separation. Make sure the cable/rod is securely connected to the engine or transmission. The rods are often threaded to screw into a fitting on the control arm, and this connection must be secure. If the connection is held by a pin through the cable terminal, the pin should be cotter-pinned and secured. It's wise to use another means (a second nut, Loctite, a cotter pin or wire) to further secure the connection. Beware, as ever, the possibility of corrosion with differing metal parts.

DRIVESHAFT

From the transmission, the driveshaft couples with the propeller shaft. Inspect this coupling carefully. To say this union is important is an understatement—should it part, the propeller shaft can be pulled aft out of the stern tube, leaving a hole open to the seas. The coupling, between two matching metal plates, must be exact. In the event of misalignment, you'll have noise, vibration, and loss of power along with undue wear on the transmission gears, transmission oil, engine, stuffing box, and cutless bearing. Focus your attention on two important aspects of the coupling—its security and its alignment.

Couplings are connected with bolts, pins, or both and should be keyed to their shafts. It's also a good idea to take measures to ensure the fixtures cannot loosen. For example, use cotter pins to hold a pin in place or wire screws to prevent them from vibrating out of position. It's imperative that this coupling does not separate.

As for driveshaft to propeller shaft alignment, the first step is to start the engine, and, after making sure all dock lines are in place, engage the transmission. If the alignment is correct, you'll have a smooth, vibration-free feel. While a mate stays in the cockpit, go below to observe the coupling and the prop shaft along its length. You should be able to spot any misalignment.

If you believe the shaft is misaligned, disassemble the coupling and, if the shaft is not a long one, support it midway with a notched wood block. If the shaft sags due to a longer run, weigh the shaft and divide by two. Add that to the coupling weight and suspend the shaft with a spring scale set at that weight. With the shaft suspended, oppose the two partners of the coupling—there should be a protrusion in the face of one that fits into a recess of the other. If any effort is necessary to bring them together, there's a problem.

Regarding proper alignment, you must also verify that the coupling faces are in perfect opposition. Use a feeler gauge to measure spaces on the top, bottom and both sides. There should be no more than 1/1000-inch per one inch of coupling diameter between any of the measurements. Assess the prop shaft by turning it 180 degrees while you hold the driveshaft coupling still. If the largest gap is still in the same place, the engine is misaligned; but if the gap has rotated, it indicates that the prop shaft is bent. A bent shaft must be taken to a machine shop to determine if it can be straightened. Also, the coupling should be checked to determine that it's precisely connected to the shaft. If not, it can be corrected.

The engine mounts must be loosened in order to move the engine to true the couplings. This is a slow, exacting process that entails a small engine movement followed by repeated coupling measurements. I, for one, prefer to have this done by a professional while I spend my time with tasks like navigation or voyage routing.

STUFFING BOX

The stuffing box is located along the aft propeller shaft as it enters the stern tube, and, although it's easily inspected, when you think about the job it performs it becomes obvious why you must keep it well maintained. The stuffing box prevents an inrushing of seawater through the stern tube and provides a secure passage for the shaft. A compromise of this barrier between the boat and the sea could result in a sinking.

For decades, the stuffing box has basically been comprised of greased flax encircling the shaft. How tightly the flax is encased within the housing is controlled by an assembly at the front end. By tightening a "packing nut," the flax is compressed more tightly around the shaft, thus making it more watertight. A product called Drip-Free Packing is now available. It's installed within the stuff-

ing box between two rings of conventional greased flax. Drip-Free has the consistency of dry Play-Doh and is easy to mold into place within the stuffing box. The manufacturer says it's simple to use, provides a dripless seal, and is guaranteed for the life of the boat.

The stuffing box is said to be well-configured when there is no water dripping through it when the shaft is not spinning, while two to four drops per minute are about right when the shaft is in motion. This small amount of water means that enough is present to lubricate the shaft, and that the stuffing is not so compressed as to hinder its motion. Of course, excess water indicates a malfunction and contributes to corrosion problems with metal components.

In the past, the stuffing box was mounted directly to the boat, with a capsule of stuffing material bolted to it. In modern designs, there is a length of hose incorporated between the two halves of the stuffing box, allowing a degree of flexibility of shaft motion. In truth, engine and shaft misalignment is the cause of most stuffing box problems, so the flexibility is only of minor benefit. In addition, the flexible hose can cause problems if it leaks or if its hose clamps fail. Inspection of the stuffing box should include a close look at the hose clamps for corrosion. As with any hose clamp, back off the screw two turns to expose any hidden signs of corrosion.

Be sure the screws of the screw clamps are oriented opposite of each other. This part of the clamp, where the screws are, is flat, and two flattened areas of hose should not be in line. Tighten the screws and inspect the hoses for cracks, slits or bulges. Should there be any sign of failure, the hose section of the stuffing box must be replaced by removing the aft section of the box from the stern tube assembly.

A grease fitting or grease cup may be present on some older stuffing box models. These usually require the regular addition of grease, typically every eight to 10 hours of running time, according to manufacturers, so make sure the grease cup doesn't run dry. You should also inspect the stuffing box for water dripping. If, with the engine running and the shaft spinning, no water drips, or if it drips more than four drops per minute, there's a problem. Shut the engine down and tighten the packing nut a quarter turn and repeat. If you end up tightening by one whole turn and the excess dripping continues, you'll need to change the packing.

In the event of no dripping, check to see if the shaft feels hot—it's normally a little warm, but if the shaft is actually hot to the touch, the packing is either old, dried out, or packed too tightly. In any case, it will probably need to be replaced. After removing the flax, grease the new packing rings with the special Teflon-based grease provided. Install the rings one at a time, making sure they are perfectly situated around the shaft and within the box. Don't compress the new rings too tightly or they will hinder the movement of the shaft. If you use Drip-Free, place it between the flax rings, making sure the joints on succeeding rings are separated.

Once the packing is installed, reassemble the box and test it again. Gradually tighten the compression nut to calibrate the rings for the appropriate amount of water seepage. The stuffing box should be serviced once a season to prevent drying of the flax, but given the difficulty in accessing the area this chore is often neglected by boat owners.

CRUISING RANGE

On any extended sailing venture, be it a cruising vacation on the Great Lakes or an offshore voyage, you'll need to address the issue of fuel consumption versus miles made good. Since available tankage, including the addition of jerry cans, provides a finite amount of fuel, conservation of that fuel and maximization of *sailing* becomes important. This exercise will help us determine those pieces of the boat directly responsible for performance under sail in order to maximize fuel efficiency and range.

In the planning stages, you can use this formula to calculate the number of miles that may be expected using the auxiliary engine:

(Miles per Gallon) x (Number of Gallons) = Fuel Range

To calculate, you need to estimate the amount of fuel in gallons that your engine burns per hour. This information is available from the boat or engine manufacturer, and also may be available at your yacht dealer or local engine servicing shop. Most marine diesel engines in sailboats consume one-half to two gallons of fuel per running hour at a conservative cruising rpm. Your expected mileage will depend on how many miles you expect to cover in that hour.

If an engine burns about three-quarters of a gallon of fuel per hour, and travels an average of 5.5 miles per hour, you can expect to travel, on average, 7.33 miles per gallon of fuel during the voyage.

$$5.5 \text{ Miles} \div (.75 \text{ Gallons}) \times (1 \text{ Hour})$$
$$= \text{Miles per Gallon}$$

$$5.5 \div .75 = \text{Miles per Gallon}$$
$$= 7.33 \text{ MPG}$$

If the fuel capacity consists of 100 gallons in the fuel tank, with another 40 gallons in jerry cans, the expected range under power is:

$$(\text{MPG}) \times (\text{Fuel Capacity}) = \text{Range}$$
$$7.33 \times 140 = \text{Range}$$
$$1,026 \text{ miles} = \text{Range}$$

Other factors

You also must take into account the factors of differing wind strengths and direction, wave action, current, and the boost achieved by motor sailing versus motoring with bare poles. These combine to confound the calculations of fuel range. Pre-voyage planning is one thing, but monitoring en route is equally important. Use your experience with this boat or time spent on similar boats to arrive at your own estimate of miles traveled per hour. I use the figure of 5.5 miles per hour for a mid-sized cruiser based on a lot of time spent on the water, and believe this to be a conservative and usable estimate for voyage planning. On a long passage, the great speeds tend to be offset by waves on the nose, so the figure has a way of evening out to around 5.5.

Don't forget that the engine must typically run at least an hour or two each day to charge the batteries, unless other means, such as solar, wind, or charging generators, are available; but running a generator will also cut into your fuel allotment. The amount of charging required depends, of course, on the nature of the electronic gear you're using, but I've never delivered a yacht that didn't require some charging of the batteries by running an engine.

Pre-voyage planning for the available fuel range is therefore an educated guess and should be made well on the conservative side when considering the amount of fuel to take to sea. Subtracting the fuel range from total distance of the passage yields the number of miles that must be sailed. This figure should represent the minimum number of miles that you can expect to cover under sail alone.

A conservative estimate of fuel range has proven to be a good guide and should result in a surplus of fuel at landfall. Using this figure encourages me to maximize boat efficiency with a clean hull, efficient sail trim and conservative engine use.

Using the waterline length (LWL), we can derive hull speed using the formula:

$$\text{Hull Speed} = 1.34 \times (\text{Square Root of LWL})$$

If you have a 58-foot sailboat with a LWL of 49 feet, then:

$$\text{Hull Speed} = 1.34 \times (\text{Square Root of 49})$$
$$\text{Hull Speed} = 1.34 \times 7$$
$$\text{Hull Speed} = 9.38 \text{ knots}$$

This figure is pertinent because we know that, with favorable winds, we should clip along at more than 9 knots, making very good time. Anyone who races knows that the bottom, mast, spars, rigging, and sails must be in reasonably good condition for a boat to sail cleanly. Efficiency under sail translates into miles made good; therefore, determining the fitness of those components is more important for an extended trip than for less rigorous day sailing.

I'll also make a plug for a lightweight downwind sail of some type to boost speed in light winds. Several days spent with the engine droning can instead be sailed with the aid of a spinnaker that makes use of those breezes. The fuel savings are significant, and the crew always enjoys sailing on calm seas, avoiding the smell, heat, and noise of running the engine.

Make note on your checklist of any problems discovered in this section, so that nothing is overlooked later.

I recommend that you stock spares of these engine and transmission components:
▪ Belts
▪ Hoses
▪ Hose clamps
▪ Engine oil, at least two gallons
▪ Transmission fluid
▪ Water pump
▪ Water pump impellers
▪ Starter solenoid
▪ Starter motor, except if a crank mechanism is available
▪ Alternator
▪ Fuel pump
▪ Fuel filters, primary and secondary
▪ Antifreeze, if in colder climates
▪ Injector lines
▪ Drip-Free or other stuffing box repair material
▪ Penetrating oil
▪ Gasket paper
▪ Engine gasket kit
▪ Gearbox oil seal
▪ Gasket compound
▪ Gas engine spare parts (points, condenser, rotor, impeller and pin, diaphragm, ignition spray, spark plugs, coil)

CHAPTER 7

ELECTRICAL SYSTEM

Inspection of a yacht's electrical system can range from a very quick verification that everything works to baffling searches for mysterious failures. To be sure, I've been content to sail without the benefit of electronics of all kinds—anemometer, knotmeter, radar, windlass, loran, GPS and various lights—but by no means is that a preference.

There are, of course, two separate electrical systems on most boats—AC and DC. A basic understanding of these very different systems is helpful as you continue the inspection.

DIRECT CURRENT SYSTEMS

A typical DC system begins at the circuit panel switch. The switch receives hot current from the battery isolation switch to the main bus bar at the panel, which then feeds the individual breakers. From the breaker positive side, the insulated wire leads to an appliance, like a light bulb. From the light socket, the negative wire leads back to the negative bus bar of the panel. Figure 7-1 illustrates a typical wiring scheme.

Electrical wiring should be kept neat and organized to facilitate inspection and troubleshooting. Wires should be bundled as they are run throughout the boat, and these bundles of wires should be secured to solid structures along their pathway. This bundled, secured wiring is often called a harness. There is a hull harness and a deck harness, feeding electrical needs in those sections of the boat.

Conduits, or wires leaving the harness much like individual nerves branching off the spinal cord, radiate throughout the boat to supply power as needed. Many boats use the engine and propeller shaft as the main path to ground. Some people feel that this leads to ground fault corrosion and that the negative wiring should feed a main ground bus to a metal keel or the hull, instead of the engine. We will discuss the grounding bus later, since it is important to our coverage of lightning protection.

I used a light bulb to illustrate my example of typical DC circuitry, but your boat has a variety of electrical appliances in several locations. The wiring, with a few exceptions, leads from the circuit panel to each electrical item and back. The main circuit breaker panel is

FIGURE 7-1
This schematic depicts a typical electrical system in a modern sailing vessel.

Courtesy of Beneteau USA

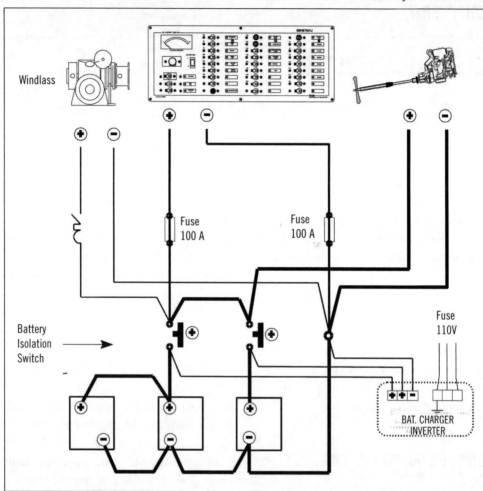

typically located near the nav station— the nerve center of the boat.

Batteries

We'll begin an inspection of the DC electrical system at the batteries, since that's where the power originates. Deep cycle batteries are best suited for marine applications. They are capable of accepting a charge after being deeply discharged (called cycling), can accept many more cycles, and are far sturdier than automotive batteries. Even if used solely to crank the engine in short bursts, automotive batteries are not suited for the rigors of marine duty and are more apt to be overcharged if they are charged along with deep cycle marine batteries used for the boat's house power.

There are two types of deep cycle batteries: wet cell and gel-cell. Most marine batteries are gel-cells—they are more efficient, require less monitoring, are able to discharge and accept charging more readily (leading to shorter charging times), and provide an adequate number of discharge cycles. Your biggest concern regarding gel-cells is that they not be overcharged. Overcharging causes a phenomenon called gassing, in which electrolytes are lost. Since gel-cell batteries are sealed, there is no way to replenish them, as you can wet cell batteries.

If you're leaving on an extended cruise, be sure the house batteries are not more than two or three years old. If you're using more than one battery, they should be the same age and type. If the batteries are wet cells, check the fluid levels—the water should be level with the bottom of the opening port. Use distilled water to replenish fluid levels and make sure you have plenty stocked on board. As mentioned, gel-cells are sealed and require no maintenance aside from cleaning the posts.

Begin a battery inspection by determining which type of battery your boat uses and be sure to inspect each battery. The batteries should be secured within a battery case and the case should be strapped down. The battery box must be well ventilated and the batteries should be kept clean at all times.

Consider how the batteries would fare if the boat were to roll over. Would they remain in position? One of the unfortunate results of a capsize is the loss of electrical power, often due to the batteries tumbling around the boat. Another consideration is keeping the batteries dry at sea. Securing them low in the boat helps with the vessel's stability, but if the boat ships water it's more likely that they'll get wet and short out. For that reason, batteries should be located above the bilge level.

In the fall of 1987 I arrived in Bermuda, having just made port after a rugged passage from New York Harbor. Almost a day out of port a supposedly weak cold front passed, bringing winds of 40-plus knots from the northwest against the Gulf Stream. For three days the wind blew violently and 30-foot waves were the norm. After landfall, while we shared a round of Dark 'n' Stormies at the White Horse Tavern, another captain related his crew's adventures during the same gale. The skipper told of a breaking wave that pooped their sturdy ketch. Seawater flooded the cockpit and splashed through the open companionway hatch to the batteries below. A loud hiss, some blue smoke, and all electronics were gone—including the loran navigation. The crew was able to locate Bermuda by maintaining their course and following the industrial overglow on some scant clouds above the island. Before continuing on to the Azores, they made sure new batteries were relocated beneath an aft quarter berth.

Check all battery posts and cable eyes. If corrosion is present, unscrew the clamp and bring the cable off the battery post evenly. Don't lever it off with a screwdriver, risking damage to the post. Clean the cable clamp and post with a wire brush, then freshen the edges with a knife to assure good connections. After replacing the cable clamps, coat them with grease or petroleum jelly to prevent corrosion, making sure the wires run fairly with no chance of chafe, kinking or damage from shifting gear.

The battery should be located close to the engine, battery isolation switch, and electric panel. Long distances call for large cables to prevent excessive voltage drops. Usually, the only cable of any length runs from the battery, and a separate isolation switch with a breaker or fuse, to the windlass. Check the battery isolation switch. The connections here are prone to corrosion, which causes major electrical problems. Remove any corrosion by carefully scraping the terminals until they're shiny, then applying grease or petroleum jelly. Check the switch operation with the dial in various positions.

A dedicated engine starting battery has cables from the positive post to the battery isolation switch and from the negative post to the engine starter motor. From that point, the negative connects either to the engine block or to a separate grounding bus to the keel or grounding plate. Check the run of these cables to ensure they're clean, and then check the attachment points. With the isolation switch in the on position and the gearshift lever in neutral, test the battery, starter, and engine by turning the ignition key. Apply grease to all connections after checking for loose clamps, bare wires and corrosion.

Battery charger

The battery charger is integral on all boats. Cables from the battery charger are run to the battery isolation switches, which are connected to the AC and DC portions of the main panel, and to the batteries. When plugged into shore power, a transformer in the battery charger changes the 120 volts (or 240 in Europe) to 12, 24 or 32 volts, depending on the system. The stepped-down voltage is then adapted from AC to DC (rectification). To keep the cable runs short, the battery charger is usually located between the electrical panel and the battery isolation switch. Check the cables and their attachment points, making sure that the charger is firmly secured within the boat. I have seen some chargers that were merely screwed into a bulkhead with small wood screws, and were easily loosened by pounding at sea. Any unit situated in a cockpit locker is especially vulnerable to corrosion.

To test the charging capability of a battery charger, plug into shore power, with the shore switch selected at the panel and the battery charger switch on. Using a voltmeter, test the output from the charger. It should read about 13 volts. If there is no output, recheck the shore power and switches. If they are in order, check the positive and negative AC terminals on the charger. If AC power arrives at the charger terminals, disconnect the charger from AC power and check the AC fuses within the charger. Also check the cables and leads from the charger to the batteries, along with any fuses or switches along the way.

I was once aboard a delivery yacht from St. Croix whose battery charger failed to charge, even though the alternator charged the batteries normally. Hurricane season was near, and the boat owner's insurance company would not insure him if we departed any later than the end of June. Despite the problem with the battery charger, I decided to sail after I was satisfied with the rest of the inspection. While en route, I checked inside the battery charger to find the remains of a small lizard that had managed to crawl inside and fry himself along with an internal fuse. Although I felt sorry for the lizard, it was reassuring to install a new fuse and find that the charger worked normally after we made landfall.

Some battery chargers have automatic shutoff switches that disable charging when the engine is running. Disconnect the wires leading to this switch and check the charging again. You can use the charger with this switch off, but must remember to turn off the charger when you start the engine.

Windlass

A separate cable from the house battery and isolation switch supplies power to the windlass. The negative cable begins at either the battery or the grounding bus. The hot side begins at the battery isolation switch, the battery itself, or the positive bus in the electrical panel. To power the windlass, a positive cable must lead to a separate fuse or breaker near the battery. The windlass requires considerable power, usually 60 to 100 amps, which calls for at least a 60-amp fuse or breaker—I highly recommend use of a breaker. Check the fuse or breaker and look for abnormalities. The cables can follow a number of pathways,

often in areas that are inaccessible for inspection, but hopefully they are within the forward hull or deck harness.

Locate the cables where they emerge forward and reach the windlass area, usually running into a sealed box. There should be a solenoid controlled by a foot or remote switch that opens and closes the circuit to the windlass. This switch should be wired to its own isolation switch that must be turned on for the windlass to operate. This protects you against inadvertent activation of the windlass. The solenoid can be situated anywhere along the positive cable, but is often forward in a chain locker since the foot pedal or hand remote is also located there. You can usually trace the wires from the foot pedal to find the solenoid. Any electrical equipment in a chain locker is exposed to moisture and direct physical abuse from anchors and chains. The solenoid should be rated to match the full-load electrical draw of the windlass and it should be protected from water and damage by whatever means necessary.

To test the windlass circuitry, place the isolation toggle on and make sure the house battery is on. Start the engine and run it at a minimum of 1,100 rpm. Make sure the anchor can move freely, then activate the remote or foot switch and observe the windlass.

Examine the rest of the DC electrical system step by step, beginning at the top and working your way down the panel. With the power on to the breaker panel, turn one breaker on at a time and check that circuit. For example, turn on the main salon circuit and examine each light, fan and piece of equipment in that circuit. A thorough inspection takes note of every electrical outlet and appliance, and any item that fails your inspection should be noted on the checklist for repair.

MULTIMETER DIAGNOSTICS

When an electrical assessment turns into an investigation, there's no tool as valuable as the multimeter. With this single tool you can test amperage, voltage, and resistance (ohms), and diagnose a variety of problems from voltage drops and equipment failures to short circuits and ground faults.

Before using any testing device on electrical circuitry, be certain you've read the manufacturer's instructions. The meter has two leads: red (positive or "hot") and black (ground or "common"). Make it a habit to touch the red to the hot wires and black to ground. The meter will read backward if the probes are reversed when taking DC voltage and amperage readings. You can access the meter's different functions by adjusting the dial or plugging the leads into different sockets on the meter.

It's difficult to get an effective measurement of amperage since the scales on many ammeters can only handle a quarter of an amp (250 milliamps) and DC circuits are much more powerful than that. If you're using an inexpensive multimeter, measurement of amperes is not usually possible since it can blow out the meter—a more expensive meter capable of handling up to 10 amps DC is required. Although this is something to

consider when shopping for a multimeter, most of the troubleshooting you'll be doing will involve the measurement of voltage and resistance.

To measure amperage, touch the red probe to the hot side and the black probe to the negative side of the circuit. To measure voltage using the voltmeter function, contact a ground with the black wire and a positive terminal or wire with the red probe. The meter reads the voltage differential between the hot and ground.

Begin testing by selecting the highest voltage scale on the meter so you won't damage the meter if you accidentally touch a wrong wire carrying far more voltage than you thought. Once you're certain you've chosen the correct wire, you can safely switch down the voltage scale to take your readings. We'll most commonly be dealing with 12 volts for marine applications.

Measuring resistance with an ohmmeter tells you how much resistance a given item provides. Resistance is the amount of opposition an electrical device (like a GPS, a wire or a switch) gives the current flowing through it. That resistance is measured in ohms, and it must be measured in the absence of voltage; in other words, the circuit must be disconnected from power. When the meter probes are touched to two points in a circuit, across a toggle switch for example, the ohms across these points are measured. An ohmmeter is particularly useful when testing a circuit that shorts out (current flows where it's not supposed to) when power is on, or a circuit whose power cannot be turned on.

Voltmeter

For a discussion of common tests that can be performed with the multimeter, we'll begin with the voltmeter function. Voltmeters are used to detect decreases in voltage across electrical equipment. When you test a 12-volt battery, touching the red to positive and black to negative posts, you should read 12.6 volts of power. If you test across a functional switch, you should still read 12.6 volts; however, if you test a corroded switch that offers resistance to electrical flow, you may get a reading of only 11 volts, indicating a reduction in flow caused by the switch. Drops in voltage are usually due to poor electrical connections or inadequate wiring somewhere in the circuit. Poor connections are often related to corrosion, but there can be other causes like wiring of inadequate size or problems with wire end terminals. In fact, it's rather common to find wire of inadequate diameter causing resistance to current flow. Anything that increases resistance in a circuit reduces the voltage.

The uppermost voltmeter in Figure 7-2 shows a zero voltage reading, which occurs when a switch is open. The middle voltmeter is connected to a normal switch, with current flowing. A voltage drop, or decreased current, is shown on the bottom voltmeter.

Although you might assume that the problem of current reduction exists only on the hot side, be aware that voltage drops can indicate unwanted resistance in the system on the positive *or* the negative side. To test electrical equipment

FIGURE 7-2

Voltmeter readings across a switch in various electrical situations.

Top – the switch is open, no voltage is registered

Middle – normal system voltage when the switch is closed

Bottom – Voltage drop due to corrosion within the switch

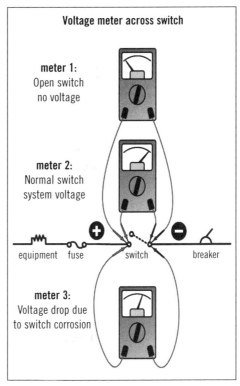

Voltage meter across switch

meter 1:
Open switch
no voltage

meter 2:
Normal switch
system voltage

equipment   fuse   switch   breaker

meter 3:
Voltage drop due
to switch corrosion

that fails to operate when current is supplied, start by making sure the circuit is on—all breakers must be in the closed position (on) and fuses must be in line and functional. Test both the hot and negative wires at their instrument terminals. If there is voltage in the circuit, the instrument is defective. If there's no voltage indicated, then the problem lies within the circuit itself, possibly with a malfunctioning breaker switch or connection within the circuit.

You may also encounter a situation where voltage is present, but below the optimum level. This could indicate low battery power, a short circuit, or a voltage drop in the circuit from unwanted resistance. Test the battery first, and, if the voltage is normal (approximately 12.5v), the fault lies in the negative wiring; but if the voltage has dropped, the positive side has the problem.

Continue the process by testing each system component on the side with the resistance. Test each length of wire and across all connections on that side of the circuit. Since these tests are performed on one side of the circuit, there should be no voltage present. If voltage is detected, it indicates the amount of voltage drop in the circuit or the location of the break.

A short circuit is an unwanted flow of current that bypasses the equipment in a circuit leading to a direct connection between the positive side and the ground side of a circuit. I once had a total electrical failure on a delivery. The batteries failed to charge adequately and lost their charge in a short time. While troubleshooting, I disconnected a positive battery cable from its terminal, and disconnected it from the battery isolation switch. Testing with a voltmeter revealed readings of .9 volts in this cable that certainly should have been dead!

Ohmmeter

The multimeter ohmmeter function measures the amount of resistance in a given length of wiring, across an item of equipment, or on one whole side of the circuit. The meter probes contact either the positive or negative side of whatever is being tested, which differs from testing with the voltmeter. *When using an ohmmeter, the circuit must always be disconnected from power.*

As shown in Figure 7-3, a break in the circuit (no current can flow) causes readings of infinite (∞) ohms (Figure 7-3a) and a specific resistance reading (indicated in the equipment manual) indicates extraneous resistance as the cause of the voltage drop. If the resistance reading is higher than the manual indicates, you've got a wiring problem or a corroded wire terminal and fitting. The excessive resistance causes a voltage drop in the circuit (Figure 7-3b). A short circuit reads as zero ohms since there is no resistance (Figure 7-3c). Resistance that's very low, but greater than zero, indicates functional equipment.

To test the circuitry of an inoperative GPS, first test the instrument itself. After making certain that all power to the instrument is off and all instrument switches are in the on position, place the leads across the instrument's electrical inputs. A very small ohm reading is normal, a reading of zero ohms indicates a short within the instrument, and ∞ means there's an open circuit inside that prevents all flow. This is very often a blown internal fuse. If the instrument tests show normal resistance, the device is cleared, and testing should proceed to the circuit itself, beginning with the positive side.

Shut off the breaker at the panel so

FIGURE 7-3

An ohmmeter is placed across one side of a circuit to an instrument.

a) A break in the circuit causes infinite resistance; no current flows

b) A specific ohms reading should be compared with the listed resistance of the appliance.

c) Zero resistance indicates a short circuit allowing current to flow between sides of the circuit.

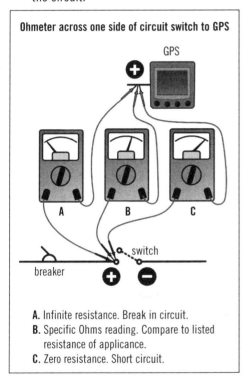

Ohmeter across one side of circuit switch to GPS

A. Infinite resistance. Break in circuit.
B. Specific Ohms reading. Compare to listed resistance of applicance.
C. Zero resistance. Short circuit.

a break in the circuit, and a high numeric reading indicates excessive resistance. Zero resistance indicates a short of some nature. Test the negative side in the same manner. Infinity reading indicates an open circuit (a blown internal light bulb or fuse, for example) but a reading of zero resistance is also abnormal and indicates a short circuit.

As I mentioned earlier, a short circuit occurs when a direct connection is made between the positive and negative sides of a circuit, and current is allowed to flow freely as it bypasses equipment. This is a dangerous situation and illustrates the need for adequate fuses or circuit breakers. Without such protection, a short circuit can cause a fire, often starting in undersized wiring within the circuit—not at the location of the short. Given its ability to locate resistance, an ohmmeter is particularly useful in tracking down a flow of current where none should exist. Two situations in which this condition occurs are short circuits and ground faults.

When equipment fails, troubleshooting usually involves looking for resistance, but when investigating a short circuit or the unwanted "leaking" of current that occurs with a ground fault, we're actually looking for the lack of resistance in a given circuit. Regarding short circuits and ground faults, you're searching for a reading of zero ohms in an area where there should be resistance—in other words, you're looking for a complete circuit where none should exist.

When a short is suspected (when the panel circuit breaker pops, for example)

that no current is flowing. Any switches or fuses in the line must be closed (on). Connect one probe of the meter to the positive end of the panel and the other probe to the instrument input. A normal, trouble-free circuit reads very low ohms, indicating a nearly resistance-free pathway. A reading of ∞ tells you there's begin your diagnosis by disconnecting the circuit from battery power and removing the wires from the equipment being tested. Test the gear and circuit as described above. If you don't get a reading of zero ohms, keep testing as described below.

Keep the power source off. Close all switches and fuses within the circuit (place them in the on position) and place one probe on the positive side of the circuit while the other touches a point on the negative side. Normally you'd see a reading of infinite ohms, as there should be no direct connection between the two sides of the circuit. Any reading besides ∞ indicates a short.

Narrow the search area by turning off a switch. If the meter reading doesn't change, the short is located between that point and the meter; but if the meter reads ∞ (break in the line) then the short must be on the other side of the meter, since there is definitely no current coming from the meter side. By following these steps, you can finally pinpoint the short—usually at connections, switches or equipment where the wire may be crimped or crushed.

The damp marine environment is hard on your boat's electrical equipment. Corrosion often allows very small amounts of current to make their way to ground wiring or ground faulting causing a slow, steady drain on batteries as well as stray current corrosion on other equipment. In many situations, wiring or equipment (like bilge pumps and float switches) are the culprits. To locate the source of such current drainage, we again turn to the multimeter.

Switch off all equipment on the boat, disconnect your solar panel or wind generators so they won't interfere with the testing, and make sure the main battery isolation switch is on. Begin with the voltmeter function. Remove the positive battery cable from its post and connect the voltmeter leads between the battery post and the removed positive cable. Because you haven't touched the negative side of the circuit, there should be no current flowing and no reading of voltage. A 12-volt reading indicates that at least one switch remains on or there is a ground leak. If you determine that no switches are on, you should use the ohmmeter to find the unwanted connection between positive and negative sides of the circuit or ground fault. Figure 7-4 shows how to test the circuit with the ohmmeter.

Switch the multimeter to the ohmmeter function and connect the meter between the disconnected positive cable clamp and the *negative battery post*. Instead of looking for voltage, the meter now detects a circuit to ground—the lower the ohms, the more serious the leak. Continue to isolate the source by using the steps outlined above.

With the ohmmeter connected to the battery's negative post and to the positive battery cable (removed from its post), evaluate the resistance.

- <10 ohms = equipment somewhere has not been turned off
- 10 – 1,000 ohms = serious ground leak
- 1,000 – 10,000 ohms = minor ground leak
- 10,000+ ohms = little to no leak at all

FIGURE 7-4

Ground faults: an ohmmeter is used to detect ground faults, or the leakage of small amounts of current to the ground side of the circuit. Here, the meter detects a connection between the ground and positive cable clamp, where no connection should exist. The lower the ohms reading, the less the resistance, and the worse the ground fault.

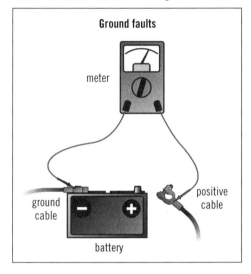

Ground faults

meter

ground cable

positive cable

battery

ALTERNATING CURRENT SYSTEMS

The AC electrical circuitry is the other component of the boat's electrical system. This system uses a generator in the boat, or on land (through the AC power cord to a source terminal), or a DC to AC inverter as its power source instead of the batteries.

AC voltage greatly exceeds DC voltage and poses far greater potential for electrical injury. For this reason, AC circuits are composed of three wires: the positive, negative and ground wires. The negative wire is connected to the ground wire. Should a short occur in an appli-

ance plugged into the outlet, the current will not flow to a person touching it, but rather to the more conductive ground wire leading back to a grounded rod buried on shore. In addition to being conducted safely away, the current flowing through the ground wire will trip the breaker and stop the current flow from its source.

During the inspection of the AC system it's convenient to test the electrical outlets first, then inspect the rest of the system using the diagrams of wiring scheme and outlet locations as an aid. You can test with a meter or simply plug an appliance into each AC outlet. There should only be three-prong electrical AC outlets on the boat. The third prong is for the grounding wire—protection that two-prong outlets don't offer. All older two-prong outlets should be converted to three-prong, with adequate grounding connected to the AC grounding bus.

Testing of the AC system is also done with a multimeter. Begin your examination of the system by connecting the AC system to shore power using the AC power cord. If a circuit breaker is located ashore, set it to the on position. At the electric panel, activate the AC system by turning the panel breaker on. The AC circuit breaker should be a two-pole breaker. These breakers discontinue both the positive and negative sides of the circuit in the event of reverse polarity (connecting the leads backwards).

Note the three-prong outlet at the dockside power supply. Using the voltmeter function on a 120-volt system, use the positive probe on both the ground and neutrals with a reading of 120 volts.

Neutral to ground should read very low, usually less than 5 volts. The voltmeter can also be used to test an unknown shore facility for reverse polarity at the power receptacle. Remember, reverse polarity occurs when the neutral wire becomes hot and the hot neutral. Test for voltage between the hot position of the receptacle and ground—the meter should read the full rated value of the power—then test between the neutral position and ground. There should be no voltage. If you find that there's no voltage in the hot position, but voltage exists in the negative, the polarity is reversed and should only be connected to the boat through an adaptor.

Testing the onboard AC circuitry is very similar to testing the DC. Any test between the hot side and ground should yield 120 volts on the meter, while testing between neutral and ground normally reads zero volts.

Inspect for short and open circuits using an ohmmeter, just as before. The power must be off, so disconnect the shore power cable, turn off the generator, and shut down the inverter. With the AC selector switch in the shore position—as opposed to generator—all AC circuit breakers on and equipment unplugged or off, it's most convenient to test the circuitry directly through an outlet.

In a typical three-prong outlet, the ground is on the bottom, neutral is on the left and hot on the right. Placing one probe in the ground and the other in the hot receptacle, there should be a reading of ∞—meaning no connection between the hot and the ground. Any voltage other than ∞ indicates a leak from hot to ground. If the ohmmeter indicates a direct connection with very low readings, a short circuit is often the cause. Readings of high resistance are more indicative of ground faults.

Moving the probe from the hot side into the neutral side, with the ground probe remaining in the ground terminal, tests the negative side of the circuit. Readings of the negative side tell the same tales as the hot side. Leakage between hot and neutral circuitry is diagnosed by placing the probes across those sites in the outlet.

Please note that it's uncommon to find circuitry disorders on the vast majority of sailing vessels, except for the ever-present threat of corrosion. Most instances of improper wiring or inadequate components occur when untrained people attempt to install equipment. Boats that have been well maintained by their owners rarely exhibit electrical problems beyond blown light bulbs or corroded connections. Having the skill to diagnose circuitry issues is invaluable, but I don't intend to give the impression that these issues occur every day.

Water heater

The water heater is a complex piece of equipment with cold water input, hot water discharge, and heating elements powered by the AC system.

The water heater receives black and white power wires, as well as a ground wire. The black and white wires screw into the thermostat from the panel bus and the ground wire screws into the designated ground terminal. There should be a reset button on the thermostat. The thermostat is wired directly to the heating element, with the wires remaining exposed to make replacing the thermostat easier.

When testing the water heater, make sure it contains water before turning on the power. The leading cause of burned out heating elements is turning on the power with an empty tank. Water should only take a few minutes to heat once the element is activated. If the element fails to heat, test the thermostat with the voltmeter. Touch the probes to the electrical inputs. If voltage is present, turn the thermostat to high and press the reset button.

If there's still no heat, the thermostat is defective and must be replaced. It's a simple process since the thermostat is simply screwed onto the face of the water heater. Turn off all power, disconnect the wires, replace the thermostat and secure the wires. If the thermostat delivers current to the heating element and there's still no heat, the problem lies with the heating element.

Inspect all other AC devices in a similar fashion—start at the individual panel breaker and examine the wiring to each appliance.

POWER REQUIREMENTS

Before sailing off, it's wise to determine how much power your boat will need during a typical day. Of course "typical" is an arbitrary term since different boats and crews consume varying amounts of energy, and it's useful to distinguish between sailing days and "anchoring" or

"dock" days. Most of my days are spent at sea, so I calculate energy requirements on that basis—they would be different were the boat anchored or docked.

Our goal is to determine the boat's electrical requirements in order to compare them to our battery's output capabilities. This in turn determines how often we'll need to run the engine or generator to charge the batteries.

Amps, volts and watts

First, let's define a few terms. *Amperage* is the amount of current flowing through the wires, *voltage* is the force that drives the amps through the wires, and *wattage* is the amount of work done by the current at its end point.

The formula **watts = amps x volts** is very useful in our calculations. Some appliances are rated on a watts basis, and others according to amps required, but using this formula makes it easy to relate the terms. Most boats use a 12-volt electrical system—in other words, there are 12 volts of power driving the current to the appliances. If the boat has a system other than 12-volt, the calculation method remains the same; just substitute the correct voltage.

To calculate the energy needed to operate a 40-watt light bulb in a typical, 12-volt electrical system, we would use this formula:

$$40 \text{ watts} = X \text{ amps times } 12 \text{ volts}$$
$$X = 3.3 \text{ amps per hour}$$

This tells us that 3.3 amps of power are required to light that bulb each hour;

multiplying by 24 gives us the amperage needed for one day.

Calculate the amps for each appliance to estimate total battery loads for each 24-hour period. Use the figure derived and your total battery storage capacity to determine daily charging requirements.

For a typical day at sea, the calculation may look like that in Table 7-1. As the table shows, this vessel will use approximately 42 amps of electricity in 24 hours. Note that our calculations take into account only house needs, not engine starting—our dedicated engine battery takes care of that.

Deep cycle batteries charge readily to about 80% of capacity, but achieving full charge takes much longer; this is a matter of battery construction. We can ex-

pect 100% charging when the engine is run for hours at a time while motor-sailing, but we should only plan on a charge of 80% when running the engine or generator for charging purposes.

It is recommended also that batteries not be discharged past 50% of capacity; routine deep-discharging shortens the working life span. With these thoughts in mind, taking 50% of 80% leaves us with only 40% of the listed total working capacity available on a routine basis. One deep-cycle 8-D house battery, with about 200 ampere hours of capacity, should only be counted on to supply about 80 amps of power daily.

Alternator

The alternator generates power for battery charging, and different alternators are rated for different charging times. The time it takes your alternator to supply the necessary amp-hours determines the duration of charging time required each day. To calculate the time required for the alternator to pull the batteries back up to charge, discharge the batteries to 50 percent of the gauge charge, and then monitor the batteries while the engine is running at a minimum of 1,000 rpm.

Most battery gauges measure the stored voltage capacity of the battery. It's also convenient to monitor the charge of the batteries with a meter wired directly into the battery cables. The meter should be installed in a highly visible location, preferably near the chart table. Digital meters that remain on and visible are preferred. I recommend the Blue

TABLE 7-1

Make a table like this to calculate your approximate electrical usage for a "typical" day to estimate battery charging times. Here, the ship uses 42.3 amps per day.

Appliance	Amps used per day
Autopilot	30.0
Knot meter	0.1
VHF	1.0
Stereo	1.0
Running lights	3.0
Radar	4.0
Depth sounder	0.2
Freshwater pump	3.0
Total	42.3

Sea DC Digital Voltmeter and the Xantrex Link 10 or Link 20 meters.

If you are outfitting for extended ocean passages or cruising, consider installing a high-output marine alternator. Charging times can be decreased by 50 to 60 percent by replacing a normal 40- or 50-amp standard alternator with a high-output alternator. This can be a complicated process, and usually requires assistance from the engine manufacturer as well as assistance with installing the alternator and regulator. It's a good idea to consult the engine manufacturer for the maximum allowable horsepower that can be taken from the front of the engine. The installation requires double alternator belts and, since belt tension is critical with the high-output alternator, you may need to construct a mounting bracket and additional pulley for the front of the engine. Having separate belts to drive the alternator and water pump is also recommended.

An external regulator will be needed to protect the batteries from overcharging, so you'll probably have to upgrade the cables from the alternator to the battery posts. Air circulation in the battery compartment becomes critical with these alternators, especially if they're used in tropical climates, so consider installing two ducted fans—one to deliver fresh air and the other located above the engine to remove hot air. The Balmar 110 and 165 amp high-output alternators have a lifetime warranty and the best reputation for dependability. I'd also recommend their Advanced Regulator System IV and Max Charge regulators.

LIGHTNING

Any discussion involving a boat at sea, electricity, and wiring will at some point turn to lightning. When you think about it, there is very little beyond our control aboard the boat. We are in charge of the boat operations, the sail trim, maintenance, navigation, crew schedules and meals. But I'm always reminded that we are at the total mercy of the elements once we leave port. No part of nature leaves a more indelible and dramatic impression than lightning as it dances around us while we're surrounded by miles of ocean. The steps required to protect your boat from a lightning strike are well worth the time and effort.

I came to that conclusion on a solo passage from Tortola to the Chesapeake Bay in the summer of 2003. The boat was recently out of charter and had no specific lightning protection. Deliveries are frequently undertaken without some of the gear or outfitting that I would prefer, and this voyage was no exception. While I would spend the extra time and money to update the lightning protection on a client's boat or my own, deliveries are often done without all the luxuries.

Sure enough, a cold front came through one evening, with nasty looking pre-frontal squall lines and ominous cloudbanks in the distance. The initial wave of clouds offered surprisingly little wind and rain and, as darkness overtook the light, I began to think this dog's bite might not be too bad.

At midnight I was stretched out on the port settee below, resting as the boat motor-sailed onward in very little wind.

Although the first flash of lightning wasn't followed by thunder, I went topsides for a look anyway. The sky was lighting up all over the horizon—sometimes only in the clouds, but other times the bolts targeted the sea with jagged streaks of bright light against the darkened sky. Over the next hour the thunder grew louder and followed closer to the flashes. I took the sails down and disconnected all electronics except the autopilot, although in retrospect, that should have come off line too. Besides rigging for rain and wind, there wasn't much else to do but have a coffee and wait. By 2 a.m., the skies were almost constantly lit up, with thunder roaring while the lightning that produced it was still visible. I went below, closed the companionway hatch, and did the only thing left to do—wait and hope to get through it.

While crossing the cabin to pour some more coffee, all my senses were stimulated at the instant the lightning hit. The blinding flash of blue-white light resembled a welder's torch; at that same instant the thunder boomed, and the smell of burning in the air was unmistakable. The autopilot started beeping as the boat spun off course, out of control as the blast of cold air slammed into the hull. I was thrown across the saloon table and onto the settee. I climbed the companionway sideways as the boat struggled to regain her feet. Reaching the cockpit, I noted that the engine ran faithfully. I hit "standby" on the autopilot, gunned the engine, and threw the wheel over toward the wind to take the onslaught on the bow.

It was a violent but short-lived squall and I was able to hoist sail within fifteen minutes. Shutting down the autopilot and turning it back on proved to be all that was needed to regain the auto function, and I was back on my way. By daylight, I was sailing on course, close reaching toward Norfolk, happy to have escaped in one piece. Lightning protection makes nights like those much less terrifying and proves well worth the inconveniences of installation.

Protection techniques

When conditions are ripe for thunderstorms, a prudent mariner starts to think about lightning. Whenever there is a movement of warm, moist air high into the atmosphere, there's the potential for lightning. Two conditions can cause the rapid movement of this warm moist air aloft: convection that occurs on hot days or the approach of a cold front. At sea we're most concerned with cold fronts. These masses of cool, dense air move close to the ocean's surface and force humid air skyward. The size and speed of the front determines how much air is displaced—the more warm air forced to the upper atmosphere, the greater tendency for turbulent weather.

In order to best protect your boat from lightning's massive amounts of voltage, you must create a low resistance path through your boat. This allows the electrical energy of the lightning bolt to follow the route that you designate instead of one that may lead to your instruments, through-hulls, or to people in contact with a metallic part of the boat.

It has been asserted by some that the aluminum mast is an adequate lightning rod. Due to negatively charged electrons accumulating on virtually everything near the surface, including the mast, the elevated position of the masthead makes it a likely site of a lightning strike. But then you run the risk of having the bolt follow the path of, say, an upper shroud, through a chainplate and then directly to the water, blowing a hole in the boat. Or perhaps the lightning finds less resistance through the backstay to a through-hull, which explodes leaving a gaping hole in the hull.

It's best to direct the lightning from the masthead, through an appropriately sized copper wire to ground. The safest and most prudent lightning protection is afforded by a lightning rod extending from the mast head at least six inches above any other structure, including the radio antenna. The rod must have a pointed end to prevent the accumulation of negatively charged electrons. An abundance of electrons on the unprotected masthead creates a greater potential for lightning to strike. Instead, you want the rod to be the focus of the lightning strike. While an aluminum mast is conductive enough to transmit the bolt downward, wooden masts need a No. 4 AWG copper cable connected to the rod to transmit down the mast.

From the mast base, the lightning pulse must be sent directly to ground—a metal hull itself can be the ground. A metal keel, centerboard or daggerboard also will make a suitable ground as long as they're not coated with fiberglass or epoxy. An alternative is to fit the hull with a corrosion-resistant copper, bronze or Monel ground plate at least one square foot in size.

To provide additional protection, use a minimum of No. 6 copper cable to connect the chainplates and any other possible pathway to ground. Keep the cable as straight as possible to provide the least resistant pathway. You can protect the engine by connecting it, using No. 6 copper cable again, directly to the external ground. In this way, you minimize the chance of a strike contacting the engine, leading to the propeller shaft and propeller. The risk of damage to the stern tube and shaft bearings is great enough to warrant this protective step. A new innovation, the Lightning Static Dissipator (LSD) is designed to prevent or reduce the intensity of lightning strikes. This device, mounted at the masthead, resembles a wire brush, with its projections facing aloft. The LSD functions on the principle that its many small bristles allow very little electron accumulation to stimulate a lightning strike. I have mounted a static dissipator on the masthead of VOYAGER.

At the conclusion of the electrical system inspection, note any defects on the checklist for later correction.

Recommended spares for the electrical system:
▪ Batteries of all sizes
▪ Bulbs of all sizes
▪ Fuses
▪ Electrical tape
▪ Copper wire of various sizes
▪ Wire strippers
▪ Ring and captive-fork wire terminals
▪ Crimper tool
▪ Soldering kit

CHAPTER 8

PLUMBING

FRESHWATER PLUMBING

Unless your boat is equipped with a water maker, the water tanks and plumbing carry one of your most important commodities—a finite supply of fresh water. Given that each crewmember typically consumes two quarts to a gallon of water daily, your supply must be monitored and conserved. A failure in any component of the water system could result in catastrophic leaking, leading to a water crisis on an extended voyage.

Tanks

Begin your inspection of this system at the water fill and waste removal fittings. The vents for water tanks and waste tanks are located on the upper hull. Examine them for obstructions at the outer ports, then proceed below and bring up the floorboards to gain access to all tankage. Remove the access ports and examine the interior of each tank. If the boat hasn't seen much use recently, there may be algae growth in the tanks. Remove this growth and clean the tanks of all debris. Empty the tanks to remove the bulk—the water filter may obstruct and need cleaning during this process—and then add water with bleach (a ratio of 1:30) to kill remaining organisms. Scrub the tank sides with a brush if possible, and pump out again.

Tanks and hoses should be sanitized at least twice a year by pouring ¼ cup of dishwashing liquid and ⅛ cup of bleach into the tanks. Add 10 gallons of warm water and turn the water pump on to distribute the solution to every tap on board. Shut off the pump and allow the solution to remain in the system for at least an hour, then empty the tanks and flush the system several times with clean water.

To filter water before pumping it aboard, I recommend the Systems IV exterior water filter. Tap filters such as the Seagull IV Water Purifier from General Ecology, on the other hand, are installed on the water faucet to purify water as it pumps through.

Fill the tanks, checking for leaks in the hoses and pipes that connect the deck fitting with the tanks. As water enters each tank, you should notice air leaving the tank at the external vent. If not, examine for blocks. While the tanks fill, check the fittings attached to the intake pipes. These are rarely inspected and leaks are easy to miss. The fittings for the vent hoses are also subject to breaking. If you're unable to examine the vent hoses, an accumulation of water in the bilge and the presence of a gurgling sound are good indications that the hoses are faulty.

Tank fill fittings are located at the top of the tanks and are attached to metal tanks by small screws through the base of the fitting. There's usually a gasket between tank and fitting, and leaks are often due to loose screws, so a simple tightening may stop the leak. If the hose moves about while the boat rolls, that motion puts a strain on the fittings, and, over time, the screws will loosen and leak.

If the tanks are fiberglass, the nipple may be part of the tank, but if it's screwed on, remove the fittings and note which screw holes are defective. Fill them in with epoxy, allow the resin to dry, drill a small pilot hole for the screw, and then bed the fitting and secure into place.

The motion of filler hoses can loosen screws on stainless steel tanks as well. In that case, remove the fill fitting, drill out the stripped threads, and enlarge the screw hole to accommodate a larger screw. To complete the repair, bed the fitting into position and screw in the old screws along with larger, self-tapping stainless screws. Secure any hose that can cause problems with the fittings.

The fitting's nipple is also subject to vibration and jostling of the attached hose. Plastic nipples do break, making it necessary to replace the entire fitting. In that case, remove the broken fitting—noting the size of the hose attached to the fitting. Get a new fitting that will accommodate that hose size and secure the new fitting using the same holes as the previous one or, if those holes don't line up, drill new holes.

Drill starter holes into the tank to match the holes in the fitting base. These must, of course, be smaller than the screw diameters. Once the holes are drilled, apply bedding compound, set the fitting into position and screw down firmly.

You should be able to detect air escaping from the vents as water fills the tanks. If not, it will be difficult to fill the tank completely. Once you've cleaned the vent, you should hear a "pop" as the metal tank expands with the water's weight. If air is not leaving the vent, there's a blockage at the outer vent orifice, in the vent hose, or at the tank fitting. Check the outer orifice first, and clean as necessary. Then check the tank fitting for clogs, which usually turn out to be algae. If none are detected, remove the hose from the tank fitting and inspect it. However, clogs in the hose are rare.

Once the water tanks have been filled, be sure to secure the observation port on top of each tank and check for leaks—they're not uncommon here. Leaks are usually the result of a worn gasket between the port lid and tank, or a loose screw-in port fitting. If a gasket is worn, replace it. If the port lid is loose, remove it, apply Teflon tape, and screw it back in securely.

On boats with more than one water tank, there are valves that determine which tank is being used at a particular time. Inspect these valves, alternating between the tanks. Check for leaks and be sure water flows to each faucet from its designated tank. Failure of water to flow indicates an obstruction in the supply line from that tank to the valve. You may be able to disconnect the hose at the valve and dislodge the obstruction by blowing into the hose. If possible, you should also check the stem extending into the tank for obstructions. If there's a screen, that's almost certainly the culprit.

Most leaks in the system are at the tank fittings, valves, or water pump hose fittings, so check for rust around the screws of hose clamps. If the clamps are made of 400 series stainless steel, they will often rust, weaken, and break. If you suspect the clamps are of this inferior steel, see if they draw a magnet—if so, remove them and throw them away. If you find rust, replace the hose clamps with those designated series 300 or 360. These are truly stainless and non-magnetic. The replacement of defective hose clamps, leaky faucets, and faulty tank fittings usually stops most water leaks.

It's a good idea to examine the entire system, whether you find leaks or not. Be sure all junctions are double hose-clamped, there's no crimping or chafe, and the pump is solidly attached to its base. Check the pump filter for debris.

Age, wear and corrosion all take their toll. In the uncommon event that a chafed or worn hose leaks water, that section of hose must be replaced.

Pumps

Water systems almost always use an electric diaphragm pump; and they won't pump if air gets in them, which sometimes happens when the pump continues running on an empty tank. You'll have to switch to a full tank, open a faucet, and wait while air is removed from the line. If at the dock, hasten the process by pumping water into that tank's water intake. That creates some line pressure and forces water into the pump. Once it regains its prime the pump will move water.

In a functional system, the pump might run for a few seconds after the faucet is closed. Once the pump achieves adequate pressure in the system, it normally shuts off. If it doesn't shut off, or runs intermittently while no water is being used, there's probably a leak in a hose, tank or valve. Starting with the water pump, look and listen as you examine the system for leaks.

In the freshwater supply application, the pump is accompanied by a check valve on the discharge side and a high-pressure switch. The switch works like a solenoid, opening the electrical circuit to the pump at a certain pressure level and closing the switch when the pressure decreases. The pressure switch is usually located on the pump itself. If the pump fails to activate, check the pressure switch by removing the switch wires and connecting them directly to the pump. Of course, any time electrical wires are handled the breaker switch should be turned off beforehand.

A pump that fails to work indicates a

problem with the electrical input, pressure switch or pump motor. Check the voltage in the wires leading to the pressure switch and the motor. If they're not receiving current, the problem is upstream, so use your multimeter to examine the wiring and circuit breaker.

If current is reaching the pressure switch, disconnect the wires from the switch and connect them to the motor. If the motor runs, the switch is defective and must be replaced—these switches are closed units and cannot be repaired. If the motor does not run, you've found the problem.

Check to see if there's a switch that disables the motor when water tank levels are low. If the tank has sufficient water, try bypassing the switch by connecting the wires directly to the pump. Some motors have a high-temperature switch that cuts the current in the event of overheating. If the motor is hot, allow it to cool then try starting it again. There should also be a reset button on the motor. If the motor is cool, hit reset and try the motor again. Should the motor still fail to work, bypass the switch and wire it directly. If the motor runs, the switch is bad and should be replaced. You could also simply bypass the switch, but you'll need to monitor the run time of the motor to prevent overheating.

Beyond this, the pump motor may be your problem. As discussed in Chapter 2, most problems with electric motors involve worn, broken or dirty brushes, as well as dirt on the commutator preventing adequate contact with brushes. See Chapter 2 for suggestions on examining and testing defective electric motors. In

reality, there are far more problems with pump mechanisms than with the motors that drive them. If the pump motor operates, but is loud and shaky, there may be an obstruction or kink in the supply line. The pump may also be loose on its bed or may require padding underneath to absorb vibrations. There could also be internal problems like missing bearings and loose pulleys or drive belts.

A pump that runs but doesn't move water indicates a clogged or leaking access line. Check the line for obstructions and listen carefully for leaks. Remember that any air in the line destroys the pump prime. Check that the water tank has water and the strainer is not plugged. A torn pump diaphragm, or debris trapped in a valve, may also be the problem.

Pressure can also be lost backward through the pump itself, indicating a bad valve at the pump discharge. In that case, the pump requires disassembly and inspection. Open the faucets to relieve system pressure and disable power to the pump at the circuit panel. For pumps with internal motors, you need to unscrew the motor from the pump head, and then unscrew the pump cover to expose the internal workings. For pumps with external motors, you need only unscrew the pump head.

Once inside the pump, you have access to the valves, drive unit and diaphragm. Inspect for obstructions or debris in the valves. Once they've been cleared, be sure to replace the valves exactly as they were positioned. The discharge fitting may have a check valve and, if it's damaged, the unit will have to be replaced. A torn diaphragm will need to be replaced as well. Just unscrew the ring holding the diaphragm in position and, when installing its replacement, be certain it is positioned exactly as the old one.

If the pump is operational, but kicks on intermittently even without water usage, a leak that allows a decrease in pressure is at fault. There can be a water leak anywhere from the tank, to the pump, to the various faucets in the boat.

I once had to deal with a difficult leak on a boat being readied for offshore. The water pump would cycle every two minutes, if the breaker was left on that long, and it worked longer than normal to build initial pressure. I traced the lines from all three tanks, and inspected the pump, tanks, hoses and all faucets; but what made the situation especially confusing was that no water ever appeared in the bilge.

Finally, I went to the cockpit and noticed water on the aft swim platform. There was the leak from the cockpit shower! The nozzles usually screw onto the hose and frequently loosen or leak. I repaired this one by wrapping Teflon tape around the threads and screwing the nozzle portion firmly to the hose. The shower is located out of the saloon area (where all the other faucets are) and is easy to overlook, so remember to include this area in your examination of the water system.

Faucets

Quite often, a faucet's gasket fails, and water begins to seep through, so replacing the gasket usually solves the problem. Just remove the faucet handle, remove the old gasket, clean the area thoroughly, and install a new gasket. I have been known to just disconnect leaky faucets as a quick fix on deliveries, but replacing them usually proves to be most effective.

WASTEWATER PLUMBING

You should also inspect the wastewater containment system. Waste from the marine head is either flushed overboard (if offshore) or into a holding tank. Typically a Y-valve is installed to direct the flushed water to the tank or out a seacock. This valve must be in the proper position, depending on the waste disposal system being used. Waste may only be dumped overboard when the boat is beyond the three-mile offshore limit. Inside of that, the Y-valve must direct waste to the holding tank. The valve must be fixed into this position and the approved methods of securing it include removal of the valve handle, attachment of a padlock, or securing with a plastic cable tie.

Alternatively, the head may pump directly to the holding tank, and a Y-valve is then positioned in the waste removal line. The waste can either be pumped overboard offshore or held in the tank for later pumping out at the dock.

The holding tank has fittings to hoses connected to the air vent and a pump-out deck fitting. It's illegal to pump waste directly overboard on any inland waterway, but boats sailing on blue water may pump overboard directly from the head or from the holding tank.

Seacocks

There is a seacock for drawing water into the head and another to pipe the waste overboard. Also located in the head, usually at the base of the lavatory vanity, are seacocks to empty water from the sink and shower. Examine each seacock, ensuring that the handles work smoothly and without leaking. Sometimes the valves are located too closely together and the hoses hamper closure of one or more valves. Check the seacocks for corrosion, indicating galvanic action (Photo 8-1). External corrosion can also indicate internal damage to the valve. If the valve doesn't open and close smoothly, or does not fully stop the flow of water, it should be replaced.

After you remove a faulty seacock, clean the area of all debris and select only an approved seacock as replacement. The unit should be made of corrosion-resistant materials and the handle easy to operate. The seacock should be strong enough to support a 500-pound weight for 30 seconds at the inboard side. To secure the external component, or mushroom fitting, coat a solid wood backing plate with bonding material—I use 3M 5200 adhesive and sealant instead of adhesive silicone—

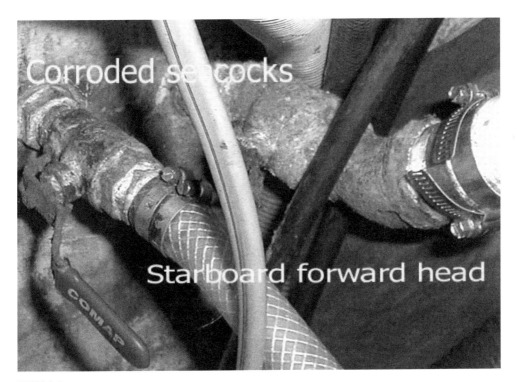

PHOTO 8-1

These seacocks were replaced before this boat sailed. Impending failure is not always this obvious, so check the handles and put pressure on the valves to assess integrity.

and position it against the interior hull. Drill holes from the outside of the hull, fill them with bonding material, and countersink machine screws through the backing plate and into the holes in the seacock base. Tighten washers and nuts onto the screws to secure the seacock into position.

A leaking through-hull should also be replaced using a method similar to that used in replacing seacocks. Begin by removing the old fitting and cleaning the area. Apply bedding compound and position the replacement through-hull against the hull exterior. Coat the wooden backing block with bedding compound and place it against the hull. Secure a screw-on fastener over the through-hull threads to finish the job. The hose barb is now ready for a double-clamped hose.

Hoses and tanks

A leaky hose or holding tank wreaks havoc with the atmosphere below decks. Noxious odors below are also a major contributor to seasickness, so this system must not leak. Work each head and observe the water being drawn in and flushed out. Trace the hose back to the holding tank and listen as the water enters the tank. All hoses should be securely double-clamped and show no sign of leaking.

Hoses used in the waste system should be designated as sanitation hoses. These hoses have a smooth interior to encourage the uninterrupted flow of waste materials. Pump out hoses are attached to a fitting near the bottom of the tank. The tank and deck waste fittings must accommodate 1.5-inch nominal hose. The hose should exit the tank, proceed upward, and form a loop above water level. That loop must be fitted with an inline anti-siphon vent.

The vent hose extends upward from the top of the tank, forming a loop with anti-siphon valve to a fitting near deck level. If the vent is too low, water can enter when the boat is heeled and cause waste to back up into the head.

Holding tanks must be secured beyond any question—even if the boat should capsize. This security is best achieved by fitting metal strapping material tightly over the tanks and screwing it into solid structural elements of the hull. Use several straps to secure the tanks in both longitudinal and lateral planes.

Pump out the holding tanks and flush the tanks and lines thoroughly with fresh water before heading offshore to reduce odors below. Have all crew use land heads before leaving, and rig the Y-valves to pump overboard.

Macerator pumps

A macerator is typically designed to pump waste directly out of the holding tanks after its electric motor powers a centrifugal pump to convert solid waste into liquid. Macerator pumps may be located on top of the holding tank, inside the tank, or anywhere along the sanitation hose. If the pump runs but doesn't move the liquid, the line may need priming. Pull off the discharge hose, pour water into the pump, and then test again.

Centrifugal pumps use an impeller

on a shaft to force liquid toward the periphery of the pump chamber where it is forced into the discharge line. Centrifugal pumps should never be run dry—that will only burn the seals and ruin the impellers. The motors are designed for intermittent usage and should not be used for extended periods. The motors can burn out, and should always be controlled by switches that must be depressed for the pump to work. If the pump fails to operate, you should test the voltage in the wires. If you detect current, I'd recommend opening the pump motor to examine the brushes, commutator, field windings and electrical connections to power.

MARINE TOILETS

Most marine heads are categorized as Type III—those that are permanently installed and pump waste overboard or into a holding tank. Both manual and electronic toilets use a double-action piston pump. Seawater drawn in through the seacock travels to the upper pump cylinder and, as the pump handle is drawn upward, is forced into the toilet bowl. The discharge hose from the toilet bowl enters the bottom of the cylinder and the down stroke of the piston pushes waste through the discharge hose, either outboard or into the holding tank.

The most common cause of head problems—obstructions created by overuse of paper products—can be easily avoided by alerting the crew to the issue and encouraging everyone to avoid placing paper in the toilet.

Inspect the toilet base and its attachment to the flooring. If the head is used while sailing in rough seas, stresses placed on the mounting screws can loosen them or cause cracks in the toilet base. A toilet with serious cracking at the base, usually around the screw holes, should be replaced. If you choose to repair the unit with epoxy, follow a procedure similar to that of delaminated fiberglass repair discussed in Chapter 2. Check the connections of all hoses to the toilet. They should be securely positioned with two stainless hose clamps, series 300 or 360.

Pumps

Leaks will eventually occur in the seal atop the cylinder where the piston rod exits. Before any disassembly of the head, be sure the seacock is closed. Replace the seal by removing the pump handle (and the yoke, depending on what type of assembly it is) from the piston rod. Then remove the faulty seal and reassemble the pump handle. These seals, along with all replaceable parts of the marine head, are available as part of complete repair kits. At least one head repair kit should be standard onboard equipment, especially when sailing offshore. I've also cannibalized one head for parts used on another head. The head that's located to leeward is the most comfortable and safest to use in most cases.

Failure of the piston to pump water may be the result of an obstruction in the discharge hose, a full holding tank, a leaking internal piston rod seal, or a loose retaining nut that has allowed the piston to fall away from the shaft. In the first two cases, the pump is difficult to operate due to increased pressure that develops in the discharge line.

It may be possible to loosen or dissolve the obstruction by allowing it to soak in water overnight. Try that, and then flush the next morning. If the obstruction persists, you'll need to remove the line from the head and locate the clog, which is commonly found at the toilet end of the hose. Remove the obstruction with a hooked length of wire and reattach the hose.

If the handle works easily without pumping, either the internal piston rod seal is leaking or the piston handle has dropped. To replace the piston rod seal, remove the hoses from the pump cylinder and unscrew the cylinder from the toilet base. Take the piston rod out of the cylinder and replace the seal. While the piston is exposed, replace the seal O-ring and reassemble. A dropped piston will require disassembly as above. Reuse the old nut, if you can find it, or install a new one, then reattach the piston to the piston shaft.

Valves

If the toilet bowl fills on its own, there is a leaky valve at the suction or discharge end allowing water to enter the cylinder. To determine which valve is leaking, use your nose. Waste leaking back from the discharge hose will have a foul odor. Otherwise, close the inlet seacock and watch the bowl's water level. If it doesn't rise, close the discharge seacock and observe. The water level should increase when one of the seacocks is open, indicating which valve is defective. Disassembly for valve replacement involves unscrewing the discharge manifold as well as the pump from its base, and inspecting each valve.

Another common cause of valve failure is the accumulation of calcium deposits in valves, seals and hoses. This is usually the case if the piston gradually becomes harder to pump, tends to clog, or if there is a tendency for backward leakage from the discharge line to the bowl. You can remove calcium by pouring a 10-percent solution of muriatic acid into the bowl. After adding the acid, wait for the fizzing to stop, then pump the bowl almost dry. Wait a few minutes, flush the head a few more strokes, and repeat until the acid works its way along the discharge hose to the holding tank. Finish by flushing thoroughly to clear the acid from the discharge line.

There are three types of valves seen in marine toilets: the ball valve, the flapper valve and the joker valve. Ball valves are held closed by a spring that pushes the valve against its seat. When water is pressurized, it forces the valve open so that water can pass. Once the pressure is relieved, the spring forces the ball back into the closed position. Pressure from the opposite direction cannot open the valve. Ball valve springs are subject to the weakening effects of corrosion and fatigue. Calcium accumulation can also interfere with valve function.

Flapper valves rest on the valve seat and open in one direction only. A weight causes the flap to fall into position when the water flow ceases. Be sure to replace a flapper valve with the weight on top, so that the valve is forced down over the seat. Joker, or duckbill, valves are slatted, rubberized cones attached to a rubber sleeve. Moving fluids enter the cone and force open the rubber slits. Flow from the other side closes the slits. This valve is commonly used at the toilet discharge with the convex portion facing the discharge. As mentioned earlier, these components are all included in toilet repair kits and should be standard equipment on board.

Open the toilet water supply seacock. Be sure the Y-valve directs flow toward the holding tank and the toilet is in the wet bowl position, then pump the pump and observe as water flows into the toilet. Flip the toilet to dry position, continue to pump, and make sure water is pumped out toward the holding tank.

Electric toilets

Electric toilets operate like their manual counterparts, but the piston is driven by an electric motor instead of by hand. Actually, the motor drives a variable-use pump that provides water for flushing, macerates the waste and pumps it into the discharge line. All of the problems associated with manual marine heads can occur with electric models, along with the possibility of electrical issues.

With the breaker in the on position, activate the toilet motor and observe its operation. If the motor does not run there's likely an electrical problem. Test the voltage at the motor. If there's no current, test the wiring, fuses, breakers and solenoid until the problem is found.

The motor may not be running at peak capacity due to stuck impellers (common at the beginning of the season after a lay up) or swollen impellers caused by chemical additives in the waste system. These problems can also cause the motor to blow fuses or breakers.

Poor flushing may be due to an electrical problem with the motor, closed seacocks, line obstruction, or loose hose connections allowing air into the motor. Anti-siphon valves at the top of hose loops can also let air into the lines. These may require a solenoid that closes the vent when the toilet motor operates.

If the pump fails altogether, it's probably due to a worn impeller or blown internal seal. In that instance, you'll need to remove the pump faceplate to examine the interior. Objects can also be trapped in the pump impeller, macerator or valves—leading to obstructed flow, loud pump noises, vibration, blown fuses or worn-out motor bearings. Never flush solid objects or heavy paper and cloth items (like tampons). Offshore you may find it wise to eliminate paper products altogether to avoid plumbing problems at sea.

Odors

Head odors should be minimized, especially when heading offshore or before any extended stay on the boat. Since the use of permeable hosing (instead of sanitary hose) contributes to head odors, every hose used for waste must be designated as sanitary. A low spot in the discharge line can cause waste to pool and essentially clog the vent. Certain marine life in the water may also cause odors, so make sure the waste system is equipped with a strainer at the inlet. It also helps to keep the toilet clean, especially at the top of the bowl where water enters. Spider webs in the vent orifice may cause obstruction of the external vent opening, or a full holding tank may back up into the vent line and cause an obstruction. A failed joker valve at the toilet outlet hose can allow seepage of waste back into the toilet—simply replacing the joker valve should solve that problem.

As always, make notations on the checklist for this segment of the inspection, noting defects or repairs that require attention before leaving port.

Suggested spares include:

- Head repair kit including all necessary replacement parts
- Sanitary hose replacements
- Hose clamps
- Hose connectors
- Silicone
- A siphon hose
- Wood bungs
- Two 50-foot potable water hoses and Systems IV water filter with garden hose connectors. Hoses that store on a reel are preferred.

CHAPTER 9

SHIPBOARD AMENITIES

This chapter will examine the equipment and accommodations below decks that make the boat serviceable and livable underway. On the surface, these may seem like secondary considerations compared to other systems like auxiliary engines and rigging, yet without safe and comfortable conditions below, the crew becomes fatigued and irritable—problematic states on any extended passage.

GALLEY

The galley, and in particular, the galley stove may be the most important item in our discussion. At least one meal per day should be warm, appealing and nourishing. Gathering the crew for meals builds camaraderie, provides a forum for communication, and keeps everyone abreast of the ship's status and latest strategies. The galley is comprised of the stove, sink and faucet, storage space, icebox, refrigerator, utensils, and (possibly) a seawater foot pump. You should assess each of these components before setting sail.

Stoves

All yachts that venture offshore, and many of those that stay close to home, are outfitted with a cooking stove. While the ability to cook is a nicety in local waters, it's a necessity at sea. The cooking arrangement must be efficient, functional and safe.

Let's begin with a discussion of the fuels: alcohol, diesel, kerosene, propane, butane and compressed natural gas (CNG). Propane and butane, known as liquefied petroleum gases (LPG), are actually interchangeable, but the tank fittings differ between British and American tanks. Propane-burning stoves dominate the marketplace due to their efficiency, availability, low cost, and clean burn during cooking. In their natural states the gases (LPG and CNG) are odorless, and therefore require additives to make them detectable by smell. In all the vessels I have sailed and delivered, the only other stoves I have seen are one alcohol, one kerosene (that was later replaced), and one electric oven.

Liquefied petroleum gases are heavier than air and will sink if leaked from the system. The gases are also explosive in the presence of oxygen and a spark. With these considerations in mind, LPG must be stored and piped safely with the utmost care within the boat. Compressed natural gas, although less commonly used, is still a good choice for cooking. It remains in a gaseous state in the tank, under high pressure, while LPG are actually liquid at the bottom and gaseous toward the top. CNG is lighter than air and rises to the cabin top if leaked—still a dangerous situation if ignited. CNG stoves are not easily interchangeable with LPG stoves because of their differences in heat output. LPG produce heat more efficiently and can flow through smaller orifices in the stove burners. To convert a stove one way or the other, the burners must be changed.

Consumers typically prefer propane to CNG, not only because of its superior efficiency in heat production, but also because of its greater availability, especially in foreign ports. LPG stoves burn both propane (widely available in the Americas) and butane (widely available in Europe). CNG, on the other hand, is available primarily in the United States. Propane is supplied and stored in tanks or cylinders of various sizes, but all must meet ABYC and DOT standards. The cylinders may be made of steel or aluminum, but aluminum is preferred for marine use because it resists corrosion.

Cooking gas cylinders are stored in dedicated lockers, separated and sealed away from the boat's interior so that no gas leaked from the tanks can reach the living compartments. The gas locker must be large enough to hold one or two tanks, but no larger—to discourage gear from being stowed alongside the tanks and equipment. The tanks must be secured to the hull in a manner that prevents them from jostling about. Straps or bungee cords, secured to the locker walls or floor, work well.

The locker should be located above the waterline and vented at the bottom to allow any leaked gas to escape at the bottom. The vent must be at least ½ inch in diameter and at least 20 inches from any access to the boat's interior. The vent must slope downward continuously to prevent accumulation of water and must provide drainage at any angle of heel. The locker lid should be situated on top of the locker and fitted with a gasket that maintains a tight seal. The locker lid should close securely yet be easily opened without tools.

LPG canisters must be equipped with an inline pressure gauge immediately down from the tank valve to measure gas pressure within the cylinder. The gauge doesn't tell how much propane is in the tank, but how much *pressure* exists in the system—tank content is determined by weight. The regulator, which reduces high pressure within the cylinder to usable pressure directed to the gas appliance, should be situated next in line followed by a shutoff solenoid valve located within the locker and wired to a lighted switch in the galley or saloon. (It's often convenient to install the switch on the main breaker panel.) This valve enables the gas flow to be shut off, after each usage, from below decks. In the event that more than one gas appliance is used onboard, all tees in the line must be located after the solenoid valve but within the gas locker.

LPG conduits are soft copper tubing and make a direct connection between the locker and the gas appliance. Quarter-inch tubing adequately supplies two-burner stoves and most small cabin heaters, but ⅜-inch tubing is best for larger stoves with ovens. Any conduit holes in the locker, bulkhead or compartment wall must be tightly sealed and tubing should be secured at least every 18 inches to prevent shifting. It's easy to use PVC pipe or flexible metal electrical conduit to protect the tubing along its entire run but, in the absence of such a safeguard, the gas tubing must be absolutely protected from kinking, abrasion or puncture due to excess movement or contact with gear. Note that the tubing should be connected to the regulator and stove/heater with flare fittings.

Another shutoff valve should be located in the galley to provide more control in the system and another layer of protection against gas leaks. Ideally, this valve would be located in a cabinet alongside the stove so that you can turn it off without reaching over the stove. After you've used the stove, always shut off the solenoid in the locker to stop the propane flow. Then shut off the manual valve and, finally, turn off the burner control on the stove. This way, gas in the line between the locker solenoid and the stove will be burned off and the line cleared.

A gas "sniffer" is an electronic safety device installed near the stove and gas line that will detect small traces of leaked gas accumulating low in the boat and sound an alarm. The device must be installed according to manufacturer's directions—totally enclosed and wired so that no sparking is possible.

It's usually convenient to begin an inspection at the cooking gas tank on deck. First, make sure its locker conforms to regulations and the tanks are secured into position. The locker should contain only the gas tanks and related hardware—no fenders, spare anchor, winch handles, six-packs, etc.

With the cylinder valve, master solenoid and manual shutoff valves open—this charges the whole circuit—check the pressure gauge. Observe the pressure gauge as it settles on a reading, then leave the gas on for a few minutes and check the gauge again. If there are any leaks in the system, you'll notice a decrease in pressure. Evidence of leaking means you'll need to search for the source, beginning at the tank itself. Since most connections are within the locker, the leak is usually there. You should be able to smell or even hear gas leaking. If no such clue is available, spray a solution of water and dish soap on all connections within the locker and any escaping gas will produce bubbles.

If you still can't find the leak, check the stove connection as well as the valve in the saloon. The leak has to be in the gas tubing if you haven't found it yet, so you should do a thorough search of the tubing from where it enters the cabin all the way to the manual shutoff and then to the stove. Since the tubing must be of one continuous piece from the regulator to the stove, any leaky tubing will have to be totally replaced.

Inspect the tank valve, pressure gauge, regulator, gas line connection, shutoff solenoid, tee joint and entrance point of the tubing into the interior, making sure the opening is sealed. Inspect connections between each component from the tank to the line as it leaves the locker, making sure there's no corrosion on any of the hardware. Corrosion signifies possible weakening of components, which then need to be disassembled, cleaned thoroughly, and assessed for damage. Anything questionable should be replaced.

You should shut off the gas cylinder valve if you detect leaks at any gas line connections within the gas locker. Disassemble the leaky connection and rid it of any grime or corrosion. Apply Teflon tape to the threaded male nipple and reconnect, then turn on the gas to test. Inspect the tubing run, as much as possible, as it makes its way forward to the stove or heater. Even the possibility of potential damage should be anticipated and prevented. Check the manual saloon shutoff valve and trace the tubing from there to the stove, making sure it connects securely.

Finally, inspect the stove itself. Note its orientation within the boat, i.e. fore and aft or athwartship. Monohulls tend to have more rolling motion than pitch, so the fore and aft arrangement of a gimbaled stove is most suitable. This is less of a factor on multihulls, which tend to roll less than monohulls. Galleys are typically located near the center of the boat, since all motion is dampened most efficiently amidships. It's also customary that galleys be located on the port side. If

hove-to on starboard (also customary to preserve right-of-way) the stove is to leeward and spills are directed away from the chef.

Stoves are gimbaled from each side with pegs secured to cabinetry. However, many of the peg brackets have no way of keeping the stove in place should the boat roll heavily or capsize. This dangerous situation can be rectified by installing a locking mechanism over the brackets to keep the stove in place.

The cabinetry's design and the stove's position within it determine which method is best for locking it down. If you have the room, mount barrel bolts or ship bolts into the cabinetry to span the gimbals and secure the stove.

Gimbaled stoves should be equipped with an approved flexible gas line that connects with the copper tubing from the shutoff. This arrangement allows the stove to move freely on its gimbals with no strain on the gas piping. Having found and repaired any leaks, check the system in operation. Open the tank valve and master solenoid valve, then open the manual valve in the saloon and depress the stove control for one of the burners. You should hear gas flowing and detect a faint odor. Light the burner and keep the control depressed a few seconds as the burner heats up, then release the control and adjust the flame. Test all burners and the oven. While you're at it, toss in a few hot dogs and break for lunch.

Refrigeration

Another prominent component of your galley is the refrigerator. I have certainly sailed on boats that had no such luxury, using only block ice in an icebox to keep things cool. One efficient way to keep food chilled is to prepare your meals ahead of time (like stews, lasagna, and hearty soups), seal them in Ziploc bags and freeze them. Just before shoving off, place the frozen dinners in the icebox—along with some block ice and anything else that needs to be kept cold. When ready, heat them in boiling water (anybody can do that!) and serve with crackers or bread for a satisfying meal.

I have often delivered boats that were outfitted with refrigeration, but elected not to use it, preferring to keep things as simple, energy efficient, and risk-free as possible. Many voyagers consider cold and/or frozen goods to be absolutely essential while at sea—different skippers, different long splices. I'm perfectly content to eat peanut butter sandwiches for breakfast, cup-o-soup for lunch, and Spam sandwiches for dinner, but I recall one voyage with a talented chef where our biggest concern was whether we'd run out of fresh basil!

Inspection of the boat's refrigeration is only effective if you have a basic knowledge of how refrigeration works. Cooling systems, whether marine, home, or automobile air conditioning and refrigeration, operate in the same general fashion:

Step 1: Take a gas vapor at atmospheric pressure.
Step 2: Compress the gas, heating it under high pressure.
Step 3: Route the hot gas to a condenser that removes the heat and changes it to a liquid.

Step 4: Introduce the cool, compressed liquid to an evaporator within the refrigerator, which is at the original low pressure. The cool, compressed liquid vaporizes and absorbs heat from the refrigerator compartment, cooling it. Then the gas vapor, at atmospheric pressure, is piped to the compressor and the cycle repeats itself.

The process of removing heat from the refrigerator and expelling it to the outside is enhanced by the addition of a cold plate. The cold plate is actually a tank filled with a solution that has a freezing point well above that of water. This makes the system much more efficient because freezing the cold plate requires less energy than freezing water.

All refrigeration systems use a refrigerant, a condenser unit, an evaporator in the icebox/refrigerator, a compressor, piping to all the units, an air or water system piped to the condenser to remove heat from the gas vapor, and a motor to run the compressor. Systems may be engine-driven or electronic.

The components of the refrigeration system are:

1. Diesel engine with drive belt to refrigeration compressor.

2. Engine-driven compressor that pressurizes cold gas into hot compressed gas. May also be powered by AC or DC electricity.

3. Condenser unit: Removes heat from hot gas and expels heat into water or air; converts the hot gas into cool, pressurized liquid after heat is absorbed.

4. Receiver/filter/drier (RFD): Filters out fine particles, absorbs water and serves as a reservoir. The sight glass is usually situated atop the RFD.

5. Expansion valve: Sprays pressurized liquid into the evaporator (in the icebox compartment), causing the liquid to vaporize into a gas and absorb latent heat from the cold plate coils, cooling the coils.

6. Evaporator coils: Chills the icebox when heat is absorbed. After absorbing heat from the coils, the low-pressure gas returns to the compressor to repeat the cycle.

In order to properly inspect the refrigeration system, first identify the system in use. The simplest type of refrigeration is identical to that which we use in our homes—AC refrigeration. The refrigerator/freezer is simply plugged into an AC power outlet on board. The AC power may come from shore power, or generated on board by a dedicated generator or AC inverter. In any case, the AC-driven compressor pump cools the cold plate.

A compressor unit connected by direct belt drive from the engine constitutes engine-driven refrigeration. At sea, this system makes perfect sense, because you need to run the engine or generator anyway to charge the batteries. All in all, this is as efficient and economical as refrigeration gets, even though battery-charging times increase when running ancillary equipment. You can identify an engine-driven system by its lack of AC power, and by the compressor unit located near the engine.

In constant-cycling DC refrigeration, the refrigeration unit is wired directly into the DC power system. When the cold plate loses cooling, the unit turns on automatically and removes heat from the icebox compartment until it has reached a designated temperature. Because DC-dependent refrigeration is wired directly to DC power, it has a breaker on the electrical panel. This system is seen on boats that are used sparingly, or those that are frequently anchored and make very good use of solar and wind power. However, the power drain on the batteries is such that they will be deep-cycled daily, sharply decreasing battery life.

Note that the primary difference between types of refrigeration is how they are powered. Once you've determined the system in use, focus your inspection on the power supply. For AC and DC systems, this means checking the wiring, breakers and other electrical components, as well as the electric motor driving the compressor. As with all electric motors, the brushes and commutator are subject to wear and failure. In addition to a visual inspection, it's a good idea to test these components with a multimeter.

The condenser is the heart of the refrigeration system. A high-pressure line enters the condenser near the top of the unit and a high-pressure liquid line exits the unit at the bottom. Water lines (in and out) also connect to the condenser in systems using water as coolant. All lines must be tight and leak-proof. The lines throughout the system must be refrigeration-grade copper, connected with flare fittings. Inefficient cooling by the refrigerator is often caused by poor flow of cooling water into the condenser.

Begin your inspection by locating the seacock and water pump. The outer seacock should have been inspected during the hull inspection. Examine and clean the seawater strainer when troubleshooting, and as part of the routine maintenance schedule. Seawater pumps in the refrigeration system work off DC power and may be either diaphragm or centrifugal pumps. They must have patent electrical circuitry, be free of debris, and be inspected for all faults common to water pumps. Refer to Chapter 2 for a discussion. Sometimes the refrigerator receives water directly from the engine water pump.

Some condensers are air-cooled and become inefficient when cool air cannot reach the fins on the condenser. The unit should be located away from the engine or any area that is exposed to high temperatures. It should also be kept free of dust and debris so that air can efficiently contact the fins. Be sure the air ducts are clear and air flow is unobstructed. Inspect the water lines, as well as the two copper high-pressure lines that enter the condenser, checking for leaks, kinks or chafing of lines, corrosion of fittings and hose clamps, obstructed air fins or restricted air flow from outside.

Refrigerant leaks will also lead to cooling problems. Leaks are most easily spotted on the liquid side of the system, from the condenser to the expansion valve where the liquid is directed back to the evaporator. See below for a thorough discussion of leak detection and system charging. Evaporation of pressurized liquid in the cold plates removes heat from the icebox or freezer. Locate the cold plate attached to the walls and inspect the pipe connections, the security of the cold plate, and any damage that may have been caused by items in the icebox.

Compressors are powered directly by the belt drive from the diesel engine, or by AC or DC power. Concerning the latter, if the electric motor fails to operate, you should test the compressor with the voltmeter. If voltage is reaching the compressor, the motor is faulty and should be tested with an ohmmeter. Open the motor to examine the brushes and commutator. Dislodged, worn, or dirty brushes, as well as dirty commutators are common motor problems. Note that some motors are permanently sealed and must be replaced if defective. Some compressors automatically shut down at high temperatures and must cool before being reset.

If voltage is not reaching the compressor, you have problems upstream and should trace the wiring back to test fuses, circuit breakers, and all electrical connections.

Engine-driven refrigeration requires a belt drive connection between compressors and the engine. Alignment of the belt is critical, and the belt should be tighter than that to the alternator or water pump. Some installations entail extended runs between engine pulley and compressor. If the belt vibrates, a separate pulley should be installed to maintain belt pressure.

Leaking refrigerant solution is the

cause of most faults and poor performance in the refrigeration system. Leaks of the gas vapor are often found near the cold plate, compressor, condenser and the pipes that connect them. If you suspect a leak of pressurized air, squirt the area with a solution of liquid soap. Bubbles will form at the point of the leak. Electronic detectors and halide leak detectors are another option.

Recharging the refrigerant: Charging a depleted system requires the use of a refrigerant gauge manifold set. This is an assembly comprised of two pressure gauges mounted atop a manifold with valves at either end controlling inlet and output hoses. The service hose is located between these two hoses and is attached to the can of replacement refrigerant. Refrigerant gauges are available at refrigeration supply or air conditioning equipment outlets.

If you're hesitant to recharge the refrigerant levels yourself, which in practice should rarely be necessary, a professional technician can do the job. This is probably the better course since marine refrigerant is still mostly Freon—a chlorofluorocarbon that's tightly controlled. Any loss of refrigerant gas is to be strictly avoided, so this maintenance is usually best handled by a professional.

When recharging, the gauge set is attached to the compressor. A red hose (high pressure) connects to the discharge side of the compressor, and a blue hose (low pressure) connects to the suction side. These connections must be airtight, and absolutely cannot allow dirt or debris into the system. Before you attach the gauge set to the compres-

sor, evacuate all air from the gauges and hoses.

If refrigerant remains in the system, begin by closing the gauge set valves, then crack open the connections between hoses and gauge manifold. Next, screw one hose onto the appropriate compressor connection. Once the connection is made, gas will flow through the hose and exit at the loose manifold connection—as long as the compressor has a Shraeder valve; if not, you'll have to open it manually. Quickly tighten the connection to keep lost gas to an absolute minimum, and then repeat the procedure on the other side. The less gas spilled into the environment, the better.

If the system is empty of refrigerant, you should purge the lines using replacement gas from a refill can. Loosely connect the service line (the middle line of the gauge set) to the replacement can, and then close the gauge valves. Connect the other two hoses at the manifold and loosely connect them to the compressor fittings, then open one of the gauge valves and the replacement can valve. As the lines fill, refrigerant will exit the hose on that side at the loose compressor connection. Tighten the connection—that side is purged. Repeat the procedure on the other side.

Once the gauge set is purged of air, you can begin refilling the system with refrigerant (charging the system). With the can of replacement gas upright so that only gas flows, keep the valves on the compressor open and both gauge valves closed. Open the can valve and the valve on the suction side of the manifold. As refrigerant fills the unit, the gauge on that side should stabilize at about 60 psi, depending on the temperature. Close the suction gauge valve once the gauge is stable. Before proceeding, you'll need to locate the sight glass.

From the condenser, the high-pressure liquid flows toward the evaporator unit. Between the condenser and the evaporator you'll find the receiver dryer (or RDF), where the refrigerant is filtered and moisture removed. The sight glass is typically found on top of the RDF. Trace the discharge line from the compressor as it reaches the condenser unit. Remember, pressurized gas enters the condenser and is cooled to a liquid.

Now start the refrigerator and observe the flow of liquid refrigerant as it passes the sight valve. The liquid will mix with gas bubbles, but, as the system fills, the gas bubbles should disappear. When the unit is full, the sight glass will appear to be clear. If the unit is not yet fully charged, you must allow it to cool. This can take up to thirty minutes if the cold plate is warm. After it has cooled (bubbles will remain in the liquid) the unit requires more refrigerant. Open the suction-side gauge valve to introduce more refrigerant while the unit continues to run. The bubbles will decrease as the unit fills—they may disappear completely or form one large bubble. In that case, close the gauge valve to stop refrigerant flow and let the unit stabilize. As it gets colder, the bubbles should disappear. If they don't, slowly top off the refrigerant to avoid overcharging the system.

When the sight glass shows only clear liquid, the system is charged. Check the compressor discharge pressure to make sure it doesn't exceed 250 psi. Check the suction line back to the compressor to make sure it's not icing up. Excess psi and/or icing of the line are indications of overcharging, and refrigerant will have to be bled off.

To recap, inspection of the refrigeration system is comprised of several steps. First, determine the type of system in use. Once you know that, consider the method used to power the system—AC, DC or motor-driven. With AC or DC, you'll need to examine the electrical components if the compressor motor fails. If the diesel engine drives the compressor, check the engine, compressor pulleys and drive belt. In this system, of course, the compressor has no independent drive motor, as in the other systems. Check each element of the refrigeration circuit, from the compressor, condenser, RDF and expansion valve, to the cold plate in the refrigerator or icebox, and back to the compressor. The connecting pipes can leak refrigerant as well and should be frequently examined.

Foot pump

In Chapter 8 we discussed the water system and faucets, so you should already have inspected those and noted any faults on your checklist. However, the galley foot pump is something new. Not all boats have one, but it certainly does come in handy. You can use seawater for cooking and washing, thereby using less of your stored fresh water.

The seawater pump is typically a simple, foot-operated diaphragm pump located beneath the galley sink. When the foot pedal is operated, it brings seawater into a dedicated faucet. In some situations, the pump is also connected to the icebox and sink drain. By closing the access seacock, the pump drains water from the icebox to the sink drain and out through the hull. Failure of the pump is usually related to a clogged hose trap or an obstructed intake valve.

When diagnosing a plumbing problem, you may have to remove a few hoses to access the pump—depending on how it's situated in a confined space—but once you've gained access, the diaphragm, pump mechanism, and valves are easy to assess and service. Be sure to check for calcium accumulation, just as in the other pumps throughout the boat.

Storage

You can't really change galley storage much on short notice, but it can be modified during more long-term outfitting. Start by considering all the storage areas available—not just in the galley but also in the saloon, bilge and berth areas. Store frequently used items in the most accessible locations, but stow lesser-used foodstuffs in more distant locations. Keep most of your provisions within the galley and saloon, since these areas are centrally located and offer the smoothest ride while underway. There is often abundant storage available forward, especially beneath the bunks, but the boat will be less stable farther forward and retrieval gets more difficult while at sea.

We were on a close reach from Norfolk heading for a coldwater eddy in the Gulf Stream, and on board was an offshore sailing student, Tom, who had done very well on his first ocean passage. VOYAGER, my Beneteau 46 teaching and family boat, loves a close reach and she powered well against the swells. After 30 hours we turned the corner at the eddy and hopped on the current's carousel toward Bermuda. With the wind just aft of the beam, VOYAGER was nicely making way in moderate seas.

Beef stew was on the menu that evening and Tom went forward to retrieve a few cans from beneath the port forward bunk. In the time it took to lift the bunk, remove the slide board and locate the stew, Tom was awash in seasickness. Noticeably pale and sweaty when he returned to the galley, his next move was to the leeward deck for some heaving-to, and then to his bunk. He was very seamanlike throughout the whole ordeal and made a nice recovery, just not in time for dinner!

It's a good idea to make sure all drawers, compartment slides, and cabinet doors have a positive locking mechanism for rough conditions. Imagine the silverware drawer flying open and tossing its contents about and you'll understand the reasoning. Barrel bolts, ship bolts, cabin door hooks, cam latches, cupboard latches, hold down clamps, button latches, flush ring latches and elbow catches are all appropriate hardware items.

Many boats are manufactured with cabinet doors that fasten when closed, and must be opened by inserting a finger through an opening to pull a lever and release the door. In many cases this mechanism is inadequate, especially if stored objects are large and heavy, like cooking pots. It's also easy to dislocate fingers in these drawers on a tossing boat. Inspect this type of door closely, and if its security is questionable it's wise to install a latch.

Keep the number of glass items on board to a minimum. Plastic is much safer, although less elegant, and safety always trumps fashion. Canned goods, valuable for their extended shelf life, should be stowed low in the boat. If they are placed in an area of the bilge, remove any paper labels, which can come off and clog the bilge pumps, and use a Sharpie to label the cans.

CABINS

Proceed to the areas of the main cabin situated centrally within the boat. The saloon is the focal point of much below deck activity and serves as a passageway between the cabins.

Keep passageways clear at all times while underway. Sails, foul weather gear, PFDs and the abandon ship bag are examples of items that tend to end up in the way if not conscientiously stowed. Anything that impedes normal traffic flow has the potential to trip someone and cause injury. Whenever a person loses balance at sea, the boat's motion only heightens the danger.

Handholds should be plentiful. There should always be something to grab hold of to assist in moving about safely, espe-

cially under rough conditions. Beamy boats sometimes have wide passages that must be traversed with no handholds. I have resorted to crawling across such expanses to avoid injury when seas ran high. In these cases, mounting strong handholds to the overhead is the best way to make the area safe.

Take note of the saloon table and how it is fixed to the sole. Determine how secure the table is. Can you count on it for support while moving about?

The navigation station should be the focal point for navigation and communication instruments. Navigation is a critical full-time job while at sea. Nothing is more fundamental to safe voyaging, so the navigator should have adequate space for all the tools required for the job.

Designate an area inside the chart table for charting equipment. Ideally, this is a partitioned area for storing things like parallel rules, triangles, dividers, protractors and pencils. A pencil sharpener should be stowed in one of the smaller compartments toward the front of the chart table. Paper charts must be stowed in waterproof cases near the chart table to keep them readily available. They should be arranged in the order in which they'll be used according to the route plan.

Many chart tables are actually too small for navigation. Quite often, charts are folded to fit on the chart table, causing unwanted creases and making them uneven and difficult to draw plots on. If it's located near the nav station, I sometimes find it more convenient to use the saloon table as my chart table.

The navigator also should be concerned with finding convenient (and dry) storage space for his or her celestial navigation tools, including a sextant, time piece, booklet to note heights and times, Universal Plotting Sheets, Work Sheets for Sight Reductions, the current Nautical Almanac, and HO249 Volume I and either HO229 or HO249 Sight Reduction Tables for the appropriate latitudes.

Communication with other vessels often entails exchanges of position information. The VHF, SSB and satellite phone should be located near the GPS and charts so that the information is at hand.

The crew's accommodations afford them a sense of privacy and a haven from the ship's activities and concerns when they're not on watch. As much as possible, the crew benefits from members having their own space. They should have adequate storage space so that all belongings are stowed neatly, conveniently and out of the way. Bunks need not be large. In fact, during rough weather, wedging into a small, confined space is the safest way to rest. Bunks should be rigged with lee cloths on the open side so that, no matter the direction of heel, it's possible to rest on the leeward side of the bunk without fear of falling.

A working stereo system with CD and cassette players is certainly not a crucial element on an offshore cruiser, but it sure helps. Music helps pass the hours at sea and is great for morale, but there should be an understanding as to what is played, when, and how loud. As much as music can help a crew, it can also cause conflict if played inconsiderately.

The electronic navigation equipment, primarily the GPS, must be at the nav station and oriented for easy viewing from the chart table—not from the main saloon. The navigator should be able to simply look up and see the GPS without any contortions. Laptop computers should be used only in areas absolutely free of seawater. There's no better way to ruin a computer's hard drive than to have an ocean wave slap onto the keyboard through an open port or leaky deck fitting. I am now on my second year of troubleshooting my laptop after just such an accident. Once the salt infiltrates the computer, it attracts moisture and is nearly impossible to completely get rid of. Again, the communication equipment must be near the computer so that weather data can be easily downloaded.

As always, note defective items on the checklist.

CHAPTER 10

THE ELEMENT OF SAFETY

The success of an offshore passage can be defined in terms of the safety of the crew. Your crew's well being is critical to safe offshore voyaging, but safety involves more than gear. Each and every crewmember must be alert to the possibility of injury and illness. The captain must not only provide training and instruction in the proper use of equipment, from fire extinguishers to life rafts, but must also teach a healthy respect for the power of the sea and the consequence of its whims. We must make them aware of the need to keep safety in mind at all times. The adage, "One hand for the ship and one hand for the sailor," sums up the concept.

EQUIPMENT

Those of us who voyage in small boats can control a great many things at sea, but aside from choosing the proper route and time of departure, there's nothing we can do to manipulate the weather. We must make our craft and crew ready for what the ocean gives us. You'll need quite a bit of safety gear to properly outfit an offshore yacht, and much of that gear is regulated by law. The United States Coast Guard mandates certain items as standard equipment aboard *all* vessels.

Assuming that most boats sailing offshore are 26 to 65 feet long, these items are:

- Personal flotation devices
  One Type I, II, or III for each person on board, and at least one Type IV throwable device.
- Fire extinguishers
  At least three B-I approved portable fire extinguishers, or at least one B-I plus one B-II-type approved unit. If a fixed fire extinguishing system is installed in machinery spaces, at least two B-I approved portable fire extinguishers, or at least one B-II approved unit.
- Ventilation
  At least two ventilator ducts fitted with cowls or their equivalent for the purpose of properly ventilating the bilges of every engine and fuel tank compartment of boats constructed or decked over after April 25, 1940 using gasoline or other fuel having a flashpoint less than 110 degrees Fahrenheit. Boats built after July 31,

1981 must have operable power blowers. This requirement does not apply to boats with diesel engines.

- Whistle
  Boats up to 39.4 feet: Any device capable of making an "efficient sound signal" audible ½ mile.
  Boats 39.4 to 65.7 feet: Device meeting technical specifications of Inland Rules Annex III, audible ½ mile.
- Bell
  Boats up to 39.4 feet: Any device capable of making an "efficient sound signal."
  Boats 39.4 to 65.7 feet: Bell meeting technical specifications of Inland Rules Annex II, mouth diameter of at least 7.9 inches.
- Backfire flame arrester
  One approved device on each carburetor of all gasoline engines installed after April 25, 1940, except outboard motors.
- Visual distress signals
  Orange flag with a black square and disc (day); and an S-O-S electric light (night); or three orange smoke signals, handheld or floating (day); or three red flares of handheld, meteor or parachute type (day/night). Note: most offshore vessels have the three red flares of various configurations. These are usually supplied in flare kits at marine hardware stores.

Although mandatory, these items comprise only a *fraction* of the necessary gear. Equipment that should also be considered mandatory is discussed below.

Life raft

Begin the deck safety inspection with the life raft. When sailing great distances from land, your boat must have a life raft that can hold all of the crew until help arrives.

Life rafts designed for offshore work have two independent inflatable tubes. Premium offshore rafts also have insulated floors, ballast bags to prevent the raft from capsizing, a drogue, a self-inflating and supportive canopy, and an entrance ramp. Offshore-capable life rafts come equipped with basic survival gear and provisions, but it is your responsibility to supplement those supplies in order to increase survivability and chances of rescue. The following is a list of equipment typically seen on offshore life rafts:

Typical Life Raft Equipment
- Floating anchor
- Thermal blanket
- Floating knife
- Life ring with line
- Bailer
- Sponges
- Repair kit
- Instruction manual
- Survival instructions
- Parachute rockets
- Signaling mirror
- Canopy lithium lamp
- Waterproof flashlight
- Whistle
- Rain-catching gear
- Rainwater collecting pouch
- Water
- Graduated cup

- Reflective canopy tape
- Food rations
- Fishing kit
- First aid kit
- Seasickness medications

A life raft is typically stored in a bag (valise) or canister. Many captains insist on having the raft contained within a canister and positioned on deck, preferably just before the cockpit for quick accessibility. Others prefer to have it in a cockpit locker within a valise, away from any possible waves. A six-person life raft can weigh over 100 pounds. Clearly, the need to deploy this amount of weight over the lifelines from a tossing boat in under 15 seconds is reason enough to have the life raft stored in an accessible location.

On deck, the raft should be stored in a rigid canister to protect it from water and UV rays, but the canister's presence is not license to use it as a stool—it should never be used to stand on. When exposed to harsh sunlight over time, even the canister cannot prevent UV damage to the raft, most notably evidenced by seam weakening. The canister may be secured in a number of ways. Although some rafts are lashed to the handrails, I recommend separate pad eyes placed specifically for the life raft.

The raft's main lanyard should be accessible through the canister. It's vital that this lanyard be lashed to the boat to prevent the raft from floating away after it is deployed. Cut the lanyard only after the crew is safely aboard the raft. A hydrostatic release mechanism can be installed to automatically deploy the raft from the canister.

A life raft is an expensive piece of equipment, so if you use your boat infrequently, it may be more cost-effective for you to rent—rather than purchase—a raft. If you opt to rent, be sure the raft was packed at an approved location by professional packers. If you're not sure about the facility, don't hesitate to ask for references. Get a list of the contents of the raft, whether leased or purchased, so that there is no confusion as to its survival gear.

Always take the time to study the survival equipment packed in the raft, and understand how it is deployed in an emergency. Go over each step with the crew so there's no question in anyone's mind what steps would be involved.

Ditch bag

The abandon ship bag should be prepared with several considerations in mind. It must complement the gear and stores available on the raft to provide communication, medications, additional foodstuffs and water, and—the most important item—at least one Emergency Position Indicating Radio Beacon (EPIRB). The size and weight of the bag should be kept to a minimum since it takes up valuable space in the boat and life raft. Take care that unnecessary items are not included. The bag itself should be durable, water-resistant, and easy to open and close.

Marine hardware outlets offer abandon ship bags specifically designed for this purpose. These handy bags float, have room for the essentials of abandoning ship, and are constructed of tough, water-resistant fabric. The sail bag that I'd used to house my supplies has finally been retired in favor of a commercial abandon ship bag. Thankfully, after many sea voyages, I have never encountered circumstances that called for readying the ditch bag for deployment. That situation is, of course, when the boat is sinking or in imminent danger of going under. Since the odds of that happening are actually quite small, the bag should be stored near the companionway but out of normal crew traffic.

Practical storage solutions include tethering the bag to the central saloon table support, storing it in a head used solely as a hanging room for wet gear, or placing it in a locker next to the companionway. The key is to make sure the bag is readily accessible in an emergency, yet stored out of the way. Your boat's layout will determine the best location. We've already discussed the gear and stores that should be packed in the life raft, so now we'll proceed to the contents of your ditch bag.

The first thing in the bag should be *at least* one EPIRB. This device, in my mind, has revolutionized offshore sailing and is a critical piece of equipment. It should have a battery well within the five-year renewal period, and should be tested frequently to make sure it functions. The entire crew should be instructed on its use.

The EPIRB transmits an internationally recognized distress signal to aircraft, satellites, land stations and rescue vessels. These signals are recognized by COSPAS/ SARSAT weather and mapping satellites that fix a location and relay it to ground stations called Local User Terminals (LUTs). LUTs are located worldwide and transmit data to Mission Control Centers (MCCs). The MCC tracks the signal and identifies the transmitting vessel using the database of registered EPIRBs; then the MCC alerts the local Rescue Control Center (RCC). This agency monitors the area of the distress EPIRB and can launch a search and rescue team.

New 406 MHz EPIRBs are quickly replacing older models. The 406 transmits on two emergency frequencies in the VHF band, 406.025 and 406.028 MHz. Older EPIRBs transmitted on 121.5 (civilian) and 243.0 (military) MHz, which the National Oceanic & Atmospheric Association (NOAA) will cease monitoring on February 1, 2009. The 406 MHz EPIRB contains a five-year lithium battery, and is available with GPS tracking and a strobe light.

It's crucial to register your EPIRB with NOAA because your name, telephone number, vessel type and description, and emergency contact information are frequently used in rescue efforts. In the event that you are sailing a boat other than your own, you may contact NOAA and inform them of that vessel's characteristics. Once the voyage is concluded, notify NOAA to return your registration information to your own boat. The people on staff at NOAA are very accommodating. Registration information and assistance is available by calling (888) 212-SAVE or (301) 457-5678.

Another breakthrough in our offshore sailing world is the satellite telephone. Along with an EPIRB, a satellite phone enables you to get help more quickly than ever. I have had excellent results with Iridium and Inmarsat phones, but poor results with the Globalstar phone. The phone should be wrapped or encased in a waterproof container and the battery should always be fully charged. If the boat has an external satellite phone antenna (highly recommended for optimum performance), be certain that the portable antenna accompanies the phone to the ditch bag.

A handheld VHF radio should complete the communications equipment in the abandon ship bag.

Although a first aid kit is installed in the life raft, it's also wise to bring along the boat's medical kit. Each crewmember should be instructed to include personal medications (like insulin or allergy treatments) that would not ordinarily be included in a standard first aid kit. You should also include sunscreen and hats to limit the sun's damage. There may only be a few liters of water supplied with the life raft, certainly not enough to sustain survivors for more than a few days, so each raft should be equipped with an osmotic water maker and a rain-catching gutter. I make it a point to have plastic jugs filled with fresh drinking water on board. These are easily tied together with a lanyard and greatly enhance the odds of survival.

Don foul weather gear or survival suits and life jackets before abandoning ship. It's also wise to bring extra food (like granola bars—no chocolate because it melts—and canned goods), a can opener, a spear gun *with spear tips covered*, a flare kit, Cyalume light sticks and space blankets. Identification of all crewmembers could become an important matter if they end up in a foreign country after rescue from the raft; keep everyone's passports together in a plastic sealable bag, along with $20, and bring them to the raft.

Additional items to include in the abandon ship bag are: a hand-bearing compass, binoculars, yacht papers and the yacht log (these can't, of course, be stored in the bag during normal proceedings).

Contents of Abandon Ship Bag
- Foul weather gear
- Survival suits
- Life jackets
- EPIRB(s)
- Satellite phone
- Waterproof VHF
- Flares
- Cyalume light sticks
- Spear gun
- Medical kit
- Duct tape
- Large black trash bag
- Hand-bearing compass
- Sunblock
- Water
- Food
- Can opener
- Passports
- Hats
- Portable water maker
- Lithium-ion batteries

I have recently added the following gear to VOYAGER's abandon ship bag contents:

- Air horn
- 2 waterproof flashlights
- Dye marker packet

- Signal mirror and whistle (even though these are contained in the liferaft survival kit)
- 1 life raft repair clamp set
- Rescue streamer
- Rescue laser
- Fishing kit
- Survival blankets
- SART (Search and Rescue Transponder). This device seeks out radar signals of search craft, and then sends out distinct pulses detectable by those vessels. The distinct series of twelve pulses appear on their radar screens aligned to the SART position.

SAFETY MEASURES

Staying in the boat

The best crew overboard technique you can teach is to prevent the situation in the first place. This fact was really driven home to me when I first single-handed a passage from Tortola to the Chesapeake. It became obvious that with nobody else on board, the only option was not going over the side. This is the message that I instill in every crewmember: Don't let yourself go overboard! It's part and parcel of the offshore mindset.

Jacklines

Rig jacklines so that they provide a strong, taut tethering point along the deck. I used line for years, and kept tripping up when it rolled underfoot, so now I use nylon webbing jacklines. They lie flat on the deck, withstand plenty of shock loading, and are easy to stow after the voyage.

Moisten them before installation on deck; once dried they'll shrink and be very tight. Use only solid pad eyes or the equivalent near the *centerline* of the boat—don't rig the jacklines outboard near the lifelines. Securely lash or shackle them to the pad eye, run them *inside* the shrouds and over the cabin top to a point just before the cockpit. Attach the front end far enough away from the bow that tethers won't extend overboard. The principle is that the tethered person is able to reach the lifelines, but could never be able to fall over them.

I prefer to secure the aft end just before the cockpit and run a separate line from the cockpit to the stern. Run the line on the other side of the boat the same way. Rig one or two aft lines, depending on the beam. Extend the jackline aft just far enough that a tethered person can reach the transom but can't go overboard.

The addition of jacklines onto the cockpit sole provides clipping points on both sides immediately upon entering the cockpit area. It's also a secure and convenient clipping point for the helmsman; much safer than the backstays that are so commonly used.

Position pad eyes fore and aft in the cockpit, so that the jacklines run along the cockpit walls. The pad eyes are fastened with bolts and adequate backing plates for security. Allow the lines to droop to the floor so that crewmembers can't trip on them. Like any pad eye, provide ample backing for strength. Our cockpit jacklines are webbing, and are attached at both ends to the pad eyes by snap hooks sewn onto the webbing by a sail loft. They could also be plastic coated wire, like that used in lifelines. Inspect the jacklines frequently for chafe, cuts or weakening from sun damage. Never trust a lifeline with your full weight; consider their purpose as prevention of gear going overboard, not people.

Harnesses

The harness should be strong enough to support a person's weight if he or she were dropped six feet or so. Most harnesses are made from heavy webbing material, and they should be adjusted to fit properly no matter how much clothing is underneath. A crotch strap ensures that a person won't slip out of the harness—even if unconscious. Many harnesses are now incorporated into the newer inflatable Personal Flotation Devices (PFDs). Most sailors prefer these inflatable PFDs, as they are not bulky and quite easy to put on, but it's important to regularly check the inflation system and the bladder for air leaks.

The tether may become your lifeline, so check it for tears, frayed stitching, ultraviolet damage or chafe. Check the stitching at the end eyes for loose or broken threads. Tethers should not be elastic, and should only be long enough to allow access to the boat's perimeter while tethered to the jacklines. Use sturdy snap hooks to ensure that you can release the tether from the harness if necessary. The tether end must include

a well-stitched eye with a safety hook or snap shackle. The hook should stay on the jackline but be easily removed if necessary—the Gibb Safety Hook is my favorite.

Harnesses should be worn *and used* in gale force winds, rough seas, fog, and from dusk until dawn. I have also asked crewmembers to hook in whenever leaving the cockpit area. Children must certainly wear a life jacket, and even a harness, when on deck. This mandate should come from the captain and must be taken seriously. For crewmembers who don't wear a combination life jacket/harness, the Type I PFD (or "Mae West") is preferred offshore for its superior buoyancy and head support. Other equipment for life jackets includes a fluorescent dye pack, whistle, and personal strobe light. Our crewmembers are equipped with overboard alarms when on watch at night. Strobe batteries should be replaced before every voyage, with plenty of spares available on board.

Keep an eye on the dye packs if the boat ships a lot of water, if it rains, or if breakers poop her from astern. Once, in just such damp circumstances, I was driving when we took two breakers over the transom. Having been in a gale for three days, we just took it in stride, but when the skipper came on watch in the morning, he thought I had jaundice! My hair and skin were yellow, matching most of the decks. The dye pack had become saturated during one of the dunkings and leaked its contents over everything. Five years later, yellow dye was still seeping from my gear.

Crew overboard pole

The crew overboard pole is a long orange pole with a flag on the top end and a weight at the bottom. A drogue is attached to prevent the pole from drifting, and an attached strobe light can define the search area at night. This pole is often the best tool for victim recovery after dark. Some sailboats have an opening in the transom in which to store the pole where it will be ready to deploy, but it may also be tied to the pushpit with slipknots. Make sure the strobe battery is fully charged and functional, and the pole deploys rapidly with no tangles. A horseshoe life ring attached to a floating light allows the victim to stay afloat during the rescue.

Crew overboard recovery

You must also have a system in place to haul an injured or unconscious victim from the water. Studies of overboard situations show that it's often easier to locate the victim than to actually retrieve him or her from the water. A life ring of some type should be available at the transom and the Lifesling is an excellent choice. It's buoyant, has a length of 125-feet of polypropylene line attached, and is effective in retrieval. The Lifesling can be thrown into the water, and the boat maneuvered to bring the Lifesling to the victim.

It is also prudent to have a block and tackle on board providing at least 4:1 mechanical advantage—one end should be a double block with cam cleat, and the other end a double block with becket or

heavy shackle for easy attachment. This piece of equipment is invaluable when assisting a victim in the water, as well as in case of vang failure or when bringing heavy items on board. It can be rigged to the outboard boom, which can be swung out over the victim. This arrangement is also perfect for occasionally suspending adventurous crewmembers above the waves and dunking them as the boat sails along during quieter times—one of the best morale boosters I've ever found.

In the event that an overboard person is unconscious, a successful rescue depends on whether the victim is already wearing a PFD that keeps his or her head out of the water—again the Type I is superior. Once you've located the victim, you must maneuver the boat close enough for the rescuer to enter the water wearing a life ring. Never allow a crewmember to enter the water without proper buoyancy or without being tethered to the boat.

Boom preventer

A boom preventer (Figure 10-1) should be rigged and used on all points of sail, even upwind. The preventer itself should be a stout, three-strand nylon line, at least ⅜-inch in diameter. It's best to rig the preventer so that it needn't be uncleated from the toe rail and led to the opposite side after a tack or jibe. Use two lines, one port and starboard, and tie the lines to a boom bridle with attachments at least two feet from the aft boom end, and a bit forward of the middle. The bridle spreads shock loading along the boom, decreasing the risk of damage.

FIGURE 10-1

This preventer system spreads shock loading over the whole boom and allows for adjustment from the cockpit. Preventer lines extend to each side of the boat from a stout ring within the boom bridle.

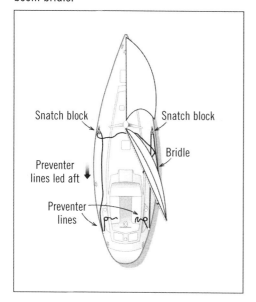

Storm sails

A principle of storm management is to bring the center of effort, or the lateral forces exerted on the boat, inward toward the main mast. This decreases the stresses on the hull and rigging as well as the tendency for yaw motion.

Boats with two masts, yawls, and ketches, have an inherent ability to manipulate the sail plan in storm conditions. Sloops, on the other hand, aren't so flexible. Most ocean sailors on sloops prefer the cutter rig, with the addition of an inner forestay, to deploy a storm staysail and control mast pumping. These also accommodate larger staysails on favorable points of sail.

From the bridle (Photo 10-1), lead the lines forward of the beam to a block on each toe rail and then aft to the cockpit. There, the windward line can be tensioned on a cleat while the leeward lazy line is stowed out of the way.

Do not run the windward line to the primary winches, because you'll be using those for the jib sheet, and the preventer will be on the same side of the boat as the loaded jib. I don't recommend taking the line across the cockpit, to use the opposing primary, because of the congestion it causes in the cockpit. The preventer need only be snugged-up manually and secured to a cleat—there's no need to winch it.

PHOTO 10-1

The preventer attaches at its midpoint to the ring within this boom bridle on VOYAGER.

Storm sails can also be constructed with a wire luff allowing the sail to be hoisted independently of a stay, from the stem fitting, with a jib halyard. Its tack can also attach to an eye bolt installed on the deck. This is a very reasonable option for the storm jib since it clears the deck when removed.

Discuss with your sailmaker adding a storm trysail to the boat's inventory. First you'll need to determine the hoist height of the sail, then the other dimensions and the length of the track. You'll need to factor in the stack height of the mainsail after it is lowered and secured to the boom, because you may not have the time or inclination to take it off the boom completely when the weather deteriorates.

A rule of thumb is that the trysail should not be longer than one-third the luff distance of the mainsail, and should approximate the square footage of your storm head sail (jib or staysail). Remember, the storm trysail serves several purposes: it's hoisted to preserve the mainsail from damaging high winds, it allows us to make way without being overpowered, it's small enough to be easily handled in a blow, and it is the preferred sail when it's time to heave-to. In light air, rolling conditions, the mainsail can be struck, flaked, and preserved from flogging with the trysail hoisted to stabilize the boat without the slatting and noise of the main.

The trysail is best kept in its sail bag tethered securely at the foot of the mast. In that position, it is always ready to run up its dedicated sail track to the port side of the main.

Of course the trysail should have a sturdy construction, with heavier sailcloth, more stitching, and more reinforcement than the mainsail. The sheets and tack line are permanently attached to the sail. The sheets run aft to blocks on either quarter, then lead to cockpit winches. All these matters should be discussed with your sailmaker to ensure a proper fit.

The storm trysail track is usually externally mounted on the port side of the mast, adjacent to the mainsail track. The tracks are stainless steel of ⅝-, ⅞-, or 1-inch stock. Tap the mast and use stainless steel machine screws to secure the track to the mast. The screws must be the correct length, depending on the widths of the track and the mast. Instead of tapping and screwing the track in place, some people choose to use rivets, but that's really a matter of personal choice. Whichever you choose, apply anti-seize thread lubricant to control corrosion.

Most skippers prefer to extend the trysail track to about a foot above deck level, so that bending on the sail is easy. When the main halyard is used to hoist a trysail, the extended distance from sail head to masthead allows for a lot of halyard slapping against the mast. This creates even more noise in a blow, and leads to chafe of the halyard and spar damage. To fix this problem, mount a cheek block on the mast to line up precisely with the trysail track. Mount it just like the trysail track—usually tapped and threaded with machine screws for a secure fit. Now you can deploy the trysail with its own halyard. When the boat will be in port for any extended time period, I replace the external trysail halyard with a feeder line; preferring that the halyard be coiled below out of the elements.

The trysail is free-footed and the clew is led to a snatch block on the rail, and then trimmed on a cockpit winch. When hove-to, the trysail sheet is adjusted as required, and then either cleated or secured at the winch. Your goal when hove-to is to balance the boat so that it maintains an approximate angle of 45 to 60 degrees to the wind. This is the safest and most comfortable position to assume when wind and waves become a threat. The boat will crab a bit to windward, then fall off to leeward, but always makes leeway and should *never* be allowed to go beam-to the seas.

When the elements overpower a sailboat, the bow will tend to fall off, exposing the beam to the waves—this is a sailboat's most vulnerable position. Should conditions begin to overpower your boat, you can maneuver the trysail and/or steer more to windward, reduce jib/staysail drive with trim or by handing them, or deploy the sea anchor.

It's customary to rig storm sails for port side deployment. That way, the boat will be on starboard tack with right of way. Check the reefing lines again to ensure that they're run and secured to the boom, with bitter ends stowed neatly in the cockpit and ready to run. See Chapter 3 for a discussion of reefing. It's always wise to uncoil sheets, halyards, and other lines to remove kinks before heading offshore.

Reducing sail

Our earlier inspection saw to the standing rigging and security of the forestay or jib furling system. Now it's time to ensure the primary jib/genoa comes down the luff slide smoothly. There should be no hesitation and no need to tug once the halyard is released. When the wind blows hard, you want your boat as stable as possible. Weight aloft counters the boat's righting moment, exaggerates roll, and makes it more difficult to recover from a deep roll or knockdown. It's far better to take safety measures before conditions deteriorate than after. When the skies, barometer, seas, and weather report forecast worsening conditions, take the genoa down, stow it safely, and put up the storm jib or storm staysail. If the bad weather passes, it's easier to redeploy the genoa in moderate conditions than to fist it down on a pitching foredeck during a blow.

The consideration of weight aloft is also a factor in my unfavorable opinion of mast-furled mainsails. Even if the sail does roll in, which is another concern entirely, the weight of the sail extending all the way up the spar is not diminished. This affects stability in the same way a furled genoa does.

Climbing the mast

I described a bosun's chair in Chapter 3, but a mention of "climbing the mast" also belongs here because it might be necessary to ascend the mast as a matter of boat safety. The chair must be solidly constructed with plenty of pocket room to accommodate tools. It should feel comfortable, and must have a crotch strap and sturdy back for support and security. Please be aware that a trip up the mast can be dangerous, and should not be attempted in heavy weather except under dire circumstances.

First put on a safety harness. Wear shoes and long pants to cut down on bruising and improve traction. Attach a halyard shackle to the chair and then tie the halyard itself to the chair rings. Next, attach a second halyard to the safety harness ring for added security. You may use sailor power or an electric winch to haul in the primary halyard, but the operator must be very attentive so that the ascending person doesn't get fouled along the way. As the primary halyard is winched in, the second halyard is hauled with the line around a second winch. Both halyards are secured with line clutches, four wraps taken around a winch, and the bitter end cleated when the person has reached the destination.

Radar

When sailing offshore, radar is a valuable tool. It extends your vision far beyond what your eyes can see. In darkness, fog, foul weather, and when ocean traffic or a squall formation nears, radar enables better decision-making. All radar units work basically the same way. The scanner (radome) is mounted high on the boat. As it rotates, it sends out radio waves in a circular pattern usually set to cover 360 degrees. When the radio waves encounter an object (another vessel, a rain squall, or even a flock of birds), they reflect the signal back to the receiving unit. This information is transmitted to an LCD display monitor. Radar systems are now capable of becoming navigational information centers—an upgrade that many yachtsmen are pleased to have.

LCD displays are best viewed head-on, as there are variations in the screen from angled positions. The screen should be located near DC power, but at least three feet from the autopilot compass. There must be enough room behind the unit for wiring to enter without being kinked. The unit should be installed in a dry, secure area away from excessive vibration and foot traffic. It must connect the scanner with the wiring runs as short and direct as possible, and all wires should be protected from motion and falling objects; cable ties work well to keep the wires out of harm's way.

The radar unit has a main power cable, as well as wiring for additional system inputs. These inputs allow for integration of navigation information, so that position, heading, waypoints, seawater temperature and MOB alarm can all be added. Radar units operate on 12- or 24-volt DC power and should have a dedicated thermal circuit breaker or fuse at the main panel.

The scanner should be mounted on the mast, or on a radar arch or post at the transom (Photo 10-2), but not so high as to be affected by the boat's motion—which increases the farther up you go. A good spot on the mast for in-

PHOTO 10-2
VOYAGER's radar, with other equipment, is positioned on a platform atop this stern post.

stallation is usually near the first spreaders—high enough to provide adequate radar coverage, but not be adversely affected by pitch and roll. That location is also fairly accessible, with the spreaders providing a degree of support for someone aloft.

The scanner should be protected against lines and sails, and you may purchase a guard assembly if necessary. Use the platform mounting kit (supplied with the scanner) and make sure it's tightly secured to the mast. I prefer to have the scanner mounted atop a sternpost away from all sails, yet readily accessible should service be necessary.

The type of hardware you use depends on the particular unit and where it's positioned. Your maintenance of the radar system should be limited to checking the electrical connections and assuring that exposed cables are not damaged. Malfunctions of the scanner, display, or cables should be repaired only by a trained professional. To test the system, simply close the main breaker to send power and turn on the display. Hold the power button down a few seconds until the unit beeps. The unit should then enter standby mode and be ready for use.

The display is connected to the scanner by an insulated vinyl-coated cable that must be protected against chafe through its entire run.

Radar reflectors

Radar reflectors enhance the echo of a radar signal sent by another vessel. It is interesting to note that the use of certain reflectors increases the returning echo by the fourth power of the diameter of the reflector. A reflector twice as large as another will provide a 16-fold increase in radar enhancement! Since sailboats at sea are tiny blips on the radar of ocean-going ships, it's to your advantage to make your ship as visible as possible, using the best radar reflector you can find. At sea, I've spotted a number of sailboats, some of them very large, with binoculars or my naked eyes that nevertheless failed to appear on radar.

In tests performed by marine retailer West Marine, the Davis Echomaster octahedron was deemed the superior overall reflector even though, at some angles to the beam, there were nulls in the return. The nature of the octahedron is such that the null periods are short and insignificant overall. Incidentally, wet sails are effective as radar beam reflectors, while dry sails don't reflect at all.

Lights

A spotlight is also considered safety gear. It can illuminate objects, serve as a distress signal, and may be the single most effective way to make your boat visible in the event of a close encounter during conditions of restricted visibility. A mainsail lit up by a spotlight has a higher visibility than one lit by a strobe light. All crewmembers should know where the spotlight is stowed and how to use it. Try not to shine the light on the shrouds, coamings, or the deck as the glare takes away night vision for a good long while.

Keep at least two flashlights in the cockpit from dusk until dawn. After use, they should be returned to their designated spots—usually coaming compartments or a designated sheet bag. There should be an assigned home for the binoculars as well, kept in their case to prevent salt accumulation. They should be readily available at all times, and always returned to the same spot after use. They may be stowed below during daylight hours, but should be in the cockpit at night. Likewise, an emergency knife should be kept in a specific location (near the companionway, or entrance to the aft deck on multihulls) readily available to the crew.

Sea anchors

Our evaluation of safety gear on deck now moves to the sea anchor. This device can be deployed as a primary means of coping with heavy weather, or used when the boat becomes overpow-

FIGURE 10-2

The sea anchor is shown deployed on its bridle.

Courtesy of ParaAnchors by Fiorentino

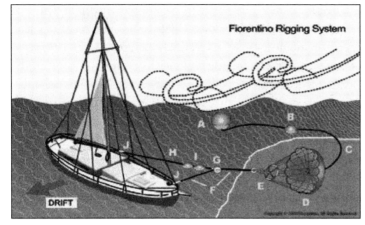

A. Retrieval float
B. Trip line support
C. Trip line
D. Parachute anchor
E. Pararing, to which the parachute lines attach, and is itself swiveled to the anchor rode
F. Anchor rode
G. Snatch block
H. Pendant line for bridle control
I. Support floats for pendant line
J. Chafe gear

ered while hove-to. As mentioned earlier, when the boat is overcome, the bow tends to drift to leeward, exposing it to beam-on seas and dangerous rolling. The sea anchor helps to keep the boat safely oriented in relation to the waves.

Rigged on a bridle, a parachute sea anchor (Figure 10-2) will help keep the bow at around 45 degrees to the wind and seas while the crew hunkers down below for some much-needed rest. There are several types of parachute sea anchors available. The anchor must be constructed of high quality nylon and webbing with reinforced seams, and it must be the proper size for your boat.

While you obviously shouldn't have an undersized sea anchor, it's a little less intuitive that it should not be oversized either. Heavy shock loading is possible in high wind and wave situations when using a sea anchor rated for larger boats. In Table 10-1, parachute anchor size is related to boat size:

TABLE 10-1

Use a chart like this to select the sea anchor most appropriate for your boat.

Boat Size	Anchor Size (Diameter)	Packed Dimensions	Weight
Up to 20'	6 Ft.	6" X 7"	6 Lbs.
Up to 25'	9 Ft.	7" X 9"	9 Lbs.
25' to 35'	12 Ft.	8" X 12"	12 Lbs.
30' to 40'	15 Ft.	10" X 15"	20 Lbs.
35' to 50'	18 Ft.	12" X 17"	25 Lbs.
50' to 90'	24 Ft.	13" X 19"	35 Lbs.
90' to 125'	32 Ft.	16" X 25"	55 Lbs.

The size and weight of the sea anchor are also provided for stowage purposes. The sea anchor is attached to its matching, appropriately sized nylon rode with a swivel shackled to an eye and thimble in the line. Inspect all items of hardware, much as you did the ground tackle in Chapter 4. Nylon rode must be of adequate size and length; consult the tables from line and sea anchor manufacturers for specifications. Typically, nylon diameter should equal that of the primary anchor rode, and the usual recommendation for parachute anchor rode length is ten feet of parachute rode per foot of vessel.

The parachute rode leads to the parachute, where it connects via shackle to the swivel.

With this arrangement, we can control the angle of the parachute rode in relation to the boat, thus keeping the boat at a safe and somewhat more comfortable angle to the weather. Also, as the boat makes leeway, the slick created tends to flatten approaching waves to provide a dampening effect.

The sea anchor is valuable on multihulls as well, but is bridled from the hulls directly off the bow.

Down below

Safety in the saloon depends on proper stowage, with all doors, lids, and drawers having proper locking mechanisms. Even the sole itself must be rigged for heavy weather. Devise a method to secure anything that could be opened by a 360-degree roll. Refer to Chapter 9 for suggested hardware. I mentioned the sole because on most boats at sea, gear, supplies, and food are stored in the bilge, and those items become dangerous when airborne. Use wood screws to secure each section of removable sole, with the exception of the sole overlying bilge pumps or other areas requiring accessibility. Those portions can be latched

to keep them in place. Make sure the cooking stove has a locking device to keep it in its gimbals in the event of a roll (see Chapter 9). There should also be a circuit breaker and gas line solenoid, along with a manual shutoff in the gas line, to prevent leaks. Each crewperson should know how to control gas valves, light the stove and properly turn it off.

Douse the stove by turning off the solenoid first, then the manual valve, which will allow the flame to burn off fuel in the gas line. Then close the stove burner knob. It's not necessary to close the external propane tank every time the stove is lit.

Draw a diagram of all through-hulls in the boat and make it available to the crew. There is usually a diagram in the owner's manual to use as a pattern. Make certain that wood bungs are tied to all seacock handles and ready for immediate use.

Have a plan in mind for securing any opening to the deck including dorade vents, slatted openings in the companionway gate, cockpit speakers, vents to the engine room, etc. Dorade vents should be turned away from the wind/waves during heavy weather situations. Should wave action threaten the boat, all water access to below decks should be secured. You may only need to stuff towels in the dorades, or duct tape openings, but you should still have a plan that everyone is aware of. There should be handholds below so that anyone traversing the saloon has something solid to grab.

One of the only elements beyond our control is striking a hard, submerged object; such as a whale or a loose cargo container. Some forethought should be given to emergency repair measures in the event of severe leaking. The bow will typically hit first, so the first action should be to cease forward motion of the boat. Assess the damage, and determine the size of the hole and degree of flooding. Plugging the hole from inside with pillows, blankets, life jackets, or settee cushions held in position with shoring will temporarily alleviate flooding. You should also activate the bilge pumps and designate crewmembers to operate the manual pump(s).

Another tactic is to externally position a collision mat of waterproof material over the damaged bow area (Figure 10-3). This mat can be a 3-foot by 3-foot piece of sail material cut in a triangular shape with grommets in the corners fitted with rope. Permanently secure lines to each corner, and stow the mat to ensure easy access. Lower the mat over the stem to cover the damaged section of bow, and then pull it tight and secure with the lines. Once rigged, the boat may resume forward motion; in fact, water pressure on the hull actually helps keep the shroud in place over the damage.

In addition to their CPR and Emergency First Aid certificates, seagoing captains should consider earning certification in open water scuba diving. This skill can come in very handy when there's a job to do under the boat. Diving

FIGURE 10-3

A collision mat is positioned with its three lines over a damaged area of the bow.

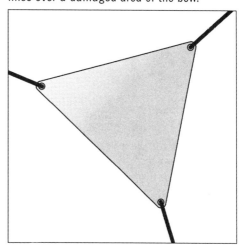

will not just enable you to examine the boat's hull, propeller, and anchor; as a sport, diving can add a great deal of enjoyment to your boating time.

MEDICAL KIT

You should assemble a medical kit with the help of a physician who can issue prescriptions and dosage instructions for some of the medications. If your doctor hesitates to comply, you may need to provide assurance that the meds will be used at sea in the absence of medical help, and only by members of your immediate crew.

Medical kit supplies
- Bandages and gauze pads in a variety of sizes
- Ace bandage wrap

- Cotton (sterile and absorbent)
- Universal arm splint
- Cast liner (padding to put under splints)
- Thermometers, including one for hypothermic patients
- Scrubbing soap pads
- Surgical knife
- Surgical blades (sealed and sterile, a No. 10 blade is best)
- Resuscitube (for CPR or mouth-to-mouth resuscitation; anyone sailing beyond medical assistance should take CPR and advanced first aid courses)
- Needle holder
- Suture material (3/0 silk with a swaged-on needle, packaged in sterile units)
- Iodine surgical scrub (to disinfect wounds before suturing or bandaging)
- Steri-Strips (an adhesive tape used instead of sutures to closed small wounds)
- Dressing materials
- Syringes (prepackaged plastic syringes with attached needle; usually 3-5 ml syringes with a 22-gauge needle)
- Forceps
- Lactated Ringer's Solution (for intravenous or subcutaneous injection; plastic bags contain one liter of solution)
- Intravenous catheters (a thin plastic tube with a removable metal component to pierce the skin and vein; used to administer intravenous fluids; experience is necessary to place an IV catheter)

All captains at sea should be certified in CPR and Emergency First Aid, and be familiar with all kit contents and their usage.

Medical kit medications

For skin ailments
- A+D ointment (for skin irritation and nosebleed prevention)
- Triple antibiotic ointment (for external skin infections or burns)
- Furacin cream (an antibacterial; apply to wound and cover with a suitable bandage)
- Lotrimin cream, Tinactin cream for athlete's foot
- Gyne-Lotrimin cream or vaginal suppositories for yeast infections
- Burrow's solution for fungal rashes
- Selsun shampoo
- Silvadene (a cream used to treat fungal infections)
- Lanacane (for skin rashes that occur due to prolonged saltwater exposure)
- Cortisone ointment (a topical remedy for severely itchy skin)
- Chiggard (a liquid applied topically to treat chigger bites)

For gastrointestinal ailments
- Lomotil (to control diarrhea; tablets for adults, liquid for children)
- Gelusil (to treat indigestion; liquid or tablets)
- Atropine sulphate (to treat bladder infections)
- Compazine (to control stomach spasms and vomiting; suppositories are considered by many to be the most reliable remedy for seasickness)

- Transderm Scop (patches to prevent seasickness)
- Pepto-Bismol for diarrhea
- Senokot (mild laxative)
- Ipecac to induce vomiting of noncorrosive poisons
- Fleet enema kits
- Flagyl (Metronidazole) 250-500 mg twice daily for 14 days to treat intestinal parasitical disorders giardia and amoebiasis; no alcohol with and for three days after administration
- Activated charcoal tablets to absorb toxins with poisoning
- Glucose and electrolyte powder (Gatorade, Pedialyte)

For infections
- Doxycycline (antibiotic capsules)
- Bactrim DS (antibiotic to treat bladder infections)
- Cortisporin otic drops for swimmer's ear (external ear infection)
- Erythromycin capsules (250 mg four times daily for staphylococcus infection)
- AP Bicillin (broad spectrum antibiotic)
- Neosporin (antibiotic ointment)
- Gentamicin ophthalmic solution
- Chiggard for mite skin infestations

For pain
- Valium (to treat anxiety, panic attacks, and insomnia)
- Tylenol #3 (pain reliever; contains codeine)
- Demerol (to treat moderate to severe pain)
- Ibuprofen (to treat mild to moderate pain, fever and inflammation)

- Cavit (temporary filling material for dental cavities)
- Pontocaine (anesthetic used before/during eye exam/surgery)

For dehydration
- Enteric-coated sodium chloride tablets (to combat dehydration during heavy perspiration)
- Pedialyte (to prevent dehydration from diarrhea and vomiting)
- Gatorade or similar sports drinks (not strictly a medication, but can help replace fluids lost during heavy perspiration, vomiting or diarrhea)

Common cold
- Sudafed or generic pseudoephedrine (30 mg tablets, two every four hours)
- Guaifenesin DM cough syrup

For anaphylactic shock
- Epinephrine HCl (to treat life-threatening allergic reactions)

For small lacerations
- Super Glue can hold small cuts closed until they heal

Heart Attack kit
These medications are to be used only under medical supervision and advice.
- Lasix (Furosemide)
- Aspirin (300 mg daily)
- Lidocaine Monoject (100 mg)
- Nitrogen patches (reduces pain and decreases heart workload)
- Percodan, for pain
- Tenormin (a beta-blocker used to control arrhythmias)
- Oxygen

Miscellaneous medications

- Injectable Lidocaine for local anesthesia
- Papaya extract (Adolph's Meat Tenderizer) for jellyfish stings
- Insect repellent
- Ammonia for stings
- Rubbing alcohol for disinfection and swimmer's ear (⅔ alcohol: ⅓ white vinegar)

In addition to the items listed above, you may need to stock things like insulin, corticosteroids, birth control pills, etc. As mentioned, the skipper must have a working knowledge of the medications and supplies in the kit. This rule applies even if a member of the crew is a doctor, since doctors can become injured or incapacitated too. For this reason, a first aid manual covering medical conditions and treatment of injuries at sea should always accompany the medical kit. The quantity of medical supplies you'll need to stock is determined largely by the intended length of the passage and the number of crewmembers on board—the larger the crew and longer the voyage, the more supplies you'll need.

Concluding this safety inspection of the boat and its gear, use the checklist to note repairs, add hardware, and supplement gear before heading out to sea. The subject of safety continues in Chapter 11, with a shift in focus from the boat to the crew.

CHAPTER 11

CREW PREPARATION

In the last chapter, we focused on examining the boat and assessing its readiness for sea. A direct extension of that discussion is crew preparation. Crewmembers with comprehensive knowledge of the boat's systems, procedures, and gear have better odds for safe and successful voyages. Gone are the days (or, at least they *should* be) when sailors are scrounged from the docks to complete the crew shortly before shoving off. Proper crew selection is a critical element of successful voyaging and cruising.

There can be times when it's advisable to sail with a skeleton crew. Ultimately, in foreign ports, the captain is responsible for each person on board, so if you aren't absolutely confident that every crewmember will serve well on board and be a good citizen once you reach your destination, it may be wise to leave some people off your crew list.

If you are unable to sail with relatives or friends, you must be vigilant. Ask for a written resume of sailing and life experiences pertinent to the voyage. Conduct a personal interview to assess honesty, fitness, motivation and future plans. Now's the time to make arrangements regarding pay, duties, expectations, contribu-

tions to the ship (such as food), and transportation home (at each crewmember's own expense). It's not unreasonable to ask someone to supply money, before sailing, to cover their airfare home. Make it absolutely clear that alcohol, drugs, tobacco, and firearms are not permitted on board your boat. Once these terms are agreed to, put them in writing, give each party a copy, and enter the agreement and date in the ship's log.

Incompatibilities offshore can be cancerous, and threaten the well-being of everyone on board. To be sure, I'd rather sail short-handed than with sailors I don't know or who have obvious behaviors that are detrimental to crew harmony. I once abandoned an Atlantic crossing delivery after learning that the owner was prone to raging episodes against crewmembers. If you know a situation isn't right, don't pursue it.

Educating each member of the team gives everyone the necessary tools to make a full and valuable contribution. People who receive ample information are confident and secure in the knowledge that they are able to handle their responsibilities and that the boat is thoroughly prepared. The value of crew personnel in this frame of mind is incalculable.

Before setting sail, I have always had what I call a "cockpit chat" with the whole crew. This chat is a discussion of what each person should know about the boat, its gear, ship's guidelines and rules, and how you intend to operate at sea. On VOYAGER, our chat has evolved into a full-blown seminar that takes an entire day, to ensure that our crews are fully versed in boat equipment and operations, ship's rules, watch schedules, night watch rules, the deck log, etc. before we leave on a teaching offshore passage.

Just as someone starting a new job benefits from a thorough understanding of the associated tasks and what is expected of them, your crew will perform at their best, and enjoy themselves as well, if you give them the information they need. This discussion, along with many other topics, is presented in the Offshore Passagemaking seminars I teach to groups interested in sailing offshore. It covers vital information that everyone on board must know.

CREW LISTS

Your preparation of the crew actually begins long before you have these discussions on the boat. Each person should get a list of necessary gear and the tasks they'll be expected to perform during the voyage. This information should be available well in advance of the launch date so everyone has time to gather their gear and become familiar

with their seagoing tasks. The lists we use on our Beneteau 46 VOYAGER are available in Appendix A.

These documents are titled:
- Checklist for Crew Clothing and Personal Gear
- Crew Responsibility List

The following is a list of procedures with which every crewmember should be familiar. It's up to the skipper and other senior sailors to educate every crewmember, and it's the crewmember's responsibility to have a good attitude and a willingness to learn. The best offshore crews are comprised of people who are eager to learn and anxious to be contributing members of the team. Everyone should be able to participate in all aspects of voyaging.

Your instructions should ensure that each crewperson understands and is able to perform the following:

- Quickly don a safety harness in dim light. Understand the jackline system and how to clip on and maneuver about. Be familiar with rules concerning the need for life jackets and harnesses.
- Ensure nothing drags behind the boat at any time.
- Start the engine.
- Use the throttle and gear shift.
- Stop the engine.
- Understand the standby and auto functions of the autopilot, how to change course, and how to immediately take manual helm control from the autopilot.

- Position the boat on a course and select the course for wind vane control. Know how to instantly disengage the wind vane clutch to regain manual steering control.
- Operate the VHF radio.
- Understand the posted watch schedule.
- Understand the cleanup procedures after meals.
- Understand the daily maintenance and monitoring of the ship's systems and gear. (See discussion below.)
- Know the location of, and how to install, the emergency tiller.
- Locate the abandon ship bag.
- Understand the EPIRB location and mode of operation.
- Read latitude, longitude, speed, heading, and track information on the GPS.
- Turn on and read bearing and distance on the radar.
- Place the radar in energy-saving mode.
- Reef the mainsail.
- Furl the headsail.
- Deploy storm sails and rig for heavy weather. (See discussion below for specific heavy weather preparations.)
- Grind and release the winches.
- Maintain proper stowage below decks.
- Operate bilge pumps—electric and manual.
- Know where the diagram of seacocks/through-hulls/fire extinguishers is located.
- Operate fire extinguishers.
- Locate the toolboxes and spares.
- Make certain that any crewmembers'

existing medical conditions are understood. This includes allergies, phobias and current medication.
- Understand seasickness and its causes, and agree on rules to limit those causes. (See discussion below.)
- Know where the collision mat is located and how to deploy it.
- Adhere to the night watch rules:

Be courteous of those off watch—no loud talking or music.

Don't drag the tether ring on deck—carry it.

Keep flashlights in their designated locations.

Keep the binoculars in their designated location.

Keep the spotlight in its designated location.

Keep toilet seat down at all times to prevent slamming.

Maintain nighttime lighting below decks.

Scan the entire horizon at least every 15 minutes.

Understand the basics of Collision Regulations (COLREG) lights and what they indicate about another vessel's course.

Know where granola bars, crackers, snacks and chewing gum are kept.

Understand how to put on and operate the Alert 2 Overboard Alarm system.

Be familiar enough with the stove to be able to heat water for warm drinks.

Make notations in the deck log once per watch.

Do not start the engine unless absolutely necessary. Inform the off-watch crew, if possible, before doing so.

If a question arises concerning vessel operation or positioning regarding another vessel, land, or any situation at sea, do not guess how to deal with the situation—wake the appropriate person.

Understand the posted watch schedule and comply with it.

Standing orders are to call the captain or first mate if (1) a vessel is sighted, (2) any unusual sound is heard, (3) a low, dark cloudbank, rain squall or waterspout is sighted to windward, (4) there is injury or a dangerous medical condition, or (5) if there is any general uncertainty or concern.

While the captain and mate have ultimate responsibility for the daily monitoring and maintenance of the vessel, everyone on board should be aware of the procedures. There are always situations where assistance is needed in performing general tasks, especially repairs, and the crew as a whole benefits from knowing how the boat is maintained.

Table 11-1 is a list of maintenance tasks to be carried out on a routine basis. See Chapter 12 for more details.

EMERGENCY PROTOCOLS

Besides general activities, the crew must be made aware of the ship's protocols. Specifically, these govern procedures followed for:

- Crew overboard situation
- Rigging for heavy weather
- Flooding emergency
- Fire emergency
- Abandoning ship

Crew overboard

Crew overboard rescue protocols used at different points of sail must be clearly laid out and understood. This conversation should end with the message that the best procedure is to make absolutely certain the overboard situation never happens.

Crew Overboard Procedure
- The first responder should yell **"CREW OVERBOARD"** to call all hands on deck.
- One person is designated as the "spotter" and **points to the victim**, never taking his or her eyes off him or her.
- Deploy the MOB pole and/or automatic floating strobe light as close to the victim as possible.
- Enter MOB on the GPS. Note position of victim and retrieval (reciprocal) course.
- Place the boat on autopilot standby or disengage the wind vane, and have one person take control of the helm and direct sail maneuvers.
- The Quick Stop method is initiated as the first preference. The second option is the Deep Beam Reach tactic.
- Heave-to if sailing downwind.
- Deploy the Lifesling as the boat maneuvers.

TABLE 11-1

The monitoring and maintenance schedule used during our VOYAGER Ocean Passages

VOYAGER Ocean Passages
Monitoring and Maintenance at Sea

Task	Schedule
State of battery charge	At least twice daily
Engine	At least every two hours while running
Belts, hoses, leaking, fluids (oil, transmission fluid, coolant, stuffing box)	At least every two hours while running
Raw water intake strainer	At least every two hours while running
Fuel reserves	At least daily, or as dictated by circumstances
Water reserves	At least daily, or as dictated by circumstances
Wet cell battery fluid levels	At least weekly
Bilges	At least twice daily
Propane reserves	At least weekly
Food preserves	At least weekly
Lights	At least once daily
Running rigging	At least twice daily
Standing rigging (masthead and spreaders with binoculars)	At least twice daily
Sails	At least twice daily
Lifelines and stanchions	At least twice daily

- Approach the victim to leeward, maneuvering the Lifesling close.
- Luff sails, check the transom for lines, and start the engine in **neutral**.
- Retrieve victim by any means necessary.

This procedure is one I believe gives the best chance of returning to and retrieving an overboard victim. Each skipper is free to choose the method he or she prefers. The most important consideration is that all crewmembers are on the same page and can work together to assist the victim. Once you've mastered the maneuvers in daylight, I strongly urge you to practice them at night; performing them in the dark is quite different and can be more difficult.

Heavy weather

Your crew discussions should also cover how to cope with heavy weather. Despite the best voyage planning, foul weather is always a possibility at sea, and you need to have procedures in place to deal with it. Preparation should start on land, well before facing a gale at sea. Along with the practical benefits of proper preparation, the crew gains valuable confidence when everyone understands that they are ready for changes in weather and capable of handling themselves in a storm.

Rig for Heavy Weather
- Reduce sail to the appropriate sail plan early.
- Make storm sails ready.
- Secure all deck gear.
- Fill fuel tanks from jerry cans.
- Close and seal companionway.
- Batten down hatches and ports.
- Don and clip on harness/tethers at all times while on deck; wear PFD and Overboard Alarm.
- Position lee cloths.
- Secure all latches below decks.
- Clear passageways.
- Prepare a warm meal and fill Thermoses with hot beverages.
- Obtain position fix and communicate fix to land base.
- Charge batteries.
- Determine storm tactics.
- Begin heavy weather watch schedule.
- Close all unnecessary through-hulls and seacocks.
- Perform the entire routine

maintenance and monitoring protocol.

This is the time that captains earn their stripes. When preparing your boat for heavy weather conditions, remember that you're leading by example. The crew is watching and taking cues from your behavior and mood. While it's important to be efficient and thorough in making ready, it's equally important to project an air of confidence and optimism. It's amazing how one person's attitude can affect others so dramatically—but it does and will. Take advantage of your position as leader and help the crew to be at their best when you need them the most.

Flooding

One emergency situation that can arise is the flooding of the boat after striking a submerged object. Stories abound of boats hitting whales as they bask on the surface or, even worse, cargo containers drifting just below the water's surface. If the boat is holed and flooded, you should follow a certain set of procedures in order to save the ship.

Flooding Emergency Protocols
- The person who discovers the flood should yell **"FLOODING AT THE BOW"** or whatever location.
- Stop forward motion of the boat. Come hove-to or shut off the engine and drift.
- Assess the damage and degree of flooding.
- Control flooding below with pillows,

sleeping bags and cushions shored against the damaged area.

- Activate all bilge pumps as needed. Use the engine water intake hose if necessary.
- Position the collision mat from the deck.
- Once the situation is fully assessed, make any necessary radio communications.
- Get underway if possible. If flooding cannot be controlled, initiate an Abandon Ship procedure.

Fire

Fires at sea can pose life-threatening risks. It is therefore important that you also discuss the procedure for extinguishing an onboard fire.

Fire emergency strategy
- The person detecting the emergency yells **"FIRE"** to alert the crew.
- All hands should know the locations of fire extinguishers.
- Use fire extinguishers immediately.
- Maneuver the boat so that the fire is to leeward.
- If the fire is in the engine compartment, turn off the engine immediately.
- Turn off the propane at the tank.
- Turn off electricity at the battery isolation switch or battery posts.
- Remove flammables from the area of fire.
- Use water buckets to aid in fighting fire, and to douse all hot embers afterward.

- If fire is uncontrollable, begin Abandon Ship procedure.

Abandon ship

If it becomes necessary to abandon ship, follow the guidelines discussed in the crew briefing. Abandoning ship is done as a last resort for survival, and only at the captain's orders.

Abandon Ship Protocols
- Person detecting the emergency **blows the horn** or calls **"EMERGENCY ON DECK"** to summon all hands.
- The boat is immediately hove-to.
- All crewmembers put on lifejackets and foul weather gear/survival suits.
- Coordinate efforts to save the boat, depending on the emergency, such as fighting a fire or stemming a serious leak.
- Make contact with land bases to inform of emergency.
- Designate two people to deploy the life raft and assure that the lanyard is tied before its release. It is put into the water in its canister or valise, to the boat's leeward side.
- The lanyard is jerked hard to inflate the raft at the captain's order. The lanyard remains tied to the boat.
- One person enters the raft, ready to receive the abandon ship bag, food, water, etc. He or she will also assist the rest of the crew in boarding.
- Once the captain decides the ship is lost, the order is given to abandon

ship. All crewmembers then enter the raft.

- Activate an EPIRB, but only one initially.
- Place all EPIRBs into the raft, along with abandon ship bag and other designated gear.
- Once all hands are aboard the raft, with all gear and supplies needed, cut the lanyard and shove away from the sinking boat.

SEASICKNESS

A discussion of safety at sea would be incomplete without covering the most common of all sea maladies—seasickness. This affliction can affect virtually everyone on board; therefore, its disabling effects are a legitimate safety concern. Overcoming seasickness is an important key to becoming a capable offshore sailor. Until you've done that, you'll never appreciate voyaging, and may elect to stop altogether.

Some people seem to have an innate "immunity" and, with increased exposure to the offshore environment, others can become less vulnerable, but the majority of people I've sailed with experience it to some degree—including myself. Everyone is predisposed to a certain level of seasickness, but we do have control over some of the dynamics that affect its onset and duration. These are the factors we must understand and work with.

Refraction of waves off coastlines causes confused, choppy seas when rebounding waves collide with those from

offshore. Many people feel the effects of seasickness shortly after beginning their journey because this type of wave action causes the boat's motion to be erratic. Recovery often begins once the boat crosses the continental shelves, allowing true ocean swells to take over and provide a rhythmic, even motion.

During one very memorable passage sailing from New York Harbor, the seas built steadily after a cold frontal wind shift. At first, the waves and boat's motion were confused and unpredictable. As the hours passed and we encountered the Gulf Stream, wind and wave action steadily increased past Force 9; but as their direction settled the boat motion became rhythmic and actually improved. However, at that point another element known to cause seasickness arose—fear—and all hands were affected.

Conditions continued to get worse, as the wind howled and the waves grew. As the hours became days, though, and confidence in the boat and crew's abilities grew, my symptoms diminished to very workable levels. This was my first, but by no means my last episode of seasickness, and it taught me valuable lessons about coping with this pesky malady.

Causes

Differences in what our eyes perceive and what our inner ear (vestibular system) senses are at the root of seasickness. If a boat's motion is primarily limited to one type, such as rolling a few degrees, the symptoms are usually minimal. But when roll is combined with pitch and yaw, or movement becomes more exaggerated, the inner ear cannot accommodate the unfamiliar motions and anyone so inclined by nature can get sick. For many people, nausea can be controlled by going on deck and watching the horizon—or, better yet, by driving the boat. Symptoms often diminish as the senses of sight and balance gradually become more in sync with reality.

On the other hand, some find relief by just giving in to the urge to vomit. This often brings relief as the emetic impulses from the brain are appeased. Still others find it helpful to head to their bunks and close their eyes or sleep, but when they arise, their first steps should be back on deck.

During the episode of seasickness I mentioned earlier, as the wind and seas built, my condition was reinforced by fear. Fear is a contributing factor that can take hold at sea *or* before leaving land. This is one aspect of a person's psyche that I always try to discover before taking them on a passage—do they have an innate fear of sailing far from land? People with that fear are more likely to give in to seasickness, a prescription for misery. For some, the only remedy comes from taking sedatives or making port.

There are often other contributing factors on board: cigarette smoke in confined quarters, odors from the head, kerosene and diesel, or the smell of onions. For many, the effects of alcohol contribute mightily, so alcohol and cigarettes are not allowed on VOYAGER. For some, Vitamin B supplements can upset the stomach and become a factor. Fatigue and dehydration are both causes and consequences of seasickness, and contribute to its severity and duration.

While a specific organism, such as a virus, is not the cause of seasickness, it is contagious all the same. When one crewmember is affected, especially by vomiting, the spread among the crew is sometimes dramatic. The psychological aspect should not be ignored.

Prevention

In your cockpit chat, you should discuss seasickness, and institute the following protocols.

Develop policies to limit or eliminate causative influences:

- No smoking on board is the best policy.
- Take care when using jerry cans to fill the fuel tank; prevent leaking of diesel fuel, and be diligent in engine inspections to prevent leaks.
- No alcoholic beverages the night before sailing or at sea.
- Begin seasickness preventative medications at least four hours before sailing, and maintain at recommended intervals. These medications can have side effects, such as dry mouth, loss of taste sensation and blurred vision. It's important to try these medications before taking an offshore voyage so that you're aware of the side effects and how they affect you.
- Keep well hydrated offshore. Increase your water intake beginning two

weeks prior to sailing. Drinking up to a gallon of water per day reduces dehydration at sea.

- Avoid coffee and other diuretics before the voyage, and *during* if dehydration becomes a problem.
- Avoid spicy foods at sea.
- Ginger is helpful for many.
- If symptoms begin, take palliative measures immediately to forestall or prevent sickness. These measures include going up on deck, driving the boat, taking medication to control vomiting, lying down with eyes closed, and limiting food and water to small amounts at a time.
- Try not to let other crewmembers witness vomiting. If vomiting occurs below, clean it up immediately.

Attempting to hasten your recovery from seasickness is part of being a good sailor. It is crucial to contributing as a crewmember and enjoying your ocean voyages. Once you recognize its symptoms, don't let seasickness over-come your resolve. If you give in and its effects linger, another condition known as Sopite syndrome can take over. Sopite syndrome causes drowsiness and the loss of all desire to eat or drink.

Dehydration can make the situation worse, so stay hydrated with small portions of electrolyte drinks such as Gatorade. Likewise, eat only small portions of food at one sitting. Begin countering seasickness by getting up on deck and gazing at the horizon. Steering the boat is a great activity, since it focuses attention away from the nausea and keeps the eyes and brain in sync.

Don't even consider missing your scheduled watches. Lingering below in the bunk, except for those with intractable vomiting, is giving in. Most episodes of seasickness occur shortly after leaving port, while people are still unaccustomed to the boat's motion. Once away from land and the awkward motion of rebound waves, most people recover within a day or two.

CHAPTER 12

PREPARING THE BOAT FOR SEA

You actually began preparing your boat for sea when you first arrived at the docks—you made notes of your First Impressions, compiled all the ship's papers, and gathered statistical information regarding fuel range, water availability, expected hull speed, draft and sail area. You have also completed the inspection process and made notes on the inspection checklists.

Once any defects have been repaired, *inspect those items again*, especially if you did not do the work yourself. Remove all glassware, update the PFDs, make sure the flare kit is current, and place lee cloths on all bunks. In short, finish all remaining tasks to make ready for sea. Also get the bottom cleaned; it improves performance and is well worthwhile.

Once at sea, establish a monitoring and maintenance program to keep all gear in working order and identify issues early before they become problems. We'll review the entire list (and more) in preparation for departure.

MAINTENANCE LIST

Engine

Let's start with the engine. Check the raw water intake filter and clean it if necessary. Proceed to the raw water pump. Remove the faceplate and, unless the impeller has been very recently replaced, pull it out and install a new one. Save the old impeller, if it's in good condition, and add it to the inventory of spare engine parts. Dip some diesel fuel from the bottom of the tank and check it for sediment. Use a flashlight to examine the inside of the tank for algae growth. Check the sediment bowl at the bottom of the tank, and if you find water or sediment, polish the fuel, and filter any brought aboard. This may seem like a lot of bother, but it's better than having your engine misfire, gurgle, then quit altogether when you're 600 miles from port.

Change the primary and secondary fuel filters, but keep the old ones if they're in good condition. Store them in sealable plastic bags along with other engine spares. Change the oil and oil filter next—noting the condition of the oil as it's drained. Take one last look at the engine bilge, keeping an eye out for water, oil, or anything that shouldn't be there.

Run your hands over the belts; feel for cracks, frayed areas or laxity. Replace all belts that don't look new, including the belt-driven refrigeration compressor, which you'll recall is tighter than most belts.

Check the coolant solution levels. There's no need to change the solution; just top it off with fresh coolant. Check the transmission fluid and top it off, if necessary. Start the engine one last time, paying close attention to how fast it kicks over and runs. Watch the smoke, check for water flowing normally from the exhaust (ensuring that you put the impeller in correctly), feel for abnormal vibrations, and listen for odd sounds. Observe all engine gauges to make sure the battery is charging and the temperature gauge reading is normal.

Making certain the dock lines (especially fore and aft springs) are on, ask a mate to slip the boat into gear while you observe from below. Watch the mechanism as it shifts from neutral to forward, and then back to neutral and into reverse. Make sure the propeller shaft's movement is smooth and free of vibration, and then do a final check of the stuffing box.

If you're using jerry cans to supplement fuel, make sure the jugs are clean inside, fill them with clean diesel fuel (filter some of it to be sure), *replace the caps tightly*, and bring them back on board. If there's room for jerry cans in the cockpit lockers, it's better to store them there, in an upright position, than lashed to the stern pushpit or anywhere else near the boat's periphery. The key is to make sure the jugs cannot be washed overboard and there is no way they can leak diesel fuel into the boat.

If your route to the ocean requires several stops, there's no need to fill the fuel tanks yet. Likewise, if the anchor is to be used before beginning the ocean passage, leave it on the bow. VOYAGER, our Beneteau 46, spends the summer on the Chesapeake Bay, near Annapolis, Maryland. When I sail with students offshore, we'll either sail directly down the bay to Norfolk, Virginia, or we may choose to stop somewhere along the way, like the Patuxent River, and drop the hook for the evening. Either way, we must wait until just before reaching the ocean to perform the final tasks. At our last stop, we stow all secondary anchors somewhere low in the boat and remove the primary anchor from the bow and secure it within the anchor well, making sure the drain hole isn't obstructed.

Cooking fuel

Remove all propane tanks and have them topped off with cooking fuel; it's more expensive in foreign ports, and you don't want to run out of fuel while cooking breakfast! After replacing the tanks, open a tank valve, and, from below, open the main solenoid so that gas can enter. Then open the manual valve in the galley so that gas is flowing throughout the entire system. Once all valves are open, check the fuel gauge for any evidence of gas leakage. After a few minutes, if you don't notice any decrease in pressure, shut the valves.

Water

If you're stocking extra jugs of water, this is the time to bring them on board. Bring as many as you can, while still leaving room for other essentials. Water can be stored in plastic milk cartons, one- or two-liter plastic soda pop jugs, or five-gallon containers. Make sure jugs are stored securely to prevent them from being jostled, broken, or punctured.

After checking the boat's water tanks for algae or dirt, enlist a crewmember to help fill them. The Systems IV inline filter, available from West Marine, pre-filters the water as it's being pumped into the tanks. This clears the water of minerals that can affect the taste. As the tanks fill, monitor the external vent for escaping air and watch the bilges for leaking water. When the tanks are being filled, flip on the water pressure switch at the panel, just to be sure water is being pumped. The "pop" of the stainless steel tanks will tell you that they're almost full. Slowly top off the tank until the water no longer disappears from the deck fitting. Secure the deck screw cap after each tank is filled.

Electronics

Check all external lights—running, stern, deck, steaming, spreader, anchor, tricolor and compass—then check all interior lighting and appliances. Activate all instruments and check the readouts to make certain they're in proper working order. Monitor the charge of all house and dedicated engine batteries. If they show low voltage, write down the voltage level and check with a voltmeter. Start the engine, place the rpms to a level that charges the batteries (usually around 1,000 or 1,100 rpm), and note the time. Make sure the battery isolation switch is set to "Both."

With the engine running, check the battery charges with a voltmeter to monitor how well the alternator brings them back to full charge. Remember, batteries charge quickly to about 80-percent of capacity, but the final 20-percent takes much longer. When the batteries are reading around 12.5 volts, take note of how long it took to charge them. If you have estimated how many amps you'll use per day (see Chapter 7), you can apply this charge time to those amps and the size of the house batteries.

Hatches

If you think the deck hatches may leak, or if a wet passage is predicted, it's wise to seal the hatches from outside. Duct tape placed around the entire rim of the hatch, bridging the hatch rim and deck, is very effective. This method does necessitate cleaning the deck and hatch rim with acetone to remove the tape glue and remnants, but it's better than having water below. Another method is to apply caulk to the gap, and, while it's still wet, tie a line firmly in the gap to prevent water intrusion. The caulk will peel off at voyage's end.

FOOD STORES

Once all deck preparations are complete, proceed below deck. The primary cook should be in charge of planning the meals and stowing the provisions. Food should be purchased based on the length of the voyage and the number of people on board. Three meals per day multiplied by the number of crewmembers yields the number of meals. In other words, a crew of five on a 14-day passage would require 70 breakfasts, lunches and dinners (as well as a number of snacks).

In my experience, most cooks tend to overstock. Remember, people at sea often eat less than they do on land due to the boat's motion, rough weather or queasiness. You should also keep in mind that meal preparation at sea is a unique challenge. Unless the cook is ready, willing, and able to produce elaborate meals, the menu should be planned with an eye to balancing the requirements of storage, preparation, nutrition, waste, and ease of serving and eating. I always recommend that the cook try a trial run of meal planning and preparation while lying at anchor or on a short local cruise with the whole crew on board. Remember, this only works if you don't go ashore for the entire length of the trial period.

Avoid perishable provisions, except eggs, potatoes, onions and other items with a substantial shelf life. Instead, take plenty of canned and dried foods, as well as flour, dried potatoes, and pasta. Be sure to include salt, pepper, mustard, sugar, and cooking oil.

These nine categories may be most useful in planning:

1. Canned goods: Easy to store and have a long shelf life.

2. Freeze-dried foods: Delicious (sometimes) and nutritious, these are convenient to store and don't require cooking.

3. Bulk foods: Flour, cereal, pasta, potatoes, and oatmeal should be stored in sealable plastic containers.

4. Dried foods: Raisins, dates, prunes, tomatoes and oranges may be added to other foods or eaten as snacks. Dried milk is a good idea even if you have refrigeration on board.

5. Bread: Can be made in a pressure cooker or bread machine while underway. Pumpernickel bread and pitas last quite a long time when wrapped and kept cool.

6. Vegetables: Canned veggies will last longer, but fresh tomatoes, potatoes, onions, green beans, carrots and cabbage are also good choices.

7. Fruits: Always select fruits that are not yet ripened and are not bruised. Store securely in a cool area where they can't be jostled. Unhusked coconuts can last several weeks. Apples can last up to a month if washed and wrapped individually in paper towels. Hard, green mangoes will last a couple of weeks, if stored properly. Green pineapples, with the stalk on, will last up to a week if stored in a cool, dark area. Watermelons also will keep with proper storage.

8. Eggs: Can keep for months if they're fresh and unwashed. Extend their shelf life by coating them individually with Vaseline and turning them over every few days.

9. Canned meats: Chicken, ham, tuna, corned beef and Spam are good choices. You should also consider cured ham—it's salt-cured, wrapped in cloth, and needs no refrigeration—but remember to rinse the salt off before cooking.

Breakfast

A complete breakfast may consist of peanut butter and jelly on bread, cereal, or oatmeal with powdered milk, fruit (for the first few days), and coffee or tea. An occasional hearty breakfast may include fried bacon, ham, or sausage with eggs. In the morning, and before night watches, it's a good idea to fill a large Thermos with a hot beverage and place it securely in a designated spot. Each crewmember should have a drinking mug with his or her name on it.

Lunch

Soups are great lunch fare. Heat-and-eat lunches in Styrofoam cups are ideal for offshore meals. You'll also find that potatoes, onions, tomatoes, beans, and stock (chicken, beef or vegetable) make great, chunky-style soups that can be prepared in large quantities in the pressure cooker. Sandwiches of canned tuna, chicken, Spam, corned beef, or ham are the foundation of quick and easy lunches.

Dinner

Dinner is often the one meal for which the whole crew gathers. People have rested from their night watches and are preparing for another round, so a nice meal is a treat. If you've taken the time to prepare pastas and stews and frozen them in Ziploc bags before the voyage, dinner will be a snap—just take a bag from the icebox, place it in boiling water, heat, and serve. Spaghetti, instant mashed potatoes, macaroni and cheese, and Dinty Moore stews are all easy to prepare and taste great.

Of course, fish, ham, or hot dogs are always options, if they're fresh. Hot dogs are easily stored in the icebox and cooked in boiling water. You can also dice hot dogs and add them to vegetable soups. Although you can't count on successful fishing, whenever fresh fish is available it adds a nice variety to the menu. You can sometimes attract flying fish by lighting the boat at night, especially if waves are more than three or four feet. The fish will often hit the sails and fall on deck to be gathered for breakfast. If only cows floated, we'd have more hamburgers at sea!

Salads make dinner a bit more nourishing and elegant, and although the ingredients are perishable, they're easy to stow. In a nutshell, canned goods, heat-and-eat soups, vegetables for the pressure cooker, eggs, crackers, and prepared boil-in-bag meals are usually your best choices.

Snacks

Snacks can include granola, energy bars, trail mix, dried fruit, and an assortment of crackers. Popcorn is a nice treat for the crew and is a good source of fiber.

Many people notice a bad taste in their mouths offshore. Queasiness, seasickness medications, and dehydration are all contributors. I've found that chewing gum is a great cure for that sour taste, and can also help you stay alert on night watches. Drinks usually include coffee, hot chocolate, tea, Gatorade and soft drinks. Be aware that carbonation can also contribute to an upset stomach, so it might be better to stock canned juices or bottled teas instead of soda. Caffeine should be avoided by anyone concerned about dehydration.

Cookware

Cookware that has proven to work well on board includes Pyrex baking dishes, nesting pots (that fit one into another), a large frying pan with high sides (no Teflon, which rusts at sea), and a stainless steel kettle for boiling water. A pressure cooker is a great addition that makes baking possible. It also allows for efficient preparation of large batches of stews and soups. Just remember—a well-fed crew is a happy crew.

VOYAGE PLANNING

Voyage planning entails consideration of timing, destinations, and routing as it pertains to weather, prevailing winds and currents; plotting of waypoints; and accumulation of all charts that will be needed along the way.

Timing of the voyage concerns the best times of year to sail a given route.

The primary consideration is weather, but prevailing winds, sea state, frequency of gales, and ocean currents must also be taken into account. The best single source for this data is the Pilot Charts for the appropriate areas of ocean.

Pilot Charts are divided into individual months of the year, and contain wind roses within each section of 30-minutes latitude by 30-minutes longitude. These wind roses indicate the average strength and frequency with which winds blow from every 45 degrees around the circle, along with the percentage of calms at that position. The charts give the set and drift of ocean currents, delineate zones where wave height exceeds 12 feet 10-, 20-, 30- and 40-percent of the time. They also provide Great Circle courses plotted between major ports, lines of equal magnetic variation, information about gale frequency, extratropical/tropical cyclones, air temperature, pressure and visibility.

Any voyage should be planned using a number of publications, the most respected being *Ocean Passages for the World*. Since 1987, I have used *The Atlantic Crossing Guide* by Philip Allen, along with *World Cruising Routes* by Jimmy Cornell, with great success. Tide tables, light lists (or "Lists of Lights"), "Notice to Mariners," navigation rules, and "Coast Pilots" for all areas of the voyage are essential.

Regarding navigation, current HO-249 Volumes I and II for the appropriate regions, and the *Nautical Almanac* are necessary for celestial navigation.

Routing and charting require the gnomonic chart for Great Circle course development. You should also include a small-scale ocean chart (1:3,500,000), along with larger scale (1:80,000) charts, depicting areas along your course that may be good storm ports. For a passage up the eastern coast of the United States from Nassau to Norfolk, for example, chart No. 11539 New River Inlet to Cape Fear, is useful. Larger scale charts (1:50,000, 1:17,500 and Harbor Charts) are required as landfall nears.

You should also keep owners' manuals, engine manuals, first aid manuals, and all equipment and gear manuals on board. Documenting your voyage is done with the medical logbook, galley logbook, deck logbook and ship's logbook. The navigator may maintain a separate workbook, with final positions plotted on the chart and entered into the ship's logbook.

Once you've decided upon your destination and the time of year you'll travel, research the most efficient course using information from the above publications along with Great Circle Plotting Charts. Plot your courses on the plotting charts, then transfer the routes to Mercator ocean charts by extracting easily transferred points on the plotting charts (say 30 degrees north latitude by 65 degrees west longitude) onto the Mercator chart and connecting them with a course line. Waypoints can then be determined from the chart and entered into the ship's GPS. Remember to write the waypoints down in the logbook or a separate navigation book.

Route planning may also be done in conjunction with a professional consulting service, such as Commanders' Weather or Jenifer Clark's Gulfstream, which monitors weather as it develops and makes suggestions for courses to steer.

Remember that plotting waypoints too far apart can prove disheartening to some crewmembers. Even though they're really only guidelines for your actual track, make it a habit to plot waypoints no farther than 250 miles apart; the achievement of each one is a point of note for the crew.

While in the area of the navigation station, check that your supply of flags includes one for each foreign country on your itinerary. When entering the port of another country, you will need the national flag of the ship's registry at the stern. Before entering customs and immigration, hoist the yellow Q (Quarantine) flag from the starboard spreader. After clearing customs, bring down the Q and hoist the host country's ensign in its place as a courtesy. It remains there on the starboard spreader until you leave port.

FLOAT PLAN

Once the voyage itinerary is determined, formulate a float plan (Figure 12-1) including:

- Names and passport numbers of all crewmembers on board

FIGURE 12-1
Complete and file your float plan once the crew is finalized, destinations selected, and sailing schedules completed. *Courtesy of VOYAGER Ocean Passages*

Voyager Float Plan

VESSEL NAME _____

SKIPPER NAME _____ PASSPORT NUMBER_____

VESSEL DESCRIPTION _____

_____

REGISTRATION NUMBERS _____

DOCUMENTATION NUMBERS _____

VESSEL CONTACT NUMBERS _____

CREW NAMES _____ PASSPORT NUMBERS

_____

_____

_____

_____

_____

VOYAGE ITINERARY

DATE   PORT OF DEPARTURE   DAYS AT SEA   DESTINATION   DATE

_____

_____

_____

_____

- Description of the vessel (46-foot cutter-rigged sloop with a white hull), registration numbers and documentation numbers
- Voyage itinerary including routing, expected days at sea, and ETA of landfalls at each port of call
- Vessel contact information (satellite phone number and SSB call number)

Fill out the float plan just before departure on an ocean voyage. Some aspects of the plan may change from year to year, or one passage to the next, as crew and registrations change, but the information should always be current and accurate. Submit the plan to ground personnel at the home port and at each destination or landfall expected on the voyage. The home port is notified with each departure and arrival, and the ground station at each succeeding destination is notified just before departure to its location. Each station should be alerted as to date of departure, expected duration of the passage, and ETA at the next port of call.

Communicate any problems en route to the appropriate ground station(s), including the nature of the problem, injuries or illnesses, damage to the boat, and any expected delays. In the event that the ground station(s) have no communication with your boat for a period of two days past the latest agreed-upon date of communication, or past the expected arrival date, they are instructed to contact the nearest coast guard or naval facility and alert them to the situation. At that point, the authorities will use their discretion as to the best course of action.

WEATHER

You can't control what develops after you're at sea, but you'd better control when you leave for sea. Weather is the single most important determinant of when to sail. You should monitor the weather at least a month before your projected sailing date, and be aware of weather systems that will affect your sailing area—if there's a risk, don't leave.

Monitor the weather at least once a day while on the water. For years I used a shortwave radio receiver, tuned to the offshore and high seas forecasts, for my offshore weather information. These broadcasts are announced by a computerized voice (Perfect Paul) and provide vital updated weather data several times each day. The broadcast schedule and frequencies are available on the NOAA Web site. Although I now download NOAA weather charts, I still keep the shortwave on board in case that method fails.

Use the information provided by NOAA to determine which broadcasts pertain to your sailing area, then construct a table to correlate the broadcasts, their times and frequencies. This way, even if all other methods of weather forecasting should fail, you can turn on your inexpensive shortwave weather radio and keep your weather forecasts current.

SSB and satellite connections to computers and weather faxes now allow for Web downloads of weather charts and predictions from a variety of sources including NOAA and professional weather and routing services.

The NOAA National Weather Service Web site (http://www.ncep.noaa.gov/) takes you to the Ocean Prediction Center. This is the page I use to monitor weather when on land and when Internet access is available. From this page you can find broadcast schedules for the shortwave broadcasts and get to the weather charts you'd like to receive.

In order to see times and shortwave frequencies for broadcast of the Coastal and High Seas forecasts, look for the link to Coastal/Offshore/High Seas Forecasts on www.nws.noaa.gov/om/marine/home .htm. Select the broadcast station closest to your sailing waters to receive the particular broadcasts you want at the specified times.

You can also view the text of the high seas and offshore radio broadcasts for the ocean zone of your choice. Under Coastal/Offshore/High Seas Forecasts, scroll down to "Marine Forecasts Text." Select either Offshore Marine Text Forecasts by Zone - Graphic Interface or High Seas Marine Text Forecasts by Area - Graphic Interface.

To view the downloadable charts available once you're on the water, return to the Ocean Prediction Center page, click on your ocean beneath "Fax Graphics With Transmission Time." This is the mother lode for ocean sailors. I use the satellite phone to load selected charts onto my computer each day at sea.

Here's a suggested list of downloads:

- 24 Hour Surface
- 24 Hour Wind & Wave
- 24 Hour 500 mb
- 48 Hour 500 mb
- 48 Hour Surface
- 48 Hour Forecast
- 96 Hour 500 mb
- 96 Hour Surface
- 96 Hour Wind & Wave
- High Seas Forecasts
- Offshore Forecasts

Once your computer is equipped with weather software that decodes incoming data, such as that provided by UUPlus, you input the script requesting your charts to the software. That message is then e-mailed to NOAA. Note that the NOAA e-mail address has very recently changed. It was at ftpmail@weather .noaa.gov, but the address is now ftp mail@ftpmail.nws.noaa.gov.

Once NOAA receives your request, the information will automatically be sent to you. Just connect to the Internet via your server and download the data whenever you want to. I use a satellite phone for receiving data as it is also convenient for land communication and can be transferred to a life raft, whereas the SSB would go down with the ship. These same NOAA chart files are also available directly from UUPlus. It is sometimes simpler, using their software, to request and almost instantaneously receive the desired weather charts.

This, along with a shortwave radio, provides a double layer of weather data availability. I stress the importance of a portable receiver, since computer, satellite phone and Internet connections are not always reliable.

While preparing for departure, I download all of the weather charts I need to gather complete information. Once offshore, though, the download times are such that I'll request only those charts that are most pertinent on a given day, depending on conditions.

Downloaded information is always combined with a series of local weather parameters to arrive at useable forecasts upon which we make routing and navigation decisions.

DOCUMENTS

Returning to our voyage preparations, the logbook should be readied, complete with all information desired for each hour of each day. Make certain that your U.S. Coast Guard Documentation certificate is current. It must be renewed annually, so before leaving on an extended cruise, notify the USCG Documentation Office of your intention to be away. Since you are subject to a substantial fine if the CGD certificate lapses, it's a good idea to ask the Coast Guard to send you a form each year (to a permanent address) that you can fill out for new documentation papers.

Most countries demand proof that you, and each member of the crew, have return airline tickets or funds available to purchase a flight home. The funds may be in the form of cash or travelers' checks, so plan on having at least $1,500 per person on board readily available. If you sail with crew not related to you, they should demonstrate that these funds exist before you allow them to join the ship's company.

The crew

Now for the crew: Assuming everyone arrived at least a couple of days in advance to allow time to shake off jet lag and handle travel problems, assemble everyone and conduct your crew orientation and information discussions.

Discuss the entire Crew Preparation Guide and make sure that everyone on board understands and accepts it, and is eager to sail. Everyone should have a bunk where their gear and clothing is stowed and sleeping bags laid out. Remind everyone to drink lots of fluids and avoid caffeine and alcohol before the departure date. A nice meal is a great way to start the crew's time together.

Finish all your final tasks, communications, and preparations in order to avoid last-minute anxiety. Replace the batteries in all flashlights, strobe lights for life jackets, light for the horseshoe ring, handheld GPS and VHF, and navigational computers, and make sure you have a good stock of replacements.

Once you reach your final stop before sea, top off the fuel and water tanks, stow the anchor, and seal the hatches. Bring blocks of ice on board if needed, and stow your pre-made frozen meals, soft drinks, and any other cold or frozen stores. Apply seasickness patches or begin taking medications at least four hours before departure. Notify the land base of your departure time. If the final weather update is favorable and the tide is headed out, start the engine, cast off the dock lines, stow the fenders, and let the adventure begin!

APPENDIX A

CREW CHECKLISTS

1. CHECKLIST FOR CREW CLOTHING AND PERSONAL GEAR

Personal Gear

- Flashlight, crew light, or head lamp, e.g. Pelican Mitylite from West Marine.
- Anti-seasickness medication of your choice
- Sunscreen
- Aspirin, ibuprofen, acetaminophen, etc.
- Harness with tether
- Lanacaine
- Personal grooming supplies
- Spare eyeglasses/sunglasses/repair kit/safety strap
- Camera and film
- Sleeping bag, lightweight with stowage bag (West Marine)
- Return flight ticket home
- Personal medications
- One bed sheet
- Two small MSR Packtowl towels (REI) or ShamWow towels
- Passport and driver's license
- Favorite CDs
- List of allergies or medical conditions
- List of contact persons and numbers
- A PIN number for your Visa or Mastercard

Warm Weather

(Select from this gear for VOYAGER Ocean Passages; none of our offshore passages are in cold weather.)

Foul Weather Gear

Light weight, breathable foulies, like Trailwizard from Helly Hansen or Equatorial Lightweight gear from West Marine. Jacket must have a hood.

Other Clothing

- Nylon lightweight shorts
- Patagonia Gi II-type pants
- 2 cotton T-shirts
- 1 lightweight, short-sleeve, collared dress shirt.
- Light-colored, lightweight, long-sleeve shirt for sun protection
- Sun cap
- Underwear, recommend sports bras for women.
- Swimsuit, or running shorts for men.

Cold Weather

Foul weather gear

West Marine's Lightweight Breathable, or Third Reef. Jackets must have a hood.

Other clothing

- Cotton T-shirts
- Helly Hansen undergarments
- A Patagonia long-sleeve top
- Patagonia fleece pullover jacket
- Patagonia long pants (Jeans are difficult to dry.)
- Fleece pants
- Polartec Orca Hat
- Ski gloves
- Underwear

Footwear

- 1 pair of white-soled boat or sneaker shoes for boat use only
- 1 pair of *non-leather*, comfortable shoes for shore excursions
- Thongs or sandals
- Waterproof, breathable socks, like Sealskinz MTV from REI
- Sport boat shoes (Sperry, West Marine)

Gear should be packed in soft canvas bags, as suitcases are difficult to store aboard. Two bags per person, plus foul weather gear. *Bags are not to weigh more than 30 pounds each.*

West Marine: 800-538-0775
Patagonia: 800-638-6464
Helly Hansen: 800-943-5594
REI: 800-426-4840

2. CREW RESPONSIBILITY LIST

General

Each member of the crew should become familiar with the location and operation of the vessel's equipment. They should be able to:

- Operate fire extinguishers
- Operate marine heads
- Understand the electrical panel
- Understand the battery isolation switch
- Operate the seacocks
- Operate the manual and electronic bilge pumps
- Put up and take down sails
- Operate the windlass
- Deploy the life raft
- Trim and reef sails
- Read GPS location
- Read the compass, depth sounder, speed indicator, and log
- Steer the course
- Operate the autopilot/wind vane
- Start and stop the engine
- Read engine gauges
- Operate engine and gear shift controls
- Understand the MOB procedures
- Operate overboard poles, Lifesling, etc.
- Light stove and oven
- Don life preserver and harness
- Operate EPIRBs
- Operate flares and flare gun
- Keep yacht Bristol
- Operate electric panel
- Understand and comply with watch schedule

- Quickly locate:
  Fire extinguishers
  Seacocks
  Medical kit
  Electrical/propane/fuel shut-off valves
  Tool kit
  Life raft
  Abandon ship bag
  Flashlights
  Binoculars
  Search light
  Storm sails
  Collision mat
  Storm sails
  Sea anchor

It is important to recognize any medical conditions that may exist well prior to the sailing date, to make certain they are handled in advance. This includes musculoskeletal pain, toothaches, cardiac abnormalities, diabetes, skin ailments requiring medication, allergies, incontinence, and phobias, etc.

All medications prescribed at the time of sailing must be brought along and included on a list along with name and dosage frequency. Please be certain you have enough to last the entire passage, and a few extras.

APPENDIX B

TOOL KIT AND SPARES

1. GENERAL TOOL KIT

Each chapter has concluded with a list of spares pertinent to that topic. In addition to those items, the ship must have tools that would make any repairs at sea possible. Recommendations for the contents of a seagoing toolbox:

Tool Kit

- Complete supply of fasteners including screws, nuts, and washers
- Duct tape
- Assortment of screwdrivers, both flat head and Phillips head, including tiny screwdrivers for repair of eyeglasses
- Pliers
- Needle nose pliers
- Wire cutters
- Wire strippers
- Soldering kit
- Grommet making kit
- Rivet gun
- Sturdy set of vise grips
- Filter removing tool
- Crescent wrenches
- Adjustable wrenches

- Monkey wrenches
- Allen wrench kit
- Grips to remove oil filters
- Hand brace and bits
- Hand drill and bits, rechargeable drill with inverter on board
- Socket set including metric sockets
- Hacksaw with spare blades
- Box cutters with spare blades
- Ruler
- Small wood saw with spare blades
- Clamps and/or a vise
- Sandpaper
- Tin snips
- Hammer
- Chisels

2. SPARES FOR THE OFFSHORE YACHT

Spares for the fiberglass hull and appurtenances:

- Resin
- Resin catalyst
- Fiberglass cloth
- Roving
- Tape
- Winch repair kits

A rigging spare parts list should include the following:

- Sail slides
- Hanks if appropriate
- Grommet kit
- Turnbuckles
- Toggles
- Cotter pins
- Clevis pins
- Shackles
- Chain or straps to lengthen standing rigging
- Cable clamps, Nicropress unit, Sta-Lock or other system for fabricating terminal eyes
- One strand of rigging wire equal in length to the longest stay on board
- Wire cutters heavy enough to cut all rigging on board.

A spare parts list for the steering system:

- Rudderhead fitting
- Replacement parts kit for electronic autopilot
- Replacement parts kit for wind vane
- Preconceived plan for rudder replacement, with portions of the rig fabricated and ready for use

A list of recommended spares for the engine and transmission:

- Replacements for all belts
- Replacements for all hoses
- Hose clamps
- Engine oil, at least two gallons
- Transmission fluid
- Water pump
- Water pump impellers

- Starter solenoid
- Starter motor, unless a crank mechanism is available
- Alternator
- Fuel pump
- Fuel filters, primary and secondary
- Antifreeze if in colder climates
- Injector lines

A list of recommended spares for the electrical system:

- Spare batteries for all sizes in use on board
- Bulbs to replace all sizes in use on board
- Fuses
- Electrical tape
- Copper wire of various sizes to repair anything on board
- Wire strippers
- Ring and captive-fork wire terminals
- Crimper tool
- Soldering kit
- Rip-Free or other stuffing box repair material
- Penetrating oil
- Gasket paper
- Engine gasket kit
- Gearbox oil seal
- Gasket compound
- Gas engine spare parts: points, condenser, rotor, impeller and pin, diaphragm, ignition spray, spark plugs, coil

A list of suggested spares for the tankage, piping, and heads:

- Head repair kit including all necessary replacement parts

READY TO SAIL

- Sanitary hose replacements
- Hose clamps
- Hose connectors
- Silicone
- A siphon hose
- Wood bungs

APPENDIX C

INSPECTION CHECKLISTS

1. THE BOAT

Make of Vessel _____ LOA _____

Year _____ LWL _____

Hull Type _____ Displacement _____

Construction Material _____ Draft _____

Port of Registry _____ Beam _____

Owner's Manual		Navigation instruments	
Documentation papers		Safety gear	
Legal registration		Liferaft	
Bill of Sale (Copy)		EPIRB	
Insurance documents		Flares	
Maintenance history		Communications equipment	
Recent work done		Condition of hull	
Sail inventory		Condition of deck	
Engine(s)		Condition of engine(s)	
Fuel capacity		Standard of maintenance	
Water capacity		Overall vessel condition	
Deck layout		Overall first impressions	

2. THE HULL AND ADJOINING STRUCTURES

Hull condition		Stern light	
Gelcoat blemishes		Compass	
Rub rail		Compass light	
Toe rail		Ports	
Cap rail		Hatches	
Cleats		Bulkheads	
Stanchions		IGU	
Lifelines		Bilges	
Pelican hooks		Bilge pumps	
Bow pulpit		Manual	
Stern pushpit		Electronic	
Deck leaking		Keel bolts	
Fuel fittings		Keel	
Water fittings		Centerboard	
Waste fittings		Daggerboard	
Vents		Delamination	
Tank fittings		Depth sounder	
Cheek blocks		Sonar	
Sheaves		Knot meter	
Cam cleats		Through hulls	
Lead blocks		Skeg	
Line clutches		Rudder(s)	
Deck organizers		Rudder post	
Lead tracks		Rudder bearings	
Handrails		Propeller(s)	
Life raft fittings		Propeller shaft	
Winches		Sacrificial zinc	
Teak decking		Cutless bearing	
Davits		Anenometer	
Dinghy		Others	
Running lights			

3. SPARS, RIGGING, SAILS, AND CANVAS

Halyards		Turnbuckles	
Sheets		Shroud eyes	
Downhauls		Stay eyes	
Topping lifts		Main reefing	
Shackles		Boom	
Feeder line		Boom vang	
Cheek blocks		Outhaul	
Turning blocks		Bails	
Fairleads		Mast bolts	
Main traveler		Mast boot	
Mizzen traveler		Wiring	
Line stoppers		Partners	
Winches		Mast position	
Mainsail		Spreaders	
Jibs		Steaming light	
Mizzen		Deck light	
Staysails		Spreader lights	
Spinnakers		Anchor light	
Other sails		Strobe light	
Telltales		Tricolor light	
Battens		Inner forestay	
Reef lines		Baby stay	
Forestay slide		Spinnaker track	
Foil		Mast tangs	
Roller reefing drum		Mast head	
Head swivel		Mast head sheaves	
Shrouds		Antennae	
Forestay		Wind instruments	
Backstay		Windex	
Running backstays		Others	
Chain plates			

4. GROUND TACKLE

Anchors		Snubber	
Thimbles		Anchor rollers	
Shackles		Windlass	
Swivels		Deck chocks	
Rodes		Other	
Bitter Ends			

5. STEERING SYSTEMS

Rudder		Wind vane	
Rudderpost		Wind vane linkage	
Lower rudder bearing		Auxiliary rudder	
Upper rudder bearing		Trim tabs	
Tiller arm		Autopilot control unit	
Rudderhead fitting		Wire connections	
Steering wheel		Autopilot compass	
Steering linkage		CPU	
Quadrant/Radial drive unit		Drive unit	
Hydraulic lines		Drive linkage	
Hydraulic drive unit		Other	
Emergency tiller			

6. PROPULSION MACHINERY

Engine room light		Fuel tank	
Engine room vent		Fuel clean	
Bilge		Fuel lines	
Primary fuel filter		Fuel gauge	
Secondary fuel filter		Engine gauges	
Oil filter		Throttle control	
Oil level		Throttle linkage	
Oil cleanliness		Solenoid	
Air filter		Starter	
Turbocharger		Starter drive belt	
Supercharger		Alternator	
Raw water seacock		Fuel tank	
Raw water strainer		Fuel lines	
Raw water hoses		Fuel valves	
Raw water pump		Observation port	
Pump drive belt		Transmission oil	
Impeller		Oil pump	
Heat exchanger		Oil filter	
Closed system pump		Water cooling	
Pump drive belt		Hydraulic lines	
Thermostat		Gearshift cables	
Expansion tank		Drive-Propeller coupling	
Coolant level		Prop shaft alignment	
Exhaust elbow		Stuffing box	
Exhaust hose		Other	
Engine mounts			

7. THE ELECTRICAL SYSTEM

Batteries		Instrument lights	
Battery isolation switch		Navigation instruments	
Grounding system		Fresh water pump	
Electrical panel		Bilge pump	
Panel breakers		Shower pump	
Running lights		Shower drain pump	
Stern light		Gas solenoid	
Anchor light		Windlass	
Steaming light		AC Main	
Deck light		Outlets	
Cabin lights		Battery charger	
Cabin fans		Water heater	
Saloon lights		Air conditioning	
VHF		Lightning protection	
Refrigeration		Others	
Stereo			

8. TANKAGE, PIPING, AND HEADS

Water fill deck fitting		Toilets	
Water tanks		Sanitation hoses	
Water tank vents		Y-valves	
Tank fittings		Anti-siphon valves	
Hoses and connections		Holding tanks	
Pipes		Holding tank vents	
Water pumps		Waste empty hoses	
Tank valves		Macerator	
Faucets			

9. SHIPBOARD AMENITIES

Cooking stove		Condenser water supply	
Gimbals		Condenser air supply	
Burners		RFD	
Gas line		Cold plate	
Gas line connections		Refrigeration tubing, connections	
Manual shut-off		Refrigeration electrical circuits	
Gas locker		Galley seawater pump	
Tank shut-off		Secure stowage	
Regulator		Workable nav station	
Solenoid		Electronics connected and secure	
Refrigeration		VHF	
Compressor motor		Sound system	
Engine driven compressor		Other	
Condenser connections			

10. THE ELEMENT OF SAFETY

PFDs		Storm sails	
Fire extinguishers		Collision mat	
Whistle		Stove operation	
Bell		Latches on drawers, cupboards, etc.	
Flare kit		Hull diagram showing seacocks, fire extinguishers	
Other visual distress signals		Handholds below	
Medical kit		VHF, SSB, Satellite phone tested	
Special medical considerations		Crew orientation	
Life raft		ship's rules, procedures	
Abandon ship bag		night watch	
EPIRBs		MOB discussion	
Crew identifications		fire discussion	
Jack lines		abandon ship discussion	
Harnesses/tethers		seasickness discussion	
Preventer		Spotlight with cockpit outlet	
Radar reflector		Emergency knife	
Man overboard pole		Binoculars	
Lifesling		Flashlights	
Sea anchor		Overboard alarm	
Reefing lines		Others	

11. VESSEL PREPARATIONS FOR SEA

Inspection completed		Instruments	
Repairs completed		Logbook	
Gear supplemented and updated		Batteries charged, filled	
Engine monitoring		Anchors stowed	
Oil and filter changed		Hatches secured against leaking	
Fuel filters changed		Provisions stored	
Fuel is certified clean		Routing	
Engine running, gauges OK		Waypoints plotted and logged	
Raw water filter		Float Plan	
Impeller changed		Weather	
Transmission fluid		Cockpit chat	
Coolant fluid		Watch schedule posted	
Cooking fuel		Hull diagram posted	
Jerry jugs secured		Holding tanks empty, flushed	
Water jugs secured		Y-valves	
Water tanks full		Final communications	
Bilges empty, pumps operational		Final land head trip	
Lights		Have fun	

ACKNOWLEDGEMENTS

This book was written with the advice and assistance of many fine people and companies from the marine industry. Each chapter reflects their input and wise counsel without which the book could not have been written. The author wishes to extend heartfelt gratitude for the drawings, diagrams, and photographs they have made available to illustrate the text.

The following have been instrumental in the writing of *Ready to Sail.*

Captain Geoffrey Williams,
   senior marine surveyor
West Indies Marine Surveyors
PO Box 540
East End
Tortola, British Virgin Islands
E-mail: info@westindiesmarine
   surveyors.com

Scanmar International
432 South 1st street
Richmond, CA 94804-2107
Tel: 510-215-2010
E-Mail: scanmar@selfsteer.com

Fiorentino Para-Anchors
1048 Irvine Avenue #489
Newport Beach, CA 92660
Tel: 800-777-0732 or 949-631-2336
Fax: 949-722-1454
www.para-anchor.com

Grunert Marine Air Systems
2000 N. Andrews Ave. Extension
Pompano Beach, FL 33069
Tel: 954-973-2477
Fax: 954-979-4414
www.marineair.com/grunert

Schaefer Marine, Inc.
158 Duchaine Blvd.,
   Industrial Park
New Bedford, MA 02754-1293
Tel: 508-995-9511
Fax: 508-995-4882
www.schaefermarine.com

Harken USA
1251 East Wisconsin Ave.
Pewaukee, WI 53072-3755
Tel: 262-691-3320
Fax: 262-691-3008
www.harken.com

Blue Water Marine Diesel Engine
　Course
30201 South River Road
Harrison Township, MI 48045
Tel: 586-468-6960
www.blue-water-marine.com

Mr. Don Casey
www.boatus.com

Fortress Marine Anchors
1386 West McNab Road
Ft. Lauderdale, FL 33309
Tel: 800-825-6289 or 954-978-9988
Fax: 954-974-5378
www.fortressanchors.com

Magnaflux
3624 West Lake Avenue
Glenview, IL 60026
Tel: 847-657-5300
Fax: 847-657-5388
www.magnaflux.com

INDEX

abandon ship
  bag, 139, 143–46, 163, 167–68, 185, 196
  protocols, 167–68
alarm
  engine, 92
  fuel filter, 83
  gas "sniffer," 131
  off-course, 70
  overboard, 147, 152, 163, 166
algae, 15, 23, 25, 65, 72, 83, 92, 118, 119, 171, 173
Allen, Philip, 176
alternator, 80, 104, 114–15, 135, 173
  brackets, 81, 91
  interference from, 74
  spare, 100, 187
aluminum
  backing plate, 60
  fuel tanks, 92
  gas cylinder, 130
  reefing extrusion, 40
  repairing frame, 6
  spars, 46, 52, 116–17
  vangs, 39
  welding weakens, 48
anchors
  bow rollers, 58–59
  hardware, 55–56
  lines/rodes, 56, 57–58, 155–56
  parachute, 155–56
  as safety gear in storms, 154–56
  sizing, 155
  snubber, 57–58
  wells, 15, 58
  wind loads, 56, 57, 58
  windlasses, 58–63

anemometer, 51, 101
Atlantic Crossing Guide, The (Allen), 176
autopilots, 70, 73–76
  backup, 70, 75
  CPU (Central Processing Unit), 73, 74–75
  drive motor, 73, 74
  fluxgate compass, 73, 74

backfire flame arrester, 142
ballast, 77, 78, 142
Balmar, 115
barnacles, 18, 23, 25, 65, 72
batteries
  charging, 99, 104–5, 114–15, 173
  dedicated engine starting, 104
  deep cycle, 102–4, 114–15, 134
  ground faults, 111
  securing, 103
bearings, 68, 69, 117, 121, 127
  cutless, 23, 24, 25–26, 82, 90, 96
  furling system, 40, 41
  rudder, 23, 66
  sheave, 8
  traveler car, 29
  winch, 9
bells, 142
Beneteau 46, 138, 162, 172
bilges, 15
  pumps, 15–17
  ventilation of, 141–42
binoculars, 145, 154, 163, 165, 185
bleach, 15, 118
Blue Sea DC Digital Voltmeter, 114–15
boom, sail, 45–46
  boom preventer, 148–49
bosun's chair, 48, 151–52

brake pads, 68
bronze, 46, 56, 117
bulkheads, 13, 74, 89, 104, 131
bunks, 138, 140, 171, 181
butane, 129, 130

cabinets, 138–39
cabins, 139–40
calcium deposits, 126, 138
canvas, 53–54
carburetor, 142
CastLok, 44
caulking, 8, 12, 173
Center of Effort (CE), 76–78
Center of Lateral Resistance (CLR), 76–78
chainplates, 43–44, 117
charts
    sailing, 139, 176–77
    weather, 179–81
clothing, 146, 162, 183–84
Coastal/Offshore/High Seas Forecasts, 180
collision, 2, 3, 7, 13, 15, 18, 20, 23
    mat, 157, 163, 167, 185
Commanders' Weather, 177
compass, 10–12, 146
    autopilot fluxgate, 73, 74
    electrical/magnetic influences, 10–11, 73
    location of, 10–11
    removal of, 68
    tuning, 11–12
compressed natural gas (CNG), 129, 130
computers, 140, 179, 181
cookware, 176
coolants, 86–88, 172
copper, 44, 68, 117, 131, 132, 134–35, 187
Cornell, Jimmy, 176
corrosion
    anchor well, 58
    autopilot, 73, 74, 75
    battery, 103, 104
    bearing, 29, 41
    chainplate, 43–44
    electrical connection, 61, 62, 91, 93, 107,
        110, 112
    engine/motor, 86, 87, 88, 90, 91, 93, 96
    ground fault, 101
    hardware, 8, 17, 26, 30, 31, 39, 41, 55, 56,
        97, 132, 135, 150
    light socket, 10, 50

propeller, 24, 25, 26
resistant, 117, 130
rigging, 31, 42, 44, 45, 46
rudder, 64, 66, 69–70, 72
stuffing box, 97
transducer, 15, 22
valve, 120, 123, 126
winch, 9
wind vane system, 73
windlass, 59, 60, 61, 62
CPR (cardiopulmonary resuscitation), 157, 158
crew
    clothing and personal gear, 183–84
    listed in Float Plan, 177–78
    overboard, 146–48, 164–65
    responsibilities, 162–64, 184–85
    return flight funds, 181
    selection/preparation, 161–70
customs and immigration, 2, 177

Dacron
    sails, 36, 38
    tape, 33–34
Davis Echomaster, 154
davits, 5–6
decking, teak, 12
    replacing non-skid, 21–22
decks, 3–13
    attachment points, 3–4, 8
dehydration, 159, 169–70, 176
delamination
    hull, 18–22
    rudder, 23–24, 64, 65, 66, 73
depth finder, 22
dinghy, 5–6
dishwashing liquid, 118, 136
distress signals, 142, 144, 154
ditch bag, 143–46, 167–68
documentation, ship, 2, 146, 179, 181
drifter-reacher, 38–39
Drip-Free Packing, 97, 98
driveshaft, 82, 83, 90, 96–97
drugs, 161
    See also medical kit: supplies list;
        medications
drum, furling, 41–42
duct tape, 34, 47, 145, 156, 173, 186
dye pack, fluorescent, 147
dye test, 43

electrical systems, 101–17
  alternating current (AC), 104, 111–13, 134, 135, 137
  DC to AC inverter, 111
  diagnostics, 106–11
  direct current (DC), 101–6, 134, 135, 137
  inspection checklist, 194
  power requirements, 113–15
  shore power, 104, 11, 112, 134
  short circuit, 62, 106, 108, 109–10, 112
  spare parts list, 117, 187
  watts = amps x volts, 113–14
  wiring. *See* wiring, electrical
emergency
  protocols, 164–68
  steering, 78–79
Emergency Position Indicating Radio Beacon (EPIRB), 143, 144, 145, 163, 168, 184
ENCHANTRESS, xi
engines, auxiliary, 80–100
  diagnostics, 82
  routine maintenance, 80–82
  smoke, 82, 88–89, 172
  vibration, 82, 90
engines, diesel, 82–93
  air, 85–86
  coolants, 86–88, 172
  exhaust, 82, 88–89, 172
  fuel, 83–84, 85, 86
  maintenance, 80–82, 171–72
  mounts, 89–91, 97
  oil, 84–85
  operation, 82–83
  refrigeration system, 133, 134
  "runaway," 86
  spare parts list, 100, 187
  starter, 93
  turbocharger, 86
  vibration, 82, 90
Etchells North American Championships, 3
exhaust, 80, 82, 83, 85, 86, 87, 88–89, 172

fiberglass
  keel, 117
  repair, 8, 12–13, 15, 18–22, 23, 24, 25, 60, 64–65, 66–67, 91, 125
  rods, 53
  spare, 26, 186
  tanks, 8, 92, 119

filters
  air, 80, 85–86
  freshwater, 118, 120, 128, 134, 173
  fuel, 80, 81, 83–84, 92, 100, 171–72, 187
  oil, 80, 81, 85, 93, 172
  raw/seawater, 80, 81, 86, 87, 88, 171
  refrigerant, 137
fire
  emergency strategy for, 164, 167
  short circuit, 109
firearms, 161
fire extinguishers, 22, 141, 163, 167, 184, 185
first aid, 143, 145, 157, 158, 160, 177
fittings, 7–8
flags, 142, 177
flooding, 166–67
food
  in abandon ship bag, 146
  stores, 138–39, 174–76
foot pump, 137–38
Freon, 136
fuel, cooking, 129, 130, 131, 172–73
fuel, diesel
  fuel, 80, 81, 83–84, 92, 100, 171–72, 187
  rate of consumption of, 98–100

galley, 129–39
gauges, 92–93, 96, 184
  battery, 114, 172
  fuel, 92, 173
  LPG pressure, 130, 131, 132
  refrigerant, 136–37
  sensor unit, 92–93
  temperature, 92, 172
  tuning, 47–48
gelcoat, 12–13, 15, 18–22, 23, 67
General Ecology, 118
generators, 99, 110, 111, 112, 113, 114, 134
Globalstar, 145
Gougeon Brothers, 65
GPS (global positioning system), 101, 163, 164, 181, 184
  course, 11
  EPIRB, 144
  inoperative, 108, 109
  location of, 140
  resistance, 106
  use in voyage planning, 177
Great Circle Plotting Charts, 176–77

handholds, 139, 157

harnesses, safety, 27, 48, 147–48, 152, 162, 166, 183, 184

hatches, 2, 4, 6, 166, 173, 181

headliners, 13–15, 21

heads. *See* toilets, marine

HO-229, 140

HO-249 Vols. I and II, 140, 176–77

hull, 3–26
 blisters, 18–19
 configuration and CLR, 76–78
 delamination, 18–19
 inner-core repairs, 19–22
 inspection checklist, 190
 spares list, 186

Hunter 28.5, 94–95

Inmarsat, 145

inspection checklists, 189–97

insurance companies, 1, 105

Internal Grid Units (IGU), 15

Iridium, 145

jacklines, 146–47, 162

Jaws, 27–28

Jenifer Clark's Gulfstream, 177

jibs
 chafing and tearing, 32
 leads, 30–31
 spare, 28
 storm, 37–38, 151
 weather helm, 78
 working, 37–38
 Yankee cut, 32

Johnson, Irving, xii

keel, 77, 78, 101, 104, 117
 bolts, 17
 keel-hull junction, 18

kerosene, 9, 86, 129, 169

knife, emergency, 154

knot log/meter
 paddlewheel, 22
 transducers, 15, 22

lee helm, 77, 78

life jackets, 141, 145, 147, 157, 162, 167, 181

lifelines, 5, 32, 143, 146, 165

life rafts, 142–43, 167–68

Lifesling, 148

lightning, 51, 115–17
 lightning rod, 51
 Lightning Static Dissipater (LSD), 51, 117

lights
 engine room, 81
 flashlights, 154
 at head box, 51
 maintenance, 173
 navigation, 10
 personal strobe, 147
 spotlights, 154
 steaming/deck/spreader, 49–50

lines
 anchor, 24, 55, 56, 57–58, 60
 reefing, 34–35, 42, 52

liquefied petroleum gas (LPG), 129–32

liquor, 161, 169

Local User Terminals (LUTs), 144

locking devices, 156–57

logbooks, 177, 181

LWL (waterline length), 100

machinery, propulsion
 inspection checklist, 193

Magnaflux Spotcheck Dye Penetrant Kit, 43

mainsail, 36–39
 furling, 37
 guidance systems, 53–54
 regular, 37
 size and storm trysail, 150

mainsheet, 28–30

man overboard. *See* crew: overboard

manuals, 177

masts, 46–48
 aluminum, and lightning, 116–17
 boot, 47
 climbing, 48–52, 151–52
 head box, 51–52
 proper positioning of, 47–48
 spreaders, 49, 51
 welded, 48, 51
 wooden, 52–53

medical kit, 146
 supplies list, 157–60

medications, 145, 157, 163, 185
 seasickness, 143, 169, 170, 176, 181
 See also medical kit: supplies list

Mercator charts, 177

mildew, 14, 15

Mission Control Centers (MCCs), 144

mold, 14–15
monitoring and maintenance schedule, 165
motors, electric, 16
   pump, 120–22
   windlass, 61–62
motors, hydraulic, 62–63
MRUD, 78
multimeter, 22, 106–12, 134

National Oceanic & Atmospheric Association
   (NOAA), 144, 179–80
National Weather Service Web site, 180
Nautical Almanac, 176–77
navigation
   lights, 10, 49–51
   station/tools, 139–40
Nicopress, 44
Norseman, 44, 45

Ocean Passages for the World, 176
ohmmeter, 10, 16, 50, 62, 93, 106, 108–11,
   112, 135
oil
   diesel engine, 84–85, 172
   filters, 80, 81, 85, 93, 172
   oil-bath air filters, 86
   spills/disposal, 85
   transmission, 94, 172
   WD-30 engine, 94

passports, 2, 146
personal flotation devices (PFDs), 141, 147,
   148
phones, satellite, 140, 144–45, 180
Pilot Charts, 139, 176–77
plates, backing, 8, 14
plumbing, 118–28
   freshwater, 118–22
   inspection checklist, 194
   marine toilets, 125–28
   spare parts list, 128, 187–88
   wastewater, 122–28
ports, 6–7
propane, 129, 130, 172–73
propeller shafts, 24–26
   driveshaft and, 96–97
   stuffing box, 97–98
   wrapped-line damage, 24, 90
pumps
   bilge, 15–17

electric diaphragm, 16–17, 120–22
engine water, 87–88, 135
freshwater, 120–22
galley foot, 137–38
macerator, 124–25
wastewater, 124–26, 127

radar, 152–54
   location of LCD display screen, 152
   reflectors, 154
   scanner, 50, 152–53
radio
   EPIRB (Emergency Position Indicating
     Radio Beacon), 143, 144
   shortwave radio receiver, 179, 180
   SSB, 140, 179, 180
   VHF, 140, 146
rails, 4–5
refrigeration, 132–37
registration papers, 2, 146, 179
Rescue Control Center (RCC), 144
rigging, running, 27–31
   inspection checklist, 191
   spare parts list, 54, 187
rigging, standing, 42–54
   fatigue cycles, 50–51
   hardware dye test, 42
   inspection checklist, 191
   spare parts list, 54, 187
   stays and shrouds, 44–45
Robertson, 73
rudders, 23–24, 64–67
   auxiliary system, 72
   bearings, 23, 66–67
   delamination, 23–24, 64–66
   emergency, 78–79
   jury-rigging, 78–79
   lap zone, 66
   minimizing movement, 76
   rudderpost fittings, 69–70

safety, 141–60
   gas "sniffer," 131
   inspection checklist, 196
   standard equipment list, 141–42
sails, 31–42
   battens, 32, 37
   Center of Effort (CE), 76–78
   controls, 39–42
   covers, 53

sails (*cont'd.*)
    foot and leech cords, 32
    forestay, 41
    genoa, 31
    headsail furler, 39–42
    hoisting, 42
    inspection checklist, 191
    inventory, 35–36
    light air, 38–39, 100, 150
    material, 32, 36, 150
    reducing, 37, 151, 166
    reefing, 34–35
    repairs, 33–34, 36
    roller reefing systems, 39–41, 52
    sailing vs. cruising, 35
    spinnakers, 28, 32, 38–39, 51, 100
    stack pack, 53
    storm, 37–38, 51, 149–52
    tears, 32, 33–34
    telltales, 32
SART (Search and Rescue Transponder), 146
Scanmar International, 78
scuba diving, 157
scudding, 24
seacocks, 2, 22, 87, 122–27, 135, 138, 156, 163,
    166, 184, 185
Seagull IV Water Purifier, 118
seasickness, 4, 124, 168–70
shower, 122, 123
SOS Emergency Rudder, 78
sound devices, 142
speed, 30–31, 99–100
speedometer, 15, 22
Sta-Lok, 44
static dissipater, 51, 117
steering
    autopilot, 70, 73–76
    balance, 76–78
    cable, 67, 68–69, 75
    chain-and-wire, 67, 68–69
    defects/failure, 69–70
    emergency, 78–79
    engine controls, 69
    gears, 68
    hydraulic, 64, 68
    inspection checklist, 192
    pedestal, 67–68
    rack and pinion, 67
    self-steering, 70–78
    spare parts list, 79, 187

    tiller, 64, 67, 78–79
    wheel, 64, 67, 70, 78
    wind vane, 70, 71–73
    See also rudders
stereo system, 140
storage
    galley, 138–39
    life raft, 143
    locking devices for, 156–57
stoves, cooking, 129–32, 156
stuffing box, 97–98
survey, marine, 1
Systems IV inline filter, 173

tachometer, 92
tackle, ground, 55–63
    inspection checklist, 192
tanks
    cooking gas, 130, 172–73
    fiberglass, 8, 92, 119
    fittings, 7–8
    freshwater, 118–20, 173
    fuel, 91–92, 171
    fullness calculation, 92
    inspection checklist, 194
    sanitizing, 118
    spare parts list, 187–88
    stainless steel, 119, 173
    ventilation, 141–42
    wastewater, 118, 124
tape
    Dacron, 33–34
    duct, 47, 173
    mast boot, 47
teak, 12
Technora, 45
thermostat
    engine, 87, 88
    water heater, 112–13
throttle, engine, 91
through-hulls, 22–23, 124, 156
tobacco, 161, 169
toilets, marine, 125–28
    electric, 127
    odors, 127–28
tools, 45, 186
trampoline, 53
transducers, 15, 22
transmissions, 93–96
    clutch, 93, 94

fluid, 94, 172
gearboxes, 93–96
hydraulic, 93, 94
shift cables, 91, 94–96
spare parts list, 100, 187
two-shaft, 93, 94
trip lines, 27–28
turbochargers, 86
turnbuckles, 5, 41, 41–43, 47–48, 54, 187

U.S. Coast Guard, 85, 181
standard equipment list, 141–42
UUPlus, 180

vangs, 39, 45, 46, 148
ventilation/vents, 15, 86, 141–42
cooking gas locker, 130
dorade, 156–57
tank, 7, 92, 118, 119, 122, 124, 127, 128, 173
voltmeter, 93, 104, 107–8, 111–12, 114–15
voyage planning, 176–79
Float Plan, 177–79
inspection checklists, 189–97
VOYAGER, 4, 138, 162, 169

water
freshwater, 118–22, 146, 173
seawater, 137–38, 171
wastewater, 118, 122–28
water heater, 112–13
waterline length (LWL), 100
waves
action and seasickness, 168–70
balanced steering and, 76–78
weather
cold front, 116
heavy, 5, 34, 152, 154–55, 156, 163, 164, 166
helm, 77, 78
software, 180

voyage planning and, 176, 179–81
West Marine, 154, 173
West System, 65
whistles, 142
winches/windlasses, 8–9, 26, 49, 58–63
electric, 61–62, 105
hydraulic, 62–63
manual, 60–61
repairing deck damage, 60
Windex, 51
winds
anchor loads and, 56, 57, 58
angle of boat to, 151
apparent, 71
balanced steering and, 76–78
detailed on Pilot Charts, 176
fuel consumption and, 99
heavy, 41, 53, 151
speed/direction indicators, 51
wind vanes
Scanner Monitor, 78
steering, 70, 71–73
wiring, electrical
AC power, 111
autopilot, 74–75
bundled/harness, 101
freshwater pump, 120–21
inadequate size, 107
instrument, 22
lights, 10, 50
reverse polarity, 112
water heater, 112–13
windlass motor, 61–62
World Cruising Routes (Cornell), 176

Xantrex Link 10/Link 20, 115

zinc
anodes, 23, 24–26, 66, 86, 94
chromate paste, 46

Of related interest:

Further Offshore
A Practical Guide for Sailors
Ed Mapes

"Mapes breaks down the process of fitting out and preparing for offshore sailing into manageable, simple to follow steps. What's more, he lets readers know what to expect once at sea, with advice on boat maintenance and handling as well as dealing with emergency situations." —*SAILING*

Handbook of Offshore Cruising
Jim Howard
Revised & Updated by Charles J. Doane

The most complete, most reliable, and most-read guide for those planning to sail across the oceans. This second edition is completely updated with reference to ever-changing technology, especially electronics.

Marine Electrical and Electronics Bible, 3E
John C. Payne

"Electrical problems are not an inevitable part of cruising and racing. An acceptable level of reliability is possible, and in fact is necessary,' says author John Payne. His *Marine Electrical and Electronics Bible* will help you achieve this reliability with detailed information on selecting, installing, maintaining and troubleshooting all the electrical and electronic systems on your boat. . . . This new edition is fully updated." —*SAIL*

Marine Diesel Engines
Maintenance and Repair Manual
Jean-Luc Pallas

"This maintenance and repair manual provides everything you need to know about diesel engines. The different engine parts are identified along with their functions. Simple maintenance tasks are covered along with problem areas and troubleshooting tables to help you diagnose problems." —*Latitudes & Attitudes*

SHERIDAN HOUSE
America's Favorite Sailing Books
www.sheridanhouse.com